Mastering the
Digital Marketplace

Mastering the Digital Marketplace

Practical Strategies for Competitiveness in the New Economy

Douglas F. Aldrich

John Wiley & Sons, Inc.

New York • Chichester • Weinheim • Brisbane • Singapore • Toronto

Published by John Wiley & Sons, Inc.
Published simultaneously in Canada.

This publication is designed to provide accurate and authoritative information in
regard to the subject matter covered. It is sold with the understanding that the publisher is not engaged in rendering professional services. If legal, accounting, medical,
psychological or any other expert assistance is required, the services of a competent
professional person should be sought.

Library of Congress Cataloging-in-Publication Data:

Aldrich, Douglas F.
    Mastering the digital marketplace : practical strategies for
competitiveness in the new economy / Douglas F. Aldrich.
        p.   cm.
    Includes bibliographical references and index.
    ISBN 0-471-34546-6 (alk. paper)
    1. Electronic commerce.   2. Intellectual property.   3. Internet
marketing.   4. Computer graphics industry—Case studies.   I. Title.
    HF5548.32.A43   1999
    658.8'00285—dc21   99-26880
                                                              CIP

Printed in the United States of America.

10 9 8 7 6 5 4 3 2 1

ACKNOWLEDGMENTS

TO SAY THAT THIS BOOK WAS A COLLABORATIVE EFFORT IS AN UNDERSTATEMENT. THE ideas expressed in this book have been developed over several years, in hundreds of conversations. Many of the topics and frameworks expressed here were first conceived in conversations with John Sifonis, Craig Lawton, Mike Grant, and Phil Osborn in the early 1990s. Since then, they've been fleshed out by many within A. T. Kearney through the development of this book and other efforts.

Much of the thought leadership that shaped the book came from a core group of officers within A. T. Kearney. Their contribution through reams of voice mails, e-mails, and even the occasional live meeting, helped push the thinking. Don St. Clair out of Hong Kong, Dave Rader out of San Francisco, Kerry Schmitt out of Costa Mesa, Peter Shadek out of Tokyo, David Donnan out of Chicago, Bill Jeffery out of New York, and Bob Ciccone out of San Francisco all made significant contributions of their previously developed works, as well as their new and original thinking.

Without great examples and supporting case work, this book would just be a jumble of unsupported ideas and for this reason, I would like to thank all of the companies that contributed to the development of supporting case materials. Specifically John Jung, David Lanciault, and Marilyn Schule with A. T. Kearney worked with Brian Baker, Joe Giordano, and Susan Carter at Mobil to develop the case study on the Mobil Speedpass product. I thank Mobil for being generous with their time and information, and I congratulate them on such an innovative product. I'd also like to thank Axel Freyberg of A. T. Kearney, along with Anders Lindquist, Lena Lundholm, and Paul Hedmann with Telia Electronic Commerce AB for their efforts in developing the Telia case study—a great example of a company working to redefine themselves and their position in the new digital marketplace.

Then, there are the dozens of individuals that contributed in small and large ways to specific topics within the book. Joe Paulsen helped in developing the diagnostic as well as read and commented on the manuscript throughout its development. Mary Dixon reviewed and helped develop the materials on intelligent markets and digital value networks. Henry Conn helped with materials on the individual employee and human aspects of the value-based organization. Will Hutchinson helped with privacy and security, as well as minor contributions throughout. Elliot Paul and Joe Meglen reviewed the manuscript and helped us improve the content and writing. Craig Hartman pushed the thinking in the entire intelligent products section. James Morehouse and Jim Farrell helped us improve the thinking on digital value networks, digital value chains, and their relationship to traditional forms of supply chain integration. Chris Dubois and others in the Consumer Products practice of A. T. Kearney contributed considerable materials in the area of intelligent products. George Droder contributed to the section on the transformation of the health care industry. Dan Rosler pulled together some of the materials on the people aspects of the value-based organization. Howard Edson, Wilson Toussaint, and Dhaval Moogimane developed the framework for the digital marketplace diagnostic along with Tami Zhu. Danielle Benson helped us with the introductory quotes, as well as research on Moore and Metcalfe. Karl Daniels at the University of Texas helped research the growth of time value and the emergence of value webs. Thomas Ross helped us with supporting materials on the new role of infomediaries. Pier Angelo Biga in Milan developed supporting materials on intelligent products. The Institute for the Future provided a significant amount of research and input on virtual value chains.

Much thanks must go to our editors. Miryam Williamson and Alice LaPlante helped give the book a final polish. In addition, I have to thank Debbie Roberts and Ken Smalling for their efforts in bringing this book to market.

I'd like to thank Hitendra Chaturvedi for his work in clarifying the ideas around intelligent markets, Brian Bleasdell for his efforts on intelligent organizations, and Lokender Bommisetty in his efforts around intelligent products. These individuals took the concepts developed in dozens of brainstorming and discussion sessions, supported them with rigorous research, and helped formulate the final product you read here. I'd also like to thank Louise Libby for her thoughtful contributions in the area of privacy and security, and her ideas on the transformation of public institutions.

I'd especially like to thank Randy Bullard for organizing the overall development of this project and driving the efforts to collect the cases and assemble the content, as well as the many hours of brainstorming sessions needed to turn ideas into readable material.

A final thanks to all of those clients who, over the years, have helped me develop these insights and have served as a laboratory for the strategies and techniques discussed.

CONTENTS

PART FOUR

Intelligent Organizations

PART FIVE

Mastering the Digital Marketplace

PART SIX

Intelligent Society

AFTERWORD

APPENDICES

PREFACE

January 5, 2002

John Dawson, until yesterday the CEO of @WarpSpeed, ran a weary hand through his hair as he surveyed his empty desk. His personal possessions were neatly packed in cardboard boxes. The walls had been stripped of his family photographs, his diplomas from Harvard and Stanford, his many industry awards. Time to head out of the office he'd practically lived in for 17 years. He was about to close his briefcase when the intercom buzzed. He pushed the button. "Yes, Megan?" he asked, trying to sound normal. Megan's voice sounded uncertain. "Ms. Caldwell is here. She wants to know if you have a moment." Heather Caldwell, formerly @WarpSpeed's senior vice president of marketing and a top-notch executive, had been named as Dawson's successor. Since yesterday's announcement, Dawson had tried to avoid his former protégé. Now, he steeled himself to shake her hand, determined to sound sincere when congratulating her on a well-deserved promotion.

It would not be easy. Dawson had been a founding member and CEO of the computer graphics manufacturer since it opened its doors in 1985. Deeply committed to the company, Dawson had rapidly built it into a global presence by strictly adhering to the original vision of the founding partners. Their strategy: To produce the highest quality products—both hardware and software—that could command premium prices even in commodity market niches. Key to this strategy was the decision to maintain rigorous control over all key technologies through creating and vigorously protecting all of @WarpSpeed's own closed proprietary designs, specifications, and processes.

Dawson kept on this path despite increasingly vocal opposition from influential members of the board of directors. Recent financial returns had been dismal, seemingly proving the point that Dawson had been wrong. However, Dawson still didn't see what he could have done differently. Hindsight is always easy, he reminded himself. He had made the best decisions he could, given the circumstances at the time. Who knew?

Corporate History

As a designer and manufacturer of high-performance graphics technology, @WarpSpeed has for nearly two decades delivered advanced computing and three-dimensional visualization capabilities to scientific, engineering, and creative professionals around the globe. Traditionally, approximately 40 percent of its revenues were derived from sales of desktop workstations; another 30 percent of revenue came from supercomputers—the most powerful in the world as @WarpSpeed had managed to acquire a small, but well-regarded, specialty manufacturer of such systems. @WarpSpeed earned the remaining 30 percent of its revenues by providing graphics-related software and consulting services to enterprise customers in a broad range of industries, including manufacturing, government, entertainment, communications, energy, the sciences, and education.

By 1998, @WarpSpeed had become the market leader in the high-performance graphics technology segment of the computer industry. Happy with @WarpSpeed's (and Dawson's) performance, the market kept upping its stock price, and Dawson was profiled as the latest Silicon Valley *wunderkind* in leading business publications such as *Forbes, Time,* and *BusinessWeek.*

In early 1999, encouraged by this success, Dawson made the decision to enter a new market, namely designing and manufacturing videogame and other home entertainment systems. Strategically, Dawson's idea seemed sound, and so the board voted its approval. After all, the digital entertainment market was widely predicted to finally explode by 2001, with new opportunities abounding in traditional video- and computer-game segments, as well as highly lucrative new niches being created as consumers became interested in virtual reality, interactive television, and emerging Internet-based entertainment forums. As @WarpSpeed dominated the high-end graphics hardware market, and possessed key software tools for rendering three-dimensional graphics on a variety of emerging platforms, including the network, the move seemed like a sure bet.

Taking care not to disrupt operations of its existing highly profitable manufacturing and service divisions, Dawson created a new organization focused on designing a new game hardware platform—one that would compete with existing (and incompatible) machines from Nintari, Mony, and Vega. Dawson personally hand-picked the people who would run this new division, giving them the budget to recruit the best and brightest engineers in the game and home entertainment industry.

In addition to developing a new game hardware platform, Dawson made the additional, and more controversial, decision to also develop the actual "content," or game software, that would run on the new machines. Perhaps more significantly, Dawson decided not to let any third-party developers create games for the new platform. His reason? He thought that the spectacular proprietary graphics at the heart of the new @WarpSpeed machine would create such a distinct competitive advantage that he couldn't take the risk of releasing its specifications to external engineers. He consequently launched a group whose sole directive was to develop the most exciting games possible for the new machine.

After much fanfare, @WarpSpeed finally launched its new system in Spring 2001, along with two games based on characters licensed from recent Hollywood hit movies. Although six months behind the scheduled launch date, @WarpSpeed was convinced that the superior graphics, lifelike animation, and superb performance of the new products would quickly win the hearts—and dollars—of notoriously fickle games consumers. Yet, although clearly technically superior, @WarpSpeed's new hardware and software products were also expensive—much more so than products from other, competing, games companies. The @WarpSpeed system retailed for just under $300; the current leader in the games market, Nintari, had just slashed its price to less than one-half that price. Perhaps more significantly, the two @WarpSpeed game titles were 25 percent more expensive than similarly themed titles designed for the Nintari system.

Dawson attributed the higher costs to several factors: the speedy organizational restructuring and personnel ramp-up necessary for launching the new platform within the projected timeframe; the additional investment in equipment, facilities, and materials required to create the new division; and the fact that Dawson was unable to leverage the vast expertise @WarpSpeed had developed over the years in its primary manufacturing operations. Contrary to Dawson's expectations, neither the engineering know-how nor the basic parts designs of their business-oriented graphics systems could be effectively scaled down to suit the requirements of a home entertainment system.

Dawson calmed his investors by promising that costs would drop over time, and he would be able to lower consumer prices—and raise margins—in the very near future.

Despite the high prices, industry analysts proclaimed that the new @WarpSpeed system posed real competition for existing market leaders. Although consumers seemed leery of purchasing a machine that could run only two games, those two games received rave reviews from leading computer magazines, and Dawson publicly promised at least 20 more titles that "will knock everyone's socks off" by the end of the year. To make good on this pledge, he hired away some of the hottest game designers in the business to come work for @WarpSpeed at astronomical compensation packages.

All was looking good until a month after the debut of @WarpSpeed's new machine, when the movie, *Adventures in the Pacific,* was released. A surprise blockbuster hit by a major Hollywood studio that earned unprecedented box office revenues, *Adventures* caused a virtual feeding frenzy of related merchandizing in a broad variety of consumer products.

The dominant player in the games market, Nintari, Inc. was quick to capitalize on this pop phenomenon. Unlike @WarpSpeed, Nintari had always depended on third-party developers, and released its technical specifications to anyone interested in creating a game for its platform. Within weeks of the movie's release, scores of third-party software firms were furiously developing Pacific Adventure–themed games for the Nintari machine. Nintari distributed limited-play copies of the various games free over the Web as a "hook" to attract consumers who had never played computer games before; it also set up Web-based sites that allowed avid Pacific game players to chat and swap tips for success on playing the various titles. Nintari encouraged competition among its developers by promising a $1-million booty to the first game developer to sell 1 million copies. Nintari didn't stop there. By contracting with the leading stars in the movie to participate in online "Webcasts" linked to the game, Nintari spurred even more interest in the game. Also, Nintari signed a contract with Kidco, Inc., to create plush bean-bag toys patterned after the main characters, that immediately became collector's items.

In contrast, @WarpSpeed was unable to react quickly to the runaway success of *Adventures in the Pacific.* Because its technology was closed to outside developers, the onus of creating new game titles fell on the shoulders of the already-overburdened programming department, who were under pressure to make good on Dawson's promise to ship 20 new titles by the end of the year. The head of @WarpSpeed's games division scrambled to put together a team to work on a Pacific game, but the project seemed doomed from the start. Programmers rebelled when asked to do double-duty on several simultaneous development products, and a number of key people quit to form their own start-up focusing on Nintari development. It was whispered throughout the games community that the @WarpSpeed Pacific product was plagued with so many technical glitches that it would sink faster than the famous ship featured in the movie. By the time @WarpSpeed released the product, it was well into 2002, and the craze for that particular movie had long subsided. Moreover, as reviewers for game magazines pointed out, the product was full of bugs and ludicrously overpriced, especially given that Nintari's Pacific titles were now being sold at remainder prices. After all, games consumers were onto the latest "big thing": Bugs.

Perhaps most damaging to @WarpSpeed's reputation, however, was that only 5 of the promised 20 new titles had been shipped by the end of 2001. By the second quarter of 2002, it was clear that @WarpSpeed had failed in its attempt to steal a significant share of the videogame market away from existing players. Dawson made a last-ditch effort by slashing prices on all @Warp-Speed hardware by 40 percent. He also cut prices in half for the entire portfolio of game titles (all seven of them). However, by this time, it was too late. There already existed a widespread perception that @WarpSpeed games were not as cool as the Nintari games. @WarpSpeed's overlong time-to-market cycle couldn't keep pace with the fickle tastes of consumers—Dawson himself realized that the titles currently under development were already out of date, and they weren't close to being released. Perhaps most fatally, consumers decided that paying twice as much for an @WarpSpeed system, despite its superior graphics and performance, was not worth it, especially when it was now obvious that there would never be a satisfactory selection of titles.

By the end of the third quarter, @WarpSpeed's board of directors decided to cut its losses and exit the videogame business. It announced to stockholders that an estimated $500 million would be charged against revenues for the fiscal year. @WarpSpeed stock took an immediate and dramatic plunge, and the board subsequently asked for, and received, John Dawson's resignation on December 12, 2002.

Back to the Present

Now Dawson's successor was waiting outside his office door. "Send her in, Megan," Dawson said, and sat down, trying to look as though he were at ease. When Caldwell entered the room, however, she appeared as uncomfortable as Dawson felt.

"I hope you know, John, this isn't personal," Caldwell began, but Dawson cut her off.

"Hey, no problem," he told her. "I gave it my best shot. It's your turn now. Good luck." With that, Dawson got up from the desk, picked up his briefcase, and headed for the door. "Megan will take care of these boxes," he said, over his shoulder.

"Look, John," Caldwell said, but when Dawson turned toward her, she seemed at a loss. "Here. You forgot something," Caldwell said finally, pointing toward the elaborately carved nine-foot antique oak bookcase Dawson had bought in the company's heydays. A single book was still lying on the bottom shelf. Caldwell picked it up, glancing at it briefly before handing it over.

"Maybe we all should have paid more attention to this," she said, ruefully.

Dawson glanced at the book cover. *Mastering the Digital Marketplace— Practical Strategies for Competitiveness in the New Economy.* He recognized it as something a highly respected CEO of a major retail conglomerate had given to him at a management summit sponsored by his alma mater, the Stanford Business School. Dawson had never gotten around to reading it. Flipping through the pages, Dawson saw chapters providing advice on understanding—and building on—core corporate competencies. Insight into the "no-time-to-market" urgency of designing consumer products in the information age. Tips on how to understand and exploit the Internet and other new distribution channels. Most interesting, he noted in-depth case studies that proved why the concept of forging value chains that create intimate and enduring partnerships between diverse businesses was so essential.

Dawson thought of his rash decision to venture into the unfamiliar consumer game market, of which @WarpSpeed knew absolutely nothing; of his inability to get a product to market within a reasonable timeframe, much less the unreasonable one demanded by games consumers; of his stubborn refusal to share technology or information at the same time his competitors flourished by enthusiastically entering into collaborative alliances with unlikely business partners.

He looked up and realized that Heather Caldwell was standing there, waiting for a response. He handed the book back to her. "I won't be needing this anymore. Perhaps if I'd read it this would still be my office and @WarpSpeed might be in better shape today. Good luck, Heather. I wish you nothing but the best."

Heather flipped the book over in her hands and browsed the cover flap. "Thanks John. And best of luck to you as well."

Dawson exited the office in a somewhat awkward silence. As he walked across the parking lot, he dissapointingly reflected on what he'd seen in the table of contents of that book. The book that had remained unread for two long—and for him, incredibly difficult—years. Two words formed in his mind, and wouldn't go away: *If only . . .*

PART
ONE

The Digital
Marketplace

The Digital Marketplace

"I think there is a world market for maybe five computers."
—*Thomas Watson (1874–1956), Chairman of IBM, 1943*

EARLY ONE FRIDAY MORNING ON THE NORTH SIDE OF CHICAGO, MARK DELANY SITS DOWN at his laptop and checks on the status of his stock portfolio. Seeing that several of his investments appreciated nicely overnight, Mark logs onto his bank's web site and sells enough shares of an international transportation fund so that he can immediately call his auto broker and order a sports car—made in Germany—containing some very cool custom features he'd always lusted after. Within an hour, workers on an assembly line in Hamburg receive the factory specifications for building a red convertible with a sunroof, leather bucket seats, quadraphonic sound, and other paraphernalia that Mark specifically asked for. Simultaneously, the fund shares that Mark sold are bought in Japan by an institutional investor who subscribes to an online financial news-alert service—and who was informed via e-mail of a sudden upsurge in sales of large-ticket transportation equipment. By noon, Chicago time, the fund has risen another 2.5 points. An Asian airline participating in the fund takes advantage of the increased valuation to order two jumbo jets from Boeing, Inc. in Seattle, Washington. The revenues from this transaction are used by Boeing to pay the salaries of several thousand of its employees, including assembly worker Mary

Delany. At 5 P.M. Pacific time, Mary knows her bank has received an electronic deposit of her week's paycheck, and so on her way home, she stops at a local florist and uses her ATM card to wire an order for a dozen roses to her brother Mark, in Chicago, who just this morning celebrated his 30th birthday by ordering the car of his dreams.

Within hours, a single man sitting in his apartment initiates a series of events that touch the economies of four countries, seven industries, and countless individuals. But what has actually been exchanged? No hard currency (dollars, yen, francs, or marks) has physically been given from one person—or institution—to another; no products (the car, airplanes, or flowers) have physically been handed over, yet. Even the less tangible—but absolutely essential—component of any economic transaction, *labor,* has yet to be performed. (The car and the airplanes are not yet built; the flowers have not yet been selected, arranged or physically delivered.)

What, then, *has* been exchanged? Information. Data flows from person to company to community; transactions execute in almost frictionless markets. Although the physical aspects of these transactions are still to be completed, even they are radically impacted by this flow of information. The assembly workers at the auto plant are making *Mark's* car with his specific requirements, not a dealer's car. The Boeing jumbo jets were selected as much for their incorporation of integrated digital entertainment and communication systems for passengers as for their flight characteristics and efficiencies. The roses that Mary is sending to her brother were cut in Tyler, Texas, this morning for distribution by a nationwide network of digitally connected florists tomorrow.

Now, multiply this scenario by the millions of similar transactions taking place in thousands of industries in every country *every second of every day,* and you can begin to comprehend why understanding the implications of what we are calling "the digital economy" tops the agenda of every right-thinking CEO in the world today.

A Brief Lesson in Economic History

Let's begin with some basic definitions that will lay the groundwork for what we'll be discussing in this book.

Economy. A systematic way of describing how goods and services are exchanged among members of a given community. Interesting note: The word can be traced back to the Greek *oikonomos,* or "one who manages a household."

Digital. Anything that can be fully expressed using digits, or numbers. Effectively, this means anything that can be translated into numerical form, and—most important—retranslated back to its original state *without losing its essential aspects.* A book, such as this one, can be expressed digitally, as can a movie, a photograph, or even the performance of a piece of music. Automobiles, hamburgers, or fresh flowers cannot be expressed digitally, as they possess physical aspects that cannot (yet) be turned into numeric form without radically altering their inherent qualities.

Reduced to its simplest terms, any macro- (meaning large, or all-encompassing) economic theory consists of explaining the interworkings of four principal components—land, labor, capital, and technology—as they facilitate the exchange of goods and services within a specific community.

Keep in mind that although all of these components are necessarily involved in all economic systems, the extent to which each one impacts a specific economy varies dramatically.

For example, the earliest economies were agricultural in nature, and were centered around producing, exchanging, and consuming products derived from working with the natural world. In agricultural communities, land and labor were understandably the most precious components for determining economic success. True, capital—or money—played a part, as did technological innovations such as the thresher, the plow, the steamboat, and the train. However, an agricultural community could subsist with a minimum of money and technology—and couldn't survive at all without land or labor.

Later, with the Industrial Revolution, technology assumed a more important role (electricity and the telephone were obviously important inventions), but because the economy was primarily driven by the ability to produce goods for the mass market, capital (possessing enough money) and labor (commanding an adequately trained workforce) were by far the most important ingredients for success.

Just as the industrial economy gradually evolved from the agricultural economy, so the industrial economy is making way for the digital economy. We see this progression, timewise, in Figure 1.1. (Note the two intermediary economic stages. In the "service" economy, the wealth created by people performing services for the first time exceeded the wealth created through the manufacturing of products. In the "global" economy, geographic and political boundaries became largely irrelevant when exchanging goods and services.)

With the advent of the digital economy, technology for the first time becomes the dominant force. With information being the driver of value and wealth creation, information technology becomes the key to success in a

FIGURE 1.1
Evolution of the digital economy.

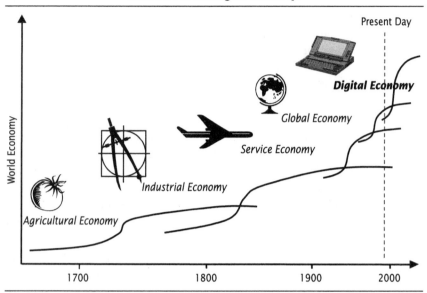

growing number of industries. Companies in the information businesses have known this for many years and have actively used information technology to great advantage. In the digital economy though, we're seeing the reach of information technology extend to even the most traditional and staid of industries. Manufacturers compete less on their manufacturing skill and more on their ability to electronically connect to suppliers and customers and implement information technology to streamline processes. Distributors compete less on their ability to manage a fleet of trucks and more on their ability to know where every widget is in transit and to optimize loading and routing through the effective use of communications and information technologies. Retailers compete less on how they pick real estate and design store layouts, and more on how they track customer buying patterns and use point-of-sale information to forge tight linkages with suppliers. Across all of these areas, information and its proper management through information technology are making the difference and separating the winners from the losers.

Here's a concrete example of the key difference between an economy based on information and one based on products. When the U.S. stock market crashed so dramatically in 1929, the industrial (i.e., manufacturing-based) economy was tossed on its head. Although labor was plentiful—there were certainly enough unemployed people eager for jobs—capital so completely dried up that there was no money to buy raw materials to make into finished products, even if there were sufficient funds to hire necessary workers. Of course, without jobs—and a full one-third of the U.S. population was unemployed—no one could afford to buy the products anyway. As a result, industrial production and the GDP sank successively lower over the next 4 years. It took more than 20 years—and World War II—before things got back on track economically.

In contrast, in 1987, when there was a serious global stock market crash, the consequences were extraordinarily mild by comparison. True, eventually a real recession hit—but not until 1990, and even then, total unemployment never rose above 7 percent. Part of the reason for this shortened recovery period was the reliance on information rather than land, labor, and particularly capital to generate wealth. Even though significant capital was lost in the market crash, the new focus on information provided an out, a way for companies to create new wealth without having to seek new capital to purchase new land/equipment and hire new labor. Information-based change can now dominate and drive success in this economy more than it ever has before—turning it into a true digital economy.

Getting a Handle on the Digital Economy

Okay—so we've attempted to provide you with a theoretical overview of the digital economy, especially as it compares with past economic models. However, giving you a practical notion of what the digital economy really smells, tastes, and feels like—especially with regard to how it will impact *your* business—is going to be a much more complex task. (As George Bernard Shaw once wittily said, "If all economists were laid end to end, they would not reach a conclusion.")

The digital economy is a weird, wild place. Much of what you have learned and practiced successfully—perhaps even marvelously successfully—in the past will no longer fly. Times have changed. Perhaps more disconcertingly, they will continue to change—and more quickly than most of us feel comfortable with. You've probably heard about how businesses in the early 1990s needed to think in terms of "Internet years," meaning that the technological advances made within a single calendar year outpaced progress that formerly took a full seven years. Get used to that sort of pace, because "digital years" will speed by even more quickly than Internet years. *That* we're sure of, even when there's so much else up for grabs.

The New Brat on the Block—The Empowered Consumer

Already, some companies have ruined it for the others. They went and built products that their customers actually wanted, delivered them when their customers wanted them, to the place their customers needed them, and even provided great after-sales service and support. Now, consumers are spoiled. They expect this treatment from everyone.

Here's an example.

A decade ago, if you needed new bathroom towels, you'd probably head over to the local department store (Macy's, Foley's, or Nordstrom's, depending on what part of the country you lived in). When one of those mega-super-bedroom-bathroom-closet-and-everything-else warehouse stores opened its doors in your area—these are called "category killers," by the way, for obvious reasons—you probably switched allegiance because of the much broader selection and lower prices you found there. Although, theoretically, there'd be hundreds of towels of varying quality, brand, and color for sale, you'd find they were often out of stock on the very ones you wanted. Therefore, you'd either take your second choice, or place an order and wait. True, it was still better than the department store, but barely.

Now, even these category killer stores are facing killer competition. That's because a 25-year-old kid from Missoula, Montana, opened his BuyThisStuff.com cyberstore last year. He offers just about every sort of thing you could ever need for your household. The prices are guaranteed to be at least 10 percent less than any superstore. Anything you order is delivered anywhere you want by the next morning (or whenever *you* choose to have it delivered). Best of all, if a product is listed on the BuyThisStuff web site, it's available; otherwise, it wouldn't be listed. Of course, you can special order anything you like. Just ask.

Within six months, BuyThisStuff had a market capitalization of $3 billion. Of course, it hasn't actually made a profit—yet. As it expands, however, from selling household goods to selling books, automotive products, groceries, and online banking services . . . (you get the idea), the market valuation will continue to climb.

Call BuyThisStuff an online retailer, an information aggregator, a consumer demand fulfiller, or a portal . . . whatever. What's more important is to see how the ability to effectively analyze and manipulate information is key to its success. The correct term is *knowledge management;* what it means is that BuyThisStuff knows how to use the latest information technology to collect, analyze, disseminate, and transform raw data into the stuff that great business decisions are made of.

BuyThisStuff knows what customers want (by performing in-depth market research based on actual online buying patterns). BuyThisStuff knows what's available, and at precisely what cost (by tapping into the inventory databases of product manufacturers). BuyThisStuff has no need to build or maintain costly physical warehouses or fleets of delivery trucks, or to employ armies of fulfillment personnel—it merely sends an electronic order to its manufacturing and transportation partners, who do all the dirty work. Most important, BuyThisStuff keeps adding to its store of information and, therefore, knowledge. Its customer databases contain everything from individual consumers' preferences for brands of toilet paper, to the time of day when a particular customer is likely to make a purchase, exponentially multiplied each fiscal quarter—whatever it takes to give the consumer *precisely* what he or she wants.

The Customer Is Always Impatient (and Right, of Course)

Of course, this example of BuyThisStuff is fictional, but just barely. It's certainly a sign of things to come. Look at Amazon.com (everyone's favorite Internet rags-to-riches story). The point: In the digital economy, the balance of power in commerce shifts inexorably to the consumer.

In the industrial economy, consumers actually had very little direct power over what goods were available. Certainly they voted with their dollars (or other relevant currency) as to what sorts of products they preferred. They bought black shoes, not red polka-dotted ones. They tended to purchase white eggs rather than brown ones. They sought solace in trusted brands when choices were limited and the real product differences were unknown.

The companies who could best anticipate what customers actually wanted did best, of course. In the end, however, it was the manufacturers themselves who had to make the hard decisions: what sorts of consumer needs they would attempt to meet; what markets they would serve; what products, and variations on products, they would offer; and what prices they would charge.

By necessity, being a consumer in the industrial era meant accepting limited choices and making frequent compromises. For instance, only the very rich could afford to have clothes custom-made to their exact measurements; the middle and lower classes needed to accept ready-made shirts, trousers, and sweaters—even when they weren't a perfect fit, or the right color, or the most desirable style. The manufacturers had the power to create; the consumer could only buy or not buy.

Information technology has shifted this balance of power, by putting unprecedented choice in the hands of the consumer. No longer can companies count on unilateral product development strategies or broad-based research to capture market share.

The consumer is making the decisions today, and he's making them based on the new buzzword in management: value. Value in the eyes of the consumer is what successful companies of the digital economy will deliver. The most obvious example of this can be seen in the disintermediation of the retail channel. Where consumers see little value being generated from the retailer and where they are comfortable using the Internet, retailers are in trouble. In the same way, products and services that don't provide value are being squeezed out. Generic or store-branded products are selling well, not because people are cheap, but because they realize there is marginal value in the brand when the stuff in the box comes from the same plant as the store brand.

How does the consumer of the digital economy assess value? There are the traditional value propositions of quality, price, and brand. These don't go away, but they have evolved and take on new meaning and significance in the digital economy. There are also new value propositions, such as the amount of time a product or service takes or gives (time-value). Consumers want to be able to use a product for many different uses, to customize it by changing its digital *content* as desired. For example, a consumer wants to buy a song (content), not a compact disc (container). They want to watch a movie (content), not a television (container). They want to play a game (software content), not a computer (container). In short, they want their containers to work with their content, their content with their containers, and they don't want to have to think about it. Companies that deliver products (be they content or container) that deliver this value will do well.

Therefore, if consumers are responding to old and new value propositions, how has this resulted in a power shift to the consumer? Companies are increasingly responding to this consumer sense of value through mass customization techniques (that is, making exactly what the consumer wants when they want it). Now that consumers have seen that PCs and even blue jeans (Levi's Personal Pair) can be made to order, they're pushing for this in the other products they buy. The companies that can deliver are the winners of tomorrow. Consumers are also informed. They're using the new power of the Internet to learn more about companies and their products and services than the companies perhaps ever wanted them to know. This informed consumer is using their new information to wield power over companies and demand value in their products and services. As indicated in Figure 1.2, the consumer's perception of value has changed dramatically since the 1950s.

FIGURE 1.2
Evolving consumer perception of value.

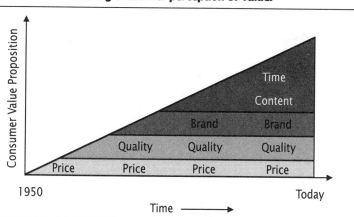

A new generation of informed consumers is beginning to enter the marketplace, and will do so in ever-increasing numbers over the next decade (a projected 88 million by the year 2000). Take a look at the average five-year-old (in the developed world), often more adept with mouse and keyboard than with pencil and paper, and you can readily see where consumer behavior is heading. Each year brings to the market a crop of increasingly savvy consumers who possess a degree of familiarity with information technology that most of today's adults did not acquire until much later in life. In his book *Growing Up Digital,*[1] Tapscott calls this the "generation lap." The younger generation cannot comprehend a world without computers and connectivity. They know how to find—and find out—what they want and can run circles around their elders when it comes to comparison shopping on the Internet.

This empowerment of the consumer has widespread repercussions. Think about it: To be competitive, companies must offer products and services that are specifically customized to meet the needs of individual consumers. They must be delivered in a timely fashion, and be reasonably priced given current standards of quality and reliability.

What does this imply? This implies that businesses in the digital age must employ product development processes that interact dynamically with customers; that they perform a more constant—and precise—monitoring of overall market trends; that cycle times get dramatically reduced; that raw materials are procured rapidly and in a cost-effective manner; and that distribution methods that suit the customer's, not the company's, convenience are put into place. In short, the free flow of information made possible in the digital age will put the customer at the center of business priorities and strategies.

To understand this more thoroughly, let's look at what drives consumer demand in the digital economy.

Pursuit of time. The world is a much wealthier place than it was in the early days of the industrial economy. With this wealth has come increased material expectations, as well as a shift from viewing work as an end in itself to seeing it as a stepping-stone to a better quality of life. Specifically, consumers are using their increased wealth to seek more—and different—ways to maximize their enjoyment of leisure time.

Pace of life. Life moves fast, and the pace is getting faster. We all know it; we acknowledge this in the way we rush through life—eating fast food; requiring elaborate planners to make it through a typical week; inventing mobile devices so we can continue working while in the car, at home, or on vacation. Because of the speed at which we move these days, there is an increased demand for products and services that allow us to work better, faster, and more productively. In short: Products or services that promise to save consumers *time*—even if they carry premium price tags—will be perceived as offering value.

Information assimilation. The digital age has given people easy access to more information than they can possibly digest. This has led to an enormous demand for tools that can help people assimilate information more quickly and make decisions more easily. (Try doing an Internet search on "maternity clothes," for example, and you will get more than 140,000 "hits," or possible relevant sites, to check out. What's an expectant mother to do?) Consumers are already hungry for products and services that help them sort through the vast reservoirs of information now becoming available.

Communication. With the universal availability of e-mail, digital telephones, pagers, and other emerging forms of electronic communication, consumers now have the unprecedented ability to provide immediate feedback to—and make more specific demands of—those businesses providing them with goods and services. Many consumers check out manufacturers' web sites as well as participate in relevant public Usenet online discussion groups before making a major purchase. They can electronically compare notes with other consumers, and communicate their questions, complaints, and frustrations directly to the manufacturer. Companies who ignore this grassroots form of consumer research do so at their peril.

A CASE IN POINT

Microsoft has shown itself to be a master of the technique of soliciting and incorporating customer comments. The company paid close attention to the Usenet newsgroups and online mailing lists devoted to Windows 95, tracked requests for clarification and technical support posted by customers on its web site, and after what was essentially a two-year debugging period for Windows 95, released Windows 98—incorporating many of the suggestions and fixing most of the bugs reported by consumers through electronic venues. Thus, digital communication technology allowed the company to turn potentially negative ongoing news as additional bugs were discovered (inevitable in an operating system as complex as Windows 95) into a way to actually improve the product, thereby increasing customer loyalty and tolerance for errors in the process.

Figure 1.3 illustrates the new interactive role that consumers will play in product design and quality improvement cycles in the digital economy.

FIGURE 1.3
Consumer role in the digital economy.

Consumer Role in the Digital Economy

- Consumer Perceives Value
- Value Drives Loyalty
- Consumer Buys In/ Commits
- Market Driven by Consumer Demand
- Market Responds with New Technology Development
- New Technology Drives New Products
- New Products/New Technology Drive the Need and Capability for New Infrastructure
- New Infrastructure Leveraged to Create New and Enhance Existing Offerings
- New Offerings Deliver Better and Faster Information and Functionality
- Faster and Better Information and Functionality Create Tangible Time Savings
- Time Savings and Information/Functionality Impact Consumer Perception of Value

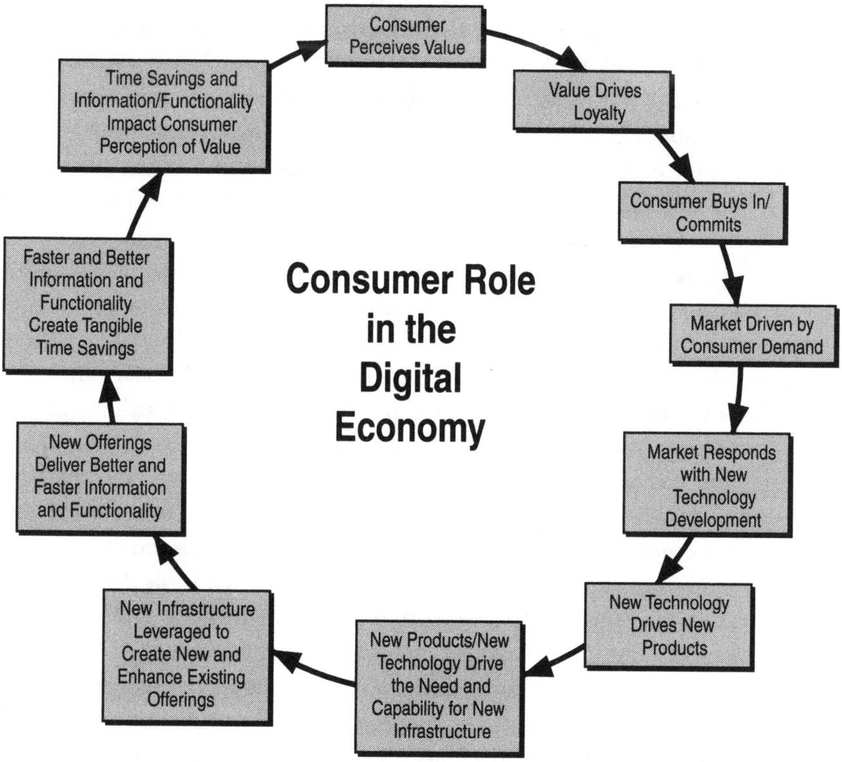

A CEO's Perspective

We spoke recently with the CEO of a leading maker of heavy-duty consumer equipment. His company is thriving: Revenue is up, profits are rising, and the current economic boom is favoring his business in unprecedented ways. Despite the rosy picture, this CEO is concerned about a technology-based trend that he believes will soon pose a significant threat to his company's business model.

What is this business-threatening trend? Simply, Internet shopping is rapidly becoming a way for consumers to bypass brick-and-mortar retailers to get the products they want at the lowest possible cost.

In this particular CEO's case, his primary "customer" *is* the retailer. That is, his company does not sell directly to consumers. It never has. Rather, the firm sells its manufactured products to retailers, who in turn provide consumers with product and after-market service. Consumers are beginning to clamor for a more direct relationship with his company. They're flooding his web site with e-mails asking for discounts if they buy direct from the factory. In addition, some of his competitors are already experimenting with direct sales to consumers via the Internet.

Now, this CEO is no fool, having been around the block more times than he can remember. He knows all the arguments in favor of eliminating the middleman from a distribution chain (efficiency of operations, cost reduction, and so forth). He feels, however, that in his case, this might be too simplistic a move.

In fact, this maverick CEO champions the contrary view that in the digital age he will actually need more, not less, help from other business partners to keep his customers happy.

True, at first glance, it might seem that much of the traditional value provided by his retailers—disseminating product information, calling in the actual orders, providing spare parts, and answering basic after-sales questions—could easily be replaced via the Web's more efficient information-sharing and transactional capabilities. He argues, however, that not all aspects of selling his company's big-ticket products can be accomplished by a remote on-line connection. After all, the products still have to be physically delivered to the consumers' homes. Also, someone must still provide after-sales service—both for routine maintenance and for emergency repairs.

Moreover, the increasing complexity of the products he sells complicates the matter. Today, each machine the company ships contains more computer technology than did a standard 1980s mainframe. The degree of digital integration that each machine involves has already required him to forge partnerships with an ever-widening array of diverse suppliers—each of whom has to successfully collaborate with all other suppliers if the end product is actually going to work. This supply web has vastly complicated postsales servicing. A single replacement part, for example, can originate with one of dozens of suppliers; the interaction of two computerized parts can obscure the diagnosis and repair of even a simple problem. Because the cost and ease of repairs have long been critical factors in determining success in the consumer appliance industry, this CEO was smart not to jettison his retailers too hastily.

In fact, this CEO is savvy enough to understand that although some middlemen (and middlewomen) in a traditional distribution chain might well be eliminated due to efficiencies of the digital age, *other* intermediaries (for lack of a better word) may be required to ensure that the customer is completely satisfied.

Redefining the Notion of Value

This executive, like all those who will survive in the digital economy, is learning to think differently about his company, its products, and its customers. He's no longer thinking in terms of distribution chains or supply chains; rather, he's thinking in terms of interlocking relationships that form a network, or value web, which has as its prime directive the goal of providing value to the customer—as the customer defines it.

The only way to do this successfully is to put yourself in your customer's place. Think about what they value most highly about your product or service. Once you've figured that out, ask yourself what you can do to enhance that value.

Obviously, it makes sense to deliver your product or service at the lowest possible cost. However, the interesting note is that you may end up charging more, not less, for your product or service after you throw in the additional value offered by your business partner(s). Your customers may line up and happily pay that extra cost. It depends on the *value* of what you (and your partners) are offering.

Of course, this flies in the face of conventional wisdom that says the age of the intermediary, or middle agent, is past. In fact, one of the goals of this book is to show you where intermediaries are indeed irrelevant—and where they are absolutely required. These new information-based intermediaries—*infomediaries*—will be discussed in detail in Chapter 6.

There are, of course, real competitive advantages to the cost-cutting tactics being implemented by leading mass-market retailers. Their strategy is a time-honored one: Go directly to the source for basic products or raw materials. Negotiate volume prices that effectively undercut traditional distributors and wholesalers. With these lower-than-wholesale prices, put smaller (and less influential) retail competitors out of business. Finally, tighten the supply-and-distribution chain until it is as tight as a drum. Look no further than Wal-Mart and Costco to see how this is done.

CEOs are beginning to understand, however, that cost containment, or operational efficiency, is not the only answer. Been there, done that. What was the business process reengineering (BPR) management craze of the 1990s but a period of intense (and much needed) focus on cost cutting throughout the value chain? Companies that successfully implemented BPR initiatives were doing the right thing—they were taking the first step toward successfully competing in the digital economy. However, it *was* just a first step. It is absolutely imperative for CEOs to realize that they cannot "save their way to prosperity."

As is evident in Figure 1.4, this puts executives at a critical crossroad. The decisions they make today will significantly impact their competitive position in the digital economy.

The good news is that they seem to be catching on. In A. T. Kearney's 1998 survey of CEO attitudes, only 10 percent said cost cutting was a "key execu-

FIGURE 1.4
Current choices faced by executives in the digital economy.

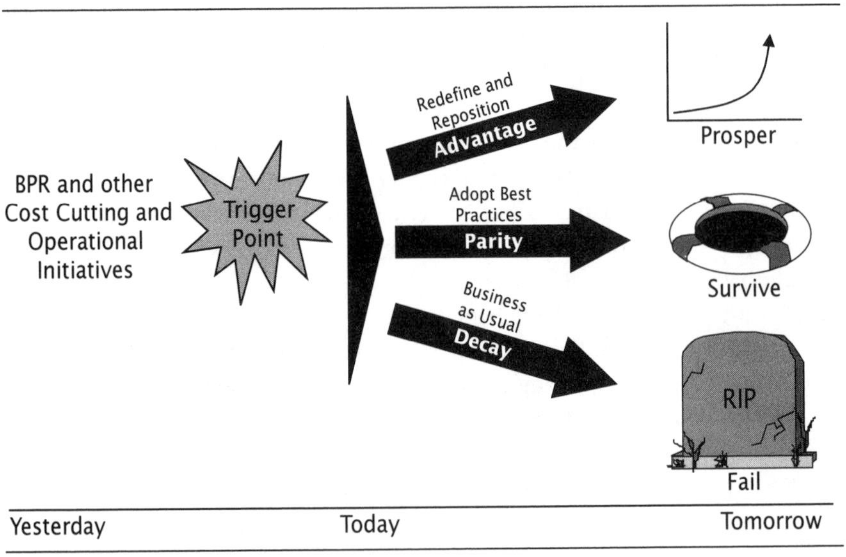

| Yesterday | Today | Tomorrow |

tive issue," down from 27 percent in 1996. Therefore, what is their new agenda? Fortunately for them (we believe), they seem to be turning attention and energy toward revenue-generating activities.

Why the Rules Have Changed So Dramatically

We believe that one of the biggest barriers to comprehending the potential impact of the digital economy is the fact that most managers (and economists) are still focused on *cost* as the principal metric of value.

Put this a different way: It is time for business leaders to abandon an "accountant mentality" in favor of a more strategic way of thinking. When you do that, you will discover the following truths:

In the digital economy, technology is the only *economic commodity that is guaranteed to cost less as time passes.* Labor, capital, land, technology—all these economic necessities have costs associated with them. Management has traditionally focused on the cost of a particular item to gauge its long-term impact on profitability; over time, the cost of investing in additional land, labor, or equipment inevitably increases. (What you bought yesterday will cost incrementally more today, except occasional economic blips.) Only with technology purchases can you be sure of getting more bang for the buck tomorrow than today.

Because of productivity gains, technology investments result in higher-than-usual returns when compared with other corporate purchases. Although the initial cost of a new technology may be quite large, most companies see dramatic improvements in productivity that more than pay for the initial investment. Manufacturers, especially, are seeing the long-term financial benefits of using technology to slash cycle times, reduce inventories, and manage plant capacities more efficiently.

The digital economy provides a free channel of information distribution. The digital economy's strength comes not from the physical movement of goods and products, with their escalating cost structures and diminishing returns, but in the geometrically increasing returns from converging ideas, knowledge, and technological change. This is far different from traditional labor or capital in which the gain in economic leverage is constant—or even, occasionally, negative. That's why Intuit has chosen to virtually give away a product like Quicken™ (a personal financial planning and tax assistance application, now preinstalled on many PCs)—to create a market. Technology's "unit cost of production" may actually approach zero, even as product revenues as a whole rise to millions, or even billions, of dollars. When you factor in the multiplier effects of transaction-based pricing, add-on services, and plug-in options, you see many ways to derive value from the "free asset"—the software base.

The digital economy eradicates many traditional barriers to entering new markets. Perhaps most important, the digital economy also leaves in the dust a central tenet of contemporary management science: that of erecting as many barriers as possible to keep competitors out of a given market. Such barriers include size (building such massive economies of scale that your prices can't be beat), geographic positioning (you've garnered the prime—or only—real estate appropriate to reach target consumers), and even legal or political coups (your territory is protected by a franchise agreement, regulation, or even legislation).

In the emerging digital economy, these barriers are providing less and less protection for companies. Newcomer Bloomberg changed the way investment news was disseminated within the securities industry; tiny Nucor Corporation (a steel manufacturer) challenged industry giants and forever changed the face of steel production; Sears countered Wal-Mart's mighty inventory-and-distribution machine by performing sophisticated analyses of customer behavior. Key players in industries ranging from transportation to health care have seen formidable new competitors arise with astonishing speed and force, and all because of digital technology.

That some companies rise and others fall is not new. What *is* new is the speed with which it now occurs—and how, in the digital age, it will be impossible for anyone to build a lasting barrier.

Perhaps most significantly, in each of these cases, the technology employed to gain competitive advantage was widely available to others. Bloomberg, Nucor, and Sears did not succeed by putting proprietary technology barriers in place. They succeeded because they creatively figured out precisely what their customers would value, and delivered it with such speed that competitors had barely a chance to blink.

A SHIFT IN ATTITUDE: SENIOR EXECUTIVES AND INFORMATION TECHNOLOGY

The principal finding from the A. T. Kearney 1998 survey of 230 CEOs: Information technology (IT) decisions are now an integral part of the corporate strategy, and technology decisions are now routinely made at the boardroom level, not by functional IT managers.

One CEO called technology "essential [to my business] in every way."[2] Proclaimed a member of the board of a multinational chemical behemoth: "[Technology is your company's] birthright. . . . Unless you use it in a way that aligns with business success, you will cease being a player." Another CEO discussed the rapid and tangible return on his technological investments: "Technology has helped my company grow faster . . . improve productivity . . . [all the while costing very little] and requiring very little manpower."

Nine out of 10 of these global companies say their technological investment is as important, if not more so, than other capital investments in helping them reach their strategic goals. They also believe their technological investments "transform customer relationships and shorten product-cycle time," as well as foster the creation of new revenue opportunities, products, processes, and organizational structures.

At a recent summit on implementing technology in the consumer products retailing industry, senior executives said they were tired of hearing glowing stories of the "nice things that happen when you invest in IT." Instead, they said they needed help understanding how technology was impacting their businesses, and expressed their concern that technology was moving so swiftly that it would forever remain beyond their comprehension.

The Changing Role of Business Leaders

The fact that technological change now drives the economy may catch many corporate leaders by surprise. They can see some signs that technology is important, perhaps even essential, to business success. However, they may not understand how completely the rules are changed. (The fact that some of the most renowned management gurus—from Alfred Chandler to Peter Drucker to Michael Porter—base their opinions on theories from the industrial economy, which has its roots in the nineteenth century, makes this message even harder to hear.)

In conference after conference, survey after survey, we hear senior executives admit that they don't know how to properly evaluate the true value of so much technological innovation. They don't know how to realistically assess the extent to which each change could impact their organization, their industry, their way of doing business. (Even the CEO of newly resurrected IBM found it necessary to publicly assure the world that in the future, *nothing* would be taken for granted.)

This book poses three fundamental questions that senior corporate leaders must be prepared to answer as they lead their companies into the digital economy:

1. *How do we understand what the consumer—our customer—truly values?* We've all heard the truism "time is money." As it turns out, time is worth a great deal of money in the digital economy. Numerous surveys prove

the point that people feel harried and rushed, and that they have much less free time than they had in the past. This is a tremendous opportunity. By providing consumers with goods and services that alleviate these loudly vocalized time constraints, businesses are assured of providing true value. (In addition, consider that consumers who claim to be most pressed for time are also those with the highest consumption patterns. Thus, what we call time-value goods and services are likely to command premium prices.)

Many companies already have begun to exploit this concept of time value. Mobil has introduced the Speedpass to save the consumer tedious time at the gas pump; American Airlines has introduced a no-wait-in-line-direct-board procedure for its most valued customers—all they have to do is scan their frequent flyer card at the gate.

In addition to time value, we will increasingly see another measure of economic value that makes a distinction between the container and content aspects of products and services. Containers are the physical things people buy (like cars or televisions). Content, on the other hand, is additional value provided, usually (but not always) in digital form. If you buy a car, for example, you have purchased a container to which you can add additional value by purchasing content, consisting of GM's OnStar satellite-based security system. Plus, we're all infinitely cognizant of the fact that purchasing a television (a container) without taking care to make sure content is available (whether through traditional broadcasts, cable, or satellite) would be foolish indeed.

As the digital economy matures, more consumer products will exude these container-plus-content characteristics. The job of business executives, therefore, is to decide how their various products fit into this paradigm—and what sorts of alliances they should be making with other businesses to create profitable container-and-content combinations.

2. *How will the digital economy change my relationships with vendors and customers?* Perhaps the most visibly dramatic effect of the digital economy is how it will undermine traditional ways of doing business—and force executives to create new, innovative transactional models. For example, Chrysler's development of a cost-effective industry *keiretsu* with its suppliers is built on sophisticated Internet-based communication. Sara Lee's decision to contract with outside firms for all-important textile and yarn manufacturing activities was made possible by an extranet that gave Sara Lee the ability to monitor quality and maintain its own high standards even for processes completed outside its corporate walls. Likewise, Heinz, the venerable tomato-product manufacturer, uses advanced information technology to outsource key aspects of product development while still monitoring quality and maintaining tight control over costs and schedules.

In short, the digital economy enables a new kind of business model that in turn requires new kinds of business relationships. Virtually all companies in the digital economy will find themselves a part of at least one extended network of complex, interrelated alliances.

Understanding the value derived from relationships, and possessing the right skills and knowledge to effectively *manage* those relationships, will be critical to achieving success in the digital economy.

3. *What will be the impact of the digital economy on my company's culture and organizational structure?* The new digital economy will demand organizations that are nimble enough to quickly adapt to ever changing consumer demands. For example, your company needs to be flexible enough to expand during times of emerging opportunities; conversely, you should be able to shrink if that is more cost-effective—or provides greater value to your customer—to outsource some aspect of creating or distributing your product to a business partner.

What This Book Is About

What this book attempts to do is provide a logical, step-by-step framework that will help senior executives lead their companies into the brave new world of the digital economy (see Figure 1.5).

Above all, this is a book about how to *win* in the digital marketplace—how to transform your products or services, your organizational culture, even your entire industry as you keep pace with the revolutionary changes taking place in society at large.

Part 2 explores how you may not only survive, but thrive, when facing consumers empowered by rapid advances in technology. This new generation of informed and intelligent consumers is demanding products that are more personal and more aligned with their particular needs—and that give them the most precious commodity of all: time.

Part 3 provides the next piece of the puzzle for mastering the digital marketplace by giving you a glimpse at a new kind of business model. This *digital value network,* or DVN, comprises a virtual community of business partners and customers who are electronically linked in such a way that the goals and needs of each participant are efficiently and speedily satisfied. Most important, the DVN model will help senior executives identify how their organizations can add value in the complex web of relationships making up the new marketplace.

The next chapters are our written response to the enormous frustration we've witnessed over the years as nontechnical senior managers try to grap-

FIGURE 1.5
The dilemma faced by senior executives.

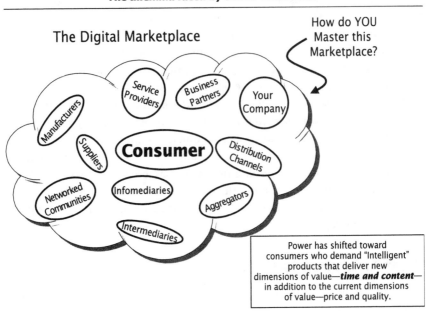

ple with the implications of the digital revolution. (One executive quipped that our recipe for getting into digital shape was similar to tempting a sedentary 400-pound man with a $1-million prize if he completed the Boston Marathon.) Thus, Part 4 is our attempt to motivate that 400-pound man to start exercising, safely, so that he can *eventually* cross that finish line. In short, you can't hope to begin designing and producing "intelligent" products, nor completely restructure the way your industry works by implementing a DVN, unless you have an organization that is nimble, flexible, modular, and value-driven. We call this a—surprise—*value-based organization* (VBO) and provide a framework to help you create it.

Part 5 pulls together all these concepts in a "dramatization" of one fictional CEO who successfully transformed her company into the lean, mean, flexible machine it needed to be to master the digital marketplace.

In Part 6, we present three case studies that prove the public sector is not immune to these dramatic forces. We examine the effects of digitization on education, health care, and the IRS. We also examine the larger social implications of rapid technical innovation, focusing especially on the effect that emerging information technologies will have on traditional law, public policy, and personal privacy—and how the role of government itself is likely to be transformed as we progress deeper into the digital economy.

The Case for a New Way of Thinking

It's said that a seasoned farmer can sniff the air and predict approaching rain, that he or she can predict crop yield by tasting the soil or that there are people who have a special intuitive talent for figuring out exactly where you should drill your well. You may have even personally had a "gut feeling" about something and taken action—even though you had no logical basis to do so.

We see this happening. We see experienced CEOs becoming wary. Savvy business executives in a broad range of industries tell us they can feel—that they *know*—big changes are coming. This is not based on data, or fact, or logical forecasts. Change of the type we're talking about defies forecasts, because forecasts are based on traditional experiences and expectations. Visionary CEOs sense this, and they are looking for help making the leap to paradigms that haven't yet been imagined, much less created.

We hope this book will help. This is our vision of what the promised digital land is likely to look like; this is our advice on how to best prepare for it. The path is still untread by human feet, however; many more books will need to be written once that has occurred.

This book is our opening salvo in a campaign to enable executives to succeed in the digital economy. A difficult goal, given that many corporate leaders have yet to recognize that such a thing even exists.

For those of you who *do* recognize what lies ahead, you may have to make radical adjustments in the current way you do business. For others, you will need to stop what you are doing—immediately—and begin anew.

A successful strategy is not about trying to maintain the status quo, even if that were possible. ("If we want everything to remain as it is, it will be necessary for everything to change," wrote Italian author Giuseppe Tomasi Di Lampedusa.) A successful strategy is not about creating barriers to entry for would-be competitors. It's not about cutting costs to maintain a marginal price advantage. It *is* about coming up with new ideas, about thinking creatively, about innovative actions that take nothing for granted.

In summary, as we enter the digital economy, we need to leave behind our twentieth-century logic and management tools and begin developing ones that will work in the twenty-first century, where nothing is sacred, nothing is given, and technology will continue to evolve beyond anything we can imagine today.

PART
TWO

Intelligent Products

2

The Value of Time

"The world is so fast that there are days when the person who says it can't be done is interrupted by the person who is doing it."

—*Anon.*

A Cautionary Tale

For generations, the *Encyclopedia Britannica* was the prime repository of knowledge that had been collected in the Western world. Schools, libraries, and, of course, any parents who could afford it, paid from $1,500 to $2,200 to purchase a single set of the distinguished multivolume encyclopedia. Owned by a trust controlled by the University of Chicago, the Encyclopaedia Britannica Company had been a highly respected and profitable business since its origin in 1768. Its brand name, *Britannica,* was synonymous with integrity, prestige, and scholarly excellence. However, in 1990, the company slammed into a brick wall.

On the surface, nothing had changed. Britannica was still producing the same comprehensive, accurate, and exceedingly high-quality product it always had. It hadn't dramatically increased its prices. The U.S. economy was healthy; the publishing industry seemed to be on track. Yet, within the span of just seven short years, the venerable Britannica experienced difficulties that challenged its very existence.

There were two key reasons for Britannica's precipitous plunge from prosperity. First, despite successfully operating for more than 200 years, Britannica had never bothered to figure out precisely what its customers valued about its product. (Odd, but true.) Second, Britannica failed because it grossly underestimated the dramatic effects that new digital technologies would have on its industry.

The instrument of Britannica's near-downfall was a product called Encarta: a digital encyclopedia published by Microsoft on CD-ROM. Consumers were thus given the choice between a $50 portable disk that could be carried from place to place, and which yielded instantaneous search results on any topic—or a $1,500 pile of books that were not even remotely transportable, and which required sifting through thousands of pages (and multiple volumes) to find desired information. Even more disastrously, although Encarta sported a retail price tag of just $50, many consumers got it free (or for a nominal fee) when purchasing a home computer or CD-ROM drive. Consumers made the obvious decision. Between 1990 and 1997, Britannica sales plummeted nearly 50 percent.[1]

Imagine the consternation in Britannica's executive suite. The company couldn't possibly drop its prices to Encarta's. After all, it cost between $200 and $300 to print, bind, and distribute a single set of the encyclopedia. In addition, it wasn't as though Microsoft was taking an enormous loss on Encarta to "buy" encyclopedia market share: It cost only $1.50 to replicate each Encarta CD-ROM.

Those were just comparative *production* costs. Britannica's ongoing expenses for continuing to develop and update the contents of its encyclopedia, although only 5 percent of its total costs, were still greater than Microsoft's. How could that be? Simply this: Microsoft had made the smart decision to "buy rather than build," and licensed Encarta's content from Britannica competitor Funk and Wagnall's for a much lower price than it would have cost to develop it in Redmond. All the illustrations, video, and audio clips that made Encarta such an appealingly multimedia experience were simply taken from the public domain. That's right—they were free.

Still, Britannica's single largest expense for getting its encyclopedias to market involved neither production- nor content-development activities. Its largest costs were those built into its distribution chain, which had traditionally used a massive direct salesforce to get printed volumes out the door and onto customers' bookshelves. (Microsoft, on the other hand, through alliances with hardware vendors, created a distribution channel in which Encarta practically walked out of retailers' doors in the boxes that contained new computers and peripherals.)

Britannica tried to fight back; however, it continued to demonstrate its appalling misunderstanding of what was really going on in the market. Sure, in 1994 it created a CD-ROM encyclopedia of its own. However, in a misguided attempt to try and salvage as much of the good old days as possible, Britannica tried to market the CD-ROM version as an "accessory" to its printed product. If you bought a complete set of its bound volumes, you received the CD-ROM version for free. If, on the other hand, you wanted to buy the CD-ROM version alone, it would cost you a whopping $1,000. In addition, you had to buy either product via existing sales channels. In short, Britannica thought it could compete in the new digital marketplace by acting in ways that protected its traditional products and ways of doing business. Clearly, the company still didn't get it.

It wasn't until the University of Chicago sold Britannica in 1996 that a $115 Britannica CD-ROM appeared on the market. Yes, it was still more than twice as expensive as Encarta. Given the sterling reputation of the Britannica brand, however, such an action might have saved the situation—at least temporarily—if taken sooner.

Britannica management's biggest mistake? They didn't understand what they were selling. Perhaps understandably, they saw their chief product as an encyclopedia, or physical set of books, that contained information. Understandably, they felt that the quality of this information, in terms of accuracy, comprehensiveness, and presentation, was what the customer valued in their product. What they missed, however, was that the bulk of their consumers—middle-class families—put down their money not to purchase the best possible collection of information, but to fulfill an emotional desire: that of doing the right thing for their children. As long as Microsoft could convince such people that they were providing decent educational tools for the homework, extracurricular, or just general curiosity needs of their kids, Encarta could easily outsell Britannica. After all, nobody who could get that feeling for $50, or less, would rationally pay $1,500 for it.

The effects that technology had on the dynamics of the encyclopedia industry were also important, because, of course, consumers immediately saw the very real (and very attractive) practical advantages of CD-ROM-based reference material. As digital information was dramatically easier to search through, and could be more cheaply and readily kept up-to-date, it was replacing print in all sorts of research-oriented publishing niches (not just encyclopedias). This wasn't just a fad. Technologically savvy consumers had left behind a company that had refused to acknowledge a true sea change in the industry that it had practically owned for more than 200 years.

New Consumer Values Emerging

The story of Britannica is not a unique one in the emerging digital market-place. Increasingly, traditional notions of consumer needs and behavior will no longer suffice. Companies need to consider—and reconsider—exactly what their customers *value* about their products and services. In addition, they have to keep a close eye on how technology is transforming their particular industry.

True, quality and price remain important. Brand names still attract consumer loyalty and confer status (witness the plethora of corporate logos on everything from baby clothing to sportswear to pickup trucks); however, two new arbiters of value—what we call *time value* and *content value*—have emerged as increasingly important drivers in consumer purchasing decisions as the digital age progresses.

Time value. Time has emerged as the most valuable commodity anyone can sell. The increased workload and stress levels experienced by most people today are evoking a newfound awareness of the value of discretionary time. This awareness translates into a desire to do things in the fastest way possible, and an intolerance of what is perceived as wasting time. One need only look at the tremendous increase over the past 10 or 20 years in the number of two-income families to appreciate how precious discretionary time has become. (Even the time available to the younger generation outside of attending school and daily chores has dropped by 10 percent since 1981, according to a November 10, 1998, report on CNN.) Add to this technology's propensity to do more things faster, and you understand why consumers expect ever-increasing speed and time savings in both products and services.

Content value. Microwave ovens that sense how long it takes to reheat last night's leftovers and clothes dryers that can tell when a load of laundry is dry enough, but not so dry as to damage fibers, are examples of the kinds of reasoning power that consumers already take for granted. The opportunity that digital technology offers to embed intelligence in products of every description is limited only by the imagination of those who are responsible for product development. In the paradigm of the digital economy, manufactured objects are containers; their content—the intelligence put into them—is often what differentiates them.

In the subsequent sections, we will discuss these new arbiters of consumer value as they relate to more traditional notions, all within the context of the digital economy. We'll also identify steps *you* can take to ensure digital preparedness for your business.

Time Value

You've heard the phrase "time equals money." When it comes to business operations, you probably have a fairly sophisticated understanding of why that has always been the case.

Time Value in Business Operations

The equation of time and money is relatively new to consumers, although businesses have always recognized it. In the Industrial Economy, the concept of time savings in business operations was driven by the push for cost reduction and improved efficiency. In the digital economy, today's consumer is demanding not only that time savings be incorporated into products and services, but also that these products and services be delivered as quickly as possible. Time consciousness has had a ripple effect through the entire value chain. Time savings across a broad variety of business operations is now seen as a primary means to improve profits by *creating value*. Reducing the time it takes to conduct business transactions allows more work to be done, decreases time to market, allows speedy reaction to market changes, reduces inventories, and increases overall productivity. For example, a business that cuts overall manufacturing time can react more speedily to changes in consumer requirements as well as reduce expensive inventories of finished goods.

Time value was introduced as a formal engineering concept as early as 1903, when Frederick W. Taylor presented his paper on the study of production operations at a meeting of the American Society of Mechanical Engineers. In 1912, Frank B. Gilbreth and Lillian Gilbreth added the concept of studying motion by taking moving pictures of workers' actions. Thus was born the field of time-and-motion study engineering, more recently called process engineering. (Is this beginning to sound familiar?)

Key to this is information technology. We increasingly see ways in which time is saved (and value created) because of advances in technology, particularly communications technologies. For example, businesses now commonly use the Internet to transact electronic commerce in which a product or service is created, configured, marketed, sold, delivered, and supported much faster than anyone would previously have dreamed possible.

GE Lighting provides a great example of this. After deciding that its existing way of buying materials from suppliers (its procurement system) took too much time, GE developed a technology-based system called TPN Post that greatly accelerated everything about the process. GE employees now issue requests for quotes (RFQs), which are processed and sent to the relevant suppliers within two hours. Suppliers make their bids electronically, which means they can be processed on the day of receipt. This has resulted in tremendous time savings for everyone involved.[2]

In his book, *Competing Against Time: How Time-Based Competition is Reshaping Global Markets,* George Stalk emphasizes the importance of saving time in business operations, and he asserts that this will result in reduced costs, better customer service, reduced inventories, and even enhanced innovation. Companies are very aware of the value of driving time delays out of their operations, and have employed several techniques (such as kanban, JIT, and BPR) to make this happen. More recently, with digitization and IT taking the business world by storm, the process of driving time out of the system has been supercharged.

However, it is important to recognize that the concept of time savings does not apply solely to business operations. The ultimate manifestation of the time-value paradigm is in the product or service that the end consumer uses. There is no doubt that getting the offering into the hands of the consumer as quickly and efficiently as possible is of value; however, getting this offering to perform its operation as quickly as possible is equally important to the consumer. The intent of the next section is to address the concept of time savings from an end-consumer perspective, and to understand how product offerings have leveraged this concept into creating consumer value.

Consumer Perception of Time Value

In a global economy in which consumer buying power is increasing and a technological environment in which speed seems to feed on itself, the aphorism "time is money" takes on a whole new meaning. Add the fact that most people today feel they have less free time than they did in the past, and it's easy to see why consumers will beat a path to the door of any company that can sell them additional time along with whatever product or service the company offers.

Look at how 3M profiles anyone who visits its web site, carefully keeping track of what they look at as well as what they actually order. Return customers are only shown the 15 or 20 products they are likely to be interested in given their past behavior; they don't need to sort through all 15,000 products posted on the web site (although, of course, they can always ask to see more). Customers say that this time-saving process is valuable in itself, and they choose 3M products over those of competitors, even when the products themselves are otherwise indistinguishable.

Peapod provides another good example. A web-based grocery delivery service, Peapod takes consumer orders over the Internet and delivers them to the customer's door or office at a selected time. The overall point of the Peapod service is, of course, to save consumer time (the time spent driving to the grocery store, putting items in a cart, standing in the checkout line, and so forth), and Peapod, recognizing this, keeps pushing the envelope further. When a customer logs onto the Peapod web site, the software automatically provides him or her with a list of items they purchased in the past, thus leading to even more time savings on the consumer's part. Recent research is proving just how smart companies like Peapod and 3M are with these kinds of strategies. A 1997 study conducted by the Families and Work Institute on a U.S. population sample turned up some interesting facts on the time demands of modern life:[3]

- Jobs have become more demanding, time-consuming, and hectic, making it increasingly difficult to achieve a balance between work and personal life. Between 1977 and 1997, the average work week for all employees working more than 20 hours per week increased 3.5 hours to 47.1 hours.

- The proportion of employees living in dual-earner families increased from 66 percent to 78 percent in the same period. Consequently, the pooled time available for child care and household work decreased.

- Employed married men and women have less time for themselves today than their counterparts did 20 years ago—54 and 42 minutes less per workday, respectively.

Another survey, conducted by Kurt Salmon Associates, corroborated these findings:[4]

- Fifty-six percent of consumers agreed they had far less leisure time than they used to have.

- Almost 40 percent of consumers responded that if given a choice between more time or more money, they would choose time.

- Consumers are spending less time on shopping and cooking in an attempt to create more leisure time for themselves.

As Figure 2.1 implies, people are willing to trade off money for leisure (or discretionary) time. Kenneth Hey and Peter Moore sum up this trend suc-

FIGURE 2.1
The reduction of consumer "free" time.

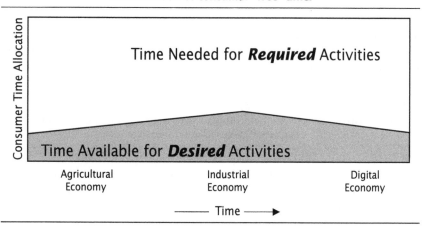

cinctly in their 1998 book, *The Caterpillar Doesn't Know,* as follows:" [Beginning in 1990, although] many consumers had plenty of money, they had less and less time to spend it. . . . Rather than accumulate greater wealth, individuals started to think about preserving time, even if that meant having less money to spend."[5]

This endemic lack of time has caused us to attempt to make optimal use of the discretionary time we *do* have, often by performing multiple activities concurrently. We take our children with us when performing our Saturday errands to have time with them while accomplishing necessary chores. This process, referred to as *time deepening,* is an attempt to cope with the *time famine* that today's environment has brought about.[6]

Figure 2.1 illustrates the distribution of time through the various economies. In the agricultural economy, work hours were long and hard, had little mechanical support, and left little time for discretionary purposes. With the industrial economy came a standardization of work hours and shifts, as well as the formation of unions to protect the workers' interests. All of this led to a stabilization of work-versus-leisure hours.

In the digital economy of today we are essentially back to the long hours of the agricultural economy. We're also seeing the same blurring of lines between our discretionary time (what we do because we want to) and the time required to complete chores—both personal and professional. On this point, the Robinson and Godbey study uncovered an interesting fact: The amount of discretionary time consumers have has actually gone *up* over the years. Yet, something about the nature and intensity of life in the digital age has created a *perception* of time famine. While this study seems to be in opposition to having less time, for the person doing the perceiving, perception is reality.

This perception is also driven by the fact that discretionary time has become more fragmented throughout the workweek. We tend to spend our weekends (the traditional uninterrupted block of discretionary time) taking care of chores, errands, and other personal responsibilities. Therefore, we never have a sense that we are truly "off"—the way previous generations did when the factory bell rang at the end of the week's shift.

Whatever the reason, companies wishing to attract the business of today's consumers must acknowledge this perception of time famine. More than that, they need to understand how great an opportunity this perception truly is. Consumers that have the highest demand for time are almost invariably those with the greatest amount of money available for discretionary spending. In the industrial economy, price and quality were drivers of customer segmentation, and time value was not considered an important factor in customer choice and behavior. In the future, all offerings will incorporate some level of digitization and time savings to remain competitive, and therefore time value will not be a key differentiator forever. *Now is the time* that companies need to focus on the consumer segments that place a definitive value on time, and those segments that are willing to pay a price premium over other products to obtain additional time. For example, given the limited PC penetration in the consumer market (approximately 35 percent of households have computers with modems as of June 1998), many financial institutions do not view online banking and self-service financial services as a real threat. However, what they do not realize is that the consumers who value these services represent the institutions' most profitable consumers. Not satisfying these customers means that they will take their money and go elsewhere.[7] Consequently, time-value-oriented goods and services will command a premium in the market. Companies that fail to incorporate the time-value proposition into their products or services face commoditization of their products and risk being put at an extreme competitive disadvantage.

Of course, there will be people who, in response to time famine, take the seemingly logical step of doing less work. Mary Loverde, author of *Stop Screaming at the Microwave: How to Connect Your Disconnected Life,* a former self-admitted workaholic, is now an eloquent advocate of increasing leisure time through simplifying your life. Similarly, Jacob Needleman, philosopher and author of *Time and the Soul,* believes that we live in a society that is rich in things, but poor in time, and that we would be well advised to reverse our priorities.

Despite this advice, the fact still remains that there are activities that are not optional and, therefore, must be performed (people must continue washing their clothes, buying diapers for their babies, and filling up their cars' gas tanks). If you can figure out ways to bundle the precious commodity of time into products used to perform these sorts of routine (but mandatory) activities, you will find ready buyers. (Until more people buy into the concept of "life simplification," you will be able to bundle time into products and services that are not only not necessary, but even overtly frivolous.) The bottom line is that digital speed is infectious—once consumers are made aware of the conveniences and expediency of digital offerings, their expectations and enthusiasm rise exponentially. Digitization is poised to meet or exceed those expectations. Increasingly, the response to the question, "Why can't I have everything today?" is "You can."

We believe that *automatic execution* will eventually prove to be the single most important aspect of any product or service that purports to provide time value to consumers. What do we mean by automatic execution? Simply, this means that the consumer will not need to spend any time at all consuming a product or service (unless, of course, there is an intrinsic social or material value in consumption).

For example, getting your car repaired when the transmission starts to go is a necessary activity that contains little intrinsic enjoyment. Most of us would like this sort of service to be completed as quickly, and with as little of our own participation, as possible. Therefore, you could schedule the repair via the Internet, drop the car off in the morning on your way to work, be given a rental car for the day, and pick up your fixed car that evening on your way home, all without having to fill out forms in triplicate, or wait in line in a garage, or even hand over a credit card (that was done electronically). *Automatic execution*—doesn't it sound great?

Taking the concept further, this activity could be automated to the point of *zero consumer* interaction to make it even more appealing. For example, your favorite auto mechanic picks up your car using his or her own key (you've naturally entrusted this to them for such purposes) and returns the repaired car to your driveway before lunchtime. It's even been washed and waxed. If this sounds too good to be true, that's because there are challenges to this sort of interaction. (For starters, how can you provide this level of automation and yet retain the customer's loyalty? After all, zero interaction implies flying below the customer's radar, being virtually imperceptible, and brand loyalty is all about visibility.) We discuss how traditional models of brand loyalty have changed in the digital economy in Chapter 4.

A CASE IN POINT: MOBIL SPEEDPASS

Throughout Chapters 2, 3, and 4, we will illustrate how an innovative offering from Mobil Corporation used these new notions of what consumers really value to enhance customer loyalty and increase market share in an industry that historically has not been driven by brand-name recognition.

Founded in 1866, Mobil Corporation was an outgrowth of the breakup of John D. Rockefeller's Standard Oil Company. Mobil today is the world's fourth largest oil, gas, and petrochemicals company, with subsidiaries in over 140 countries worldwide. Exxon, the world's second largest oil company, has agreed to buy Mobil, creating Exxon Mobil and making the world's largest oil company. Mobil competes along the entire energy value chain, including exploration, production, refining, supply, distribution, and marketing. The company sells gasoline at 15,000 retail stations around the world, half of which are in the United States.

The Challenge

Gasoline retailing is a highly competitive business in which product differentiation is difficult, brand-name recognition is practically useless, and customer loyalty is fleeting. Even independent gas retailers quickly identify and respond to any significant strategic action taken by competitors—large or small. This is why street corners are filled with generic gasoline retailers who provide clean, well-lit, and conveniently located service stations selling reputable grades of gasoline. Also, this is why most offer a colocated convenience store, pay-at-the-pump payment option, a car wash facility, competitive prices, and sometimes even a loyalty program. Not much has been overlooked in the effort to acquire business. Retaining customers, however, is another matter entirely.

On most people's pleasure scales, filling up with gasoline ranks a hair above taking out the garbage. To many consumers, a gas station is a necessary evil: Making a transaction there requires an annoying expenditure of time and money, and it is done solely to avoid the penalty of immobility. In short, there is no intrinsic satisfaction in the replenishment of a tank of gas. (The pleasure or relief a motorist may feel on seeing a gas station when the car's fuel gauge needle is hovering over the red zone is hardly the stuff on which brand loyalty is based.) People buy gasoline wherever they may be when the need arises. In the gas station business, conventional wisdom says that even the most loyal customers are unlikely to spend more than half their gasoline budget with any particular supplier.

Mobil was interested in figuring out if there was any way it could offer sufficient additional value to consumers to create brand loyalty in spite of these factors. After much trial and error, the company came up with Speedpass (Speedpass is explained in greater detail later) (Speedpass, Mobil Speedpass, and Speedpay™ are registered trademarks of Mobil Oil Corporation). Shortly after its introduction of Speedpass, Mobil saw a dramatic rise in customer loyalty across all customer segments, as well as having the satisfaction of turning the entire industry on its head. *The Journal of Petroleum Marketing* called Mobil Speedpass "the fastest-growing new development in fueling." Media excitement was unprecedented, and it was not limited to the gasoline retailing industry. Forrester Research stated, "Mobil Speedpass will marginalize the benefit of smart cards," and *USA Today* wrote, "Speedpass is In for 1998."

The Evidence

To identify possible new opportunities, Mobil first divided customers into different segments, based on such things as demographics (age, sex, geographic location), consumption patterns (how much and what kind of gasoline products were purchased), and microeconomics (sensitivity to price). Examination of these segments revealed that the most profitable, and therefore most attractive, customers were also the ones who responded to new Mobil offerings that emphasized speed and convenience. (In short, they were most interested in time-value propositions.) Furthermore, Mobil concluded that despite marketplace advances, these needs remained largely unfilled and that latent in the customer base was significant hidden loyalty that could be captured—if the appropriate value was delivered.

The Mobil Speedpass project was based on the concept of meeting these unserved needs in the marketplace. It's important to note that Mobil wasn't ignoring traditional standards of value that had existed for decades in the industry—it was simply *enhancing* the value of its offerings by acting on these new findings.

"We felt that while most traditional customer levers were important—such as location, price and quality—these were simply basic elements to have in our overall value proposition and would not lend great opportunity for sustainable differentiation with competitors," said Brian Baker, Mobil's president of North American Marketing and Refining, in an interview with A. T. Kearney. "Instead, to achieve competitive differentiation and customer loyalty within our target market, we chose to focus our strategy on customer service based on speed and convenience."

By 1986, Mobil had already been a pioneer in installing customer-oriented electronic payment systems, including pay-at-the-pump fueling terminals, which embedded point-of-sale (POS) technology directly into gasoline pumps. By offering the option of paying for gas at the fueling terminals, Mobil saved time for (and improved the safety of) consumers while freeing up human attendants to work in the convenience store without interruption, or to help customers with other, more complicated aspects of automotive service. The reduced time it took for any particular customer to purchase gasoline also increased the effective capacity of fueling stations (more cars could be filled in the same amount of time) as well as reduced the likelihood that a customer would have to wait in line before a pump was available.

Interestingly, although the actual time saved at the pump when using the Speedpass is typically less than a minute, the perception of time saved coupled with the greater ease of paying for the purchase pleases even people who felt perfectly happy with first-generation pay-at-the-pump methods. Mobil discovered this opportunity by conducting detailed time-and-motion studies to analyze the conventional pay-at-the-pump payment process, in which the customer:

1. Takes out his or her wallet or purse.
2. Decides which card to use for payment and pulls out the card.

3. Locates the card reader on the pump and figures out the correct orientation of the card relative to the magnetic stripe reader.
4. Inserts and removes the card, often repeatedly to get it to read correctly.
5. Returns the card to wallet or purse.
6. Replaces the wallet or purse in a pocket or in the car. (Customers who place the wallet or purse on top of the car risk losing it.)
7. Responds to pump prompts about whether a receipt is desired.
8. Reads instructions to activate the appropriate gas grade pump.

The Mobil Speedpass system eliminates these steps and requires only that the customer fill the gas tank. Mobil is currently examining the use of robots to do the actual physical fueling, thus eliminating altogether the driver's need to get out of the vehicle. The company also plans to make Mobil Speedpass available for purchases made in its convenience stores. Other current leading-edge payment systems that Mobil offers include prepaid gas cards, bank debit cards, and a hand-held payment program called Speedpay™, which can be used at full-service gas stations.

Innovators Abound

Other companies are taking advantage of advances in digital technologies to better serve the needs of their customers. In each of the following examples, time was the basic value delivered by the new product or service offering.

Mini Case 1: Northstar-at-Tahoe Ski Resort

Since 1991, the California ski resort Northstar-at-Tahoe[8,9] has invested more than $13 million in numerous information technology initiatives. For example, it was the first resort in the United States to offer an electronic map of its ski trails. More recently, its electronic frequent skier program, called Vertical Plus, has kept it a step ahead of competitors.

Conventional frequent skier programs focus mainly on cost reduction—discounts on tickets, food, and lodging. Vertical Plus, on the other hand, builds customer loyalty by offering the extremely valuable commodity of additional time to its members.

Vertical Plus members wear preprogrammed microchip wristbands, personalized with their photographs, that give them the right to pass through special electronically guarded entrances to each lift. (Think of the empty car pool lane on the expressway during a killer morning commute, and you get the idea of how attractive an idea this is.) The microchip uses bar code technology to scan electronic markers embedded throughout the resort, and automatically records the number of vertical feet the member has skied. Additional prizes and discounts are awarded as that number increases. Members can charge lift tickets, food, beverages, ski lessons, and even child care via their wristbands. They can even send and receive electronic messages while skiing. All these innovations are designed to maximize what the skiers are there for: the actual time spent skiing.

Yet, the consumer is not the only beneficiary of this technology. For its part, Northstar gets instantaneous feedback on what aspects of the resort skiers like and don't like; which ski trails are the most popular, and which ones are avoided; Northstar can even use its precise knowledge of ski traffic patterns to schedule staff and plan for future expansion. Since Vertical Plus was launched in 1992, Northstar has seen an upsurge in return business by members as well as increased expenditures on other resort products and services. All told, Northstar estimates Vertical Plus alone has brought in an additional $2 million in revenues in its first 7 years—a number that increases annually.

Mini Case 2: The U.S. Postal Service

The 223-year-old United States Postal Service may not seem like a digital innovator.[10] However, even the USPS is tapping into the opportunities of the digital era as evidenced by recent innovations. Though it may not have been the first organization in the shipping industry to adopt digital technology, the USPS exemplifies the adage "Better late than never."

- *Online mail.* Currently being tested in Tampa, Florida, and Hartford, Connecticut, this service would allow consumers to send electronic documents to the post office, where postal workers will then print the message out and either fax or mail it to the intended recipients.
- *Online shipping.* To save the consumers the time wasted waiting in long lines at their local post office, mailing labels and stamps can now be purchased via the Internet.
- *Electronic courier service.* Top-secret documents can be sent securely online for a small additional fee. (This includes international transmissions.)

The USPS has also entered the online package tracking arena. Customers of its Express Mail package service can track the status of a package online via the USPS web page (*http://www.usps.gov*). Additional quick-access features at the site include a postage rate calculator, a zip code finder, downloadable forms, and a frequently asked questions (FAQ) page.

Other Leaders Emerging

Numerous other companies and industries have incorporated time value propositions into their service offerings, either directly or indirectly. For example, most major airlines have recognized the increasing importance of time to their passengers and introduced a no-wait-in-line, direct-board procedure enabled by the digitized scanning of the passenger's frequent flyer card at the gate area. The Hertz Gold Club program is another time-saving consumer product. Travelers can avoid the tedious time formerly spent waiting in queues at the car rental counter. Instead, a Gold member walks directly up to his or her waiting car and drives away. (At airports where the winters are especially harsh, the car will even be running with the heater on.)

Being able to shop for everything from books to flowers to major appliances via the Internet is putting significant time back into the hands of the consumer, as evidenced by a study showing that the average shopping trip was reduced from 1 hour 40 minutes to 40 minutes—a savings of 60 percent—when done via the Internet versus the standard brick-and-mortar retail store. Figure 2.2 provides an illustration of time conservation through online shopping.

FIGURE 2.2
Time spent in the online shopping experience.

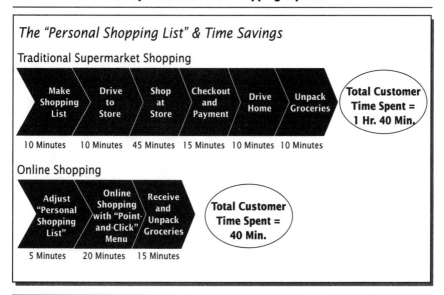

Although Internet shopping is widely regarded as a major time-saver by many consumers, there is one part of the process that is considered tedious—checkout. By some estimates, more than two-thirds of Internet virtual shopping carts are left at the virtual checkout counter.

Now, this is odd: The customer has browsed through all the products available online, has selected what he or she wants to purchase, but then has abandoned the whole effort at the final stage of the transaction? Although it could be that the consumer was just browsing and never intended to purchase anything, it is more likely that most online checkout processes are difficult and too time consuming. After all, the virtual checkout counter is where consumers are required to type in credit card numbers, shipping addresses, phone numbers, as well as select desired shipping options, and answer follow-up questions. This is very time-consuming stuff for something that is supposed to save them time.

Several Internet shopping services today are addressing this problem by offering online "wallets" that capture and store important basic data on each customer (name, address, credit card info) the first time they visit the site. This allows return customers to quickly complete any additional purchases. Amazon.com pioneered this way of doing online business with its "one-click shopping" feature that never asks a repeat customer to enter the same information twice. Now, many other sites are following suit. It's a good thing, too: Time clearly *is* money when the majority of your potential customers are walking out of the store empty-handed simply because the virtual checkout line is too long.

Digital Containers and Content

"Everything that can be invented has been invented."
—*Charles H. Duell, Commissioner, U.S. Office of Patents, 1899*

WE'VE JUST DESCRIBED THE ENORMOUS VALUE TIME WILL CREATE IN FUTURE PRODUCTS AND services. Now it's time to turn our sights toward the second major value proposition of the digital age: *content.*

Evolution of Content Value

In the industrial economy in which manufacturing activities dominated, competitive advantage was held by those businesses that could build the highest-quality products at the lowest possible cost. These products were generally designed and built using mass-production methods. Manufacturers were understandably focused on getting an acceptable, low-cost product to the largest number of consumers possible. Minimal thought was given to tailoring the product to suit the individual needs of each consumer.

The service industry was initially created to provide basic services that could support and service such mass-manufactured products. For example, automotive repair shops began appearing everywhere to service the increasing number of cars appearing (and breaking down) on the newly built roads. As time went on, there was a gradual shift in the focus of people who were providing these services: They moved from concentrating on the needs of the products (such as selling them, or fixing them when they broke) to attending to the needs of the *consumer.* As time value became more important for consumers, such things as financial advisory services, dry cleaning stores, and fast food became more popular—it was a natural and direct consequence of the increased discretionary spending ability of consumers, their desire for more leisure time, and their enhanced appreciation of convenience.

In the digital economy, it is essential to understand how these two economic elements, previously thought of separately as "products" and "services," come together to create a distinctly new type of offering. Think of it this way: Almost anything you can purchase contains both a tangible *container* element (typically a physical product) and an intangible *content* element (typically the accompanying information, knowledge, or service that adds additional value to the container).

Clearly, the degree to which something is either container or content can vary enormously. An ordinary hammer contains practically zero content. A computer microprocessor contains an extraordinarily high degree of content. It is important not to confuse content with what is simply an increased efficiency of the container. Technological improvements have resulted in making most containers capable of executing their core functionality more efficiently. However, *content* enhancement means extending the core functionality of the offering into other domains that were not traditionally a part of the product.

This is best explained using an example. Consider an ordinary $50 watch that you buy at your local retailer. Compare this with a 17-jewel-precision Swiss-made watch that sells for around $10,000. Obviously, the Swiss watch is much more stylish and elegantly superior compared with the $50 one. If we think of a watch as a "container," then the Swiss watch certainly represents a highly evolved version of that particular sort of container. However, the basic functionality of that $10,000 watch is the same as the $50 one. They both tell the time of day, and there is no added *content value* in the Swiss watch. Now consider, instead, a digital watch that keeps the time, day and date, and includes a calculator, compass, memory for storing numbers, an alarm, and other features. The basic functionality of the watch has been enhanced to include new characteristics that were not traditionally in the domain of the watch's functionality. In other words, much more content has been added to the traditional container.

Here's another example. Motorola was very successful with its StarTac cellular phones in the analog cell phone market. However, when digital wireless technology became available, Motorola was slow to react, and it allowed competitors Nokia and L.M.Ericsson to seize significant market share (40 percent and 20 percent, respectively, as of 1998). Although Motorola may have been able to make improvements to its basic container (the cellular phone) such as reducing its size and weight, enhancing its durability, and providing clearer analog transmissions, its ability to add *content* (such as paging, caller ID, and e-mail features) was severely limited due to the technology used.

Not surprisingly, companies are employing digitization to come up with new ways to use products, creating new applications that take advantage of existing content, and new ways to meet consumer expectations to attract consumers of the future. We can foresee the exploitation of digitized content (mostly information) within almost every conceivable market offering.

Consumers are beginning to appreciate containers that include additional content (even if they wouldn't use these terms). For example, 3Com's basic Palm Pilot handheld computing device can now be fitted with a pager module so that the owner of the device can receive wireless messages. Clearly, this is additional content that makes the container more valuable to consumers. Similarly, Global Positioning Satellite (GPS) systems were originally developed by the U.S. Department of Defense in the 1960s for military purposes. Yet, when coupled with the commercially available NAVSTAR navigation software, the content provided by GPS systems has been used to enhance consumer containers ranging from automobiles, trucks, camping equipment—even Palm Pilots—and other products used in travel or transportation. After companies like Mapsco sprang up to provide electronic topologies, a plethora of new nonmilitary opportunities for creating hiking, personal protection, automobile navigation, ambulance dispatch, and even air traffic control products and services emerged that combined this new GPS content with existing containers. This concept of creating products that are hybrids of existing content and containers is not a new idea. For example, the minivan was created by combining a panel truck (container) with the features and feel of a passenger automobile (content), and the home entertainment system was created by combining a television with hi-fi stereo equipment.

What *is* new is that, with the advent of sophisticated new digital tools, the content of any container can now be tailored to address the individual needs and requirements of each consumer. This was simply not feasible before. Prior to the digital age, generic offerings were mass-produced and aimed at broad markets; specialized offerings were targeted at the smaller segments that could afford customization. Technology is changing all that, allowing us to do the previously unimaginable—mass customization of products.

One of the earliest precursors of mass customization occurred in the automobile industry, when manufacturers introduced the concept of mass production, but with certain options. In 1903, when it sold its first car, the Ford Motor Company allowed buyers to pick the car's color. However, when Ford shifted production to the assembly line in 1914, a tremendous technology development in itself, the company told buyers they could choose any color they wanted as long as they chose black. (Black paint dried faster and thus allowed the line to move faster.) In 1925, Ford resumed the provision of optional colors.[1] Along the way, car manufacturers gradually began to allow buyers to choose not only color, but also engine type and size, manual or automatic transmission, and accessories such as radios and roof racks.

Of course, the majority of consumers still picked a car from the dealer's inventory, but the dealer could accommodate a prospective customer by special-ordering a car configured precisely to his or her specifications. As long as the buyer was willing to wait, that is. We foresee mass customization in the auto industry evolving to a point at which not only will the consumer be able to custom-order his or her car, but will aggressively use information technologies to specify desired performance levels, required features, and even quote a price for his purchase, based on knowledge provided by third-party agents and other infomediaries. (See Chapter 6 for a discussion on info-mediaries.)

THE EVIDENCE

The Mobil Speedpass condenses the former multiple steps involved in purchasing gas into a single consumer action. All the consumer has to do is hold the Speedpass next to the reader on the pump (see Figure 3.1). Mobil did this by using "toll tags," or a radio frequency–based technology traditionally used by electronic toll booth payment systems. Speedpass holders have a miniature transponder device attached to their key chain or affixed to their car window. With this they can activate a pump, fill up their gas tank, and drive away without producing a credit card or cash. Thus, the "value" of stopping at a Mobil station has shifted from merely acquiring a physical product (gasoline, which was virtually indistinguishable from the gasoline sold at competing retailers) to a sophisticated combination of container *and* content (the gasoline itself, plus automatic selection of payment method, authorization of the credit card, activation of the gas pump, and printing of the receipt).

Mobil Case Study: Results

At the time this book went into print, Mobil was still rolling out its Speedpass. Yet, it had already seen a tremendous increase in sales—both in terms of gasoline sales per existing customer and sales to new customers attracted to the intriguing, time-saving notion. In fact, sales per customer enrolled in Mobil Speedpass increased by more than 20 percent (1998 annualized). Furthermore, the program has delivered a 2.8 percent increase (1998 annualized) in overall sales, despite the incomplete rollout. This increase in sales volume is observed across all customer segments.

FIGURE 3.1
Mobil Speedpass.

Mobil®
Speedpass™
The fastest way to get gas.

Whether you have the key tag or the car tag.
Speedpass uses an electronic system located
in the pump to "talk" with a miniature
radio-like device (a transponder).

Together, these electronic devices provide
"instant" access to gasoline by automatically
charging fuel purchases to the credit card
you selected when you enrolled.

The Speedpass system operates on a dedicated transponder identification code.
Your credit card code remains outside the Speedpass signal system, maintaining
the confidentiality of that information and protecting your account from
unauthorized use.

Mobil Speedpass is a testament to the company's ability to thrive in the digital economy. The company was chosen as the 1997 "Innovator of the Year" in the credit card industry. Lou Noto, Mobil's chairman and CEO, was declared "technology-savvy chairman of the year" by *PC Week*. In addition, Speedpass has generated widespread interest outside the retail gasoline market, and Mobil is currently planning to license the core technology to nongasoline retailers.

Mini Case 3: Evolution in Trucking

In the trucking industry, a truck was historically viewed as nothing more than a physical means of delivering goods to the next link in the supply chain. Lately however, this pure *container* way of thinking of the basic truck has been radically changing. As digital technology becomes more widely deployed, numerous important *content* enhancements have been made to the basic truck. Along the way, sophisticated digital routing, communication, tracking, and diagnostic functionality have dramatically transformed the entire trucking industry.

At least 60 percent of U.S. private fleets now use computerized routing and scheduling in their daily operations. Manufacturers are installing satellite, telephone, and fax communications inside the truck console, creating a mini-office environment. Devices that monitor mechanical reliability and fuel consumption, and that provide real-time diagnostics of the engine are being placed under the front hood. Proprietary software installed on the onboard computer allows truck drivers to communicate directly with dispatch control when problems arise, receiving immediate interactive support. Dispatch offices can instantly determine the location of their vehicles using a combination of GPS systems and georeferenced travel information databases that provide up-to-the-minute information on food, fuel, and service locations; detailed city maps; and electronic address locators. Dispatch controllers across the United States can inform drivers of weather conditions, closed roads, scheduling changes, and other critical information.

Addition of such content to the industry's most basic container—yes, we're still talking about trucks—has created benefits that percolate throughout the entire supply chain. Trucking services can reduce loss by using satellites to track down stolen equipment or freight. Consumers are better served because they can obtain real-time information on the status of goods in transit. In-cab communication systems result in better carrier performance due to the ability of the driver to respond to last-minute changes in routing or scheduling. Improved driver satisfaction leads to better on-time performance. Real-time tracking of the trucked goods gives precise estimates on arrival times and allows more efficient inventory planning, a key to today's just-in-time operations. These factors drive profitability across the supply chain.

The Cemex Cement Company, based in Guadalajara, Mexico, provides another example of how a company has successfully applied information technology to trucking operations. As recently as 1995, the company's delivery process was unpunctual and unreliable. The process was vulnerable to equipment failure, last-minute customer cancellations, and weather delays. Today, however, all Cemex trucks are linked together by a GPS system and onboard computers that allow the dispatcher to plan and communicate the truck's routing instructions for the day. The system alerts the dispatcher to the possibility of last-minute cancellations, and enables the dynamic rerouting of trucks in the case of such cancellations.[2]

Mini Case 4: GM OnStar

General Motors began placing OnStar systems in its 1996 Cadillacs and has never looked back.[3,4] Now available in more than 20 GM-manufactured cars and trucks, the OnStar system represents a significant "content" addition to the basic transportation "container."

Of course, we've seen how satellite-based navigation systems, once seen as "gee-whiz" gadgets for the wealthy, have rapidly become standard features in cars and trucks. What differentiates OnStar from other commercial GPS-based systems is the *convenience* it offers. Based on a marriage of GPS and hands-free cellular phone technologies, OnStar offers the vehicle's operator several nontraditional options.

For starters, the driver never has to look at a monitor to determine his or her location. Instead, the touch of a red button puts the driver in touch with a human operator at the OnStar communications hub. An OnStar representative answers the call—operators are available 24 hours a day, 365 days a year—and can immediately ascertain the exact location of the car and provide the driver with instructions to the desired address or to the nearest gas station, restaurant, or hotel. (This feat is performed with the help of a database that contained more than 3.2 million listings as of the end of 1998.)

The remote OnStar operator also has the ability to lock and unlock the car or beep the horn. For example, if the keys get locked in the car, all the driver has to do is call the operator from another phone and pass the requisite security test to regain access to the vehicle.

OnStar also has more conventional features, such as the ability to notify police and/or ambulance services if the airbags are deployed and the driver does not respond to an operator query. (The OnStar command center will know instantly if the air bags are activated and will place a call to the vehicle.) OnStar-equipped cars are not easy to steal, but if they are, they can be located immediately.

OnStar makes the driving experience a much less stressful endeavor. You don't have to worry about whether your directions are accurate, or running out of gas because you can't locate an open station, or summoning emergency medical help when you need it most. OnStar integrates all these services into one cohesive offering.

When Is a Silo Not a Silo?

We've now seen several examples of how "containers" are being enhanced by various new digital content. However, to prove the point that just about *any* product or service can be enhanced in a similar way, let's look at something most people would consider truly nontechnological. Let's look at grain storage. Yes, as in silos. Those odd, vertical structures you see when driving through Illinois, Kansas, or Nebraska.

As always, our first step is to consider the basic function of the container itself. What have its primary customers (farmers and agricultural wholesalers) traditionally valued in silo products they purchase? Traditionally, a grain silo's primary function was to store grain. As such, its capability to store grain in such a way that would protect it from the elements, from thieves, from vermin, and other potential hazards ranked paramount in how much value it offered to its customers. So far so good.

It isn't difficult, however, to envision how this simple (and relatively low-value) usage could easily evolve into something much more sophisticated if the proper content were added. It is simply a matter of taking the next step: to creatively add content to a basic container that makes the combined product much more valuable to its target customer.

For example, wouldn't it be more valuable to a farmer if his silo contained special mechanical features that streamlined the loading and unloading of grain? How about a silo that gave him up-to-the-minute readings on how much grain it contained? (Yes, we're talking inventory management here.) You can imagine the rest—a silo that automatically receives a customer order for a certain quantity of grain, and sends that quantity to the delivery dock; a silo that automatically invoices customers; and so on.

In fact, grain silos are already evolving into sophisticated information-processing members of the agricultural value chain. They have mass customization and inventory management capabilities, computerized stored-grain management systems, and digital links both upstream and downstream (see Figure 3.2). We have already seen digital technologies applied to the stored-grain management industry with the use of PC-controlled grain-conditioning systems that control grain aeration and humidity, electronically based on input from devices that sense ambient conditions as well as moisture sensors in the actual grain mass.[5] So this hypothetical vision of future grain storage is probably not so far off.

The point we're trying to make here is less about silos or grain storage per se, and more about a universal trend just now perceptible as the digital age commences. No product or service offering—and no business in any industry—can safely ignore the far-reaching effects of digitization.

Leading innovators are already busy converting such hypothetical visions into reality. Automotive companies in conjunction with Microsoft have adapted the Windows CE operating system to work with the Auto PC, an integrated automobile audio and navigation system. Auto PC enables drivers to issue voice commands for directions, adjust the stereo, or even tap into the first few lines of incoming e-mail. The functionality of a car is thus expanded, making it more like a mobile office. Another example of a conventional con-

FIGURE 3.2
The smart grain silo.

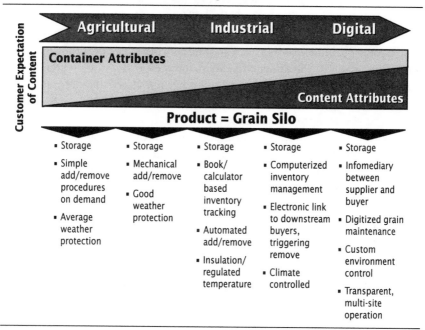

tainer that uses digital technology to expand its functionality is in the proposed Electroflux Screenfridge refrigerator, due for launch in early 2000. This device allows the user to scan cartons and cans of provisions that are running at near-empty levels, and a signal is sent over the Internet to a designated grocery store, which then delivers the requisite groceries to the consumer's doorstep. This refrigerator not only performs its basic function (keeping things cold), but now adds some inventory management capabilities into its operation.[6]

Companies in the container business obviously desire some kind of standardization in the content business. For example, the manufacturers of DVDs today have to deal with multiple formats of content; cellular phone manufacturers have to deal with multiple worldwide standards—obvious inefficiencies that inhibit economies of scale. Similarly, content-focused companies would be the happiest with standard containers, so as to prevent having to make multiple versions of their product that can run on different platforms. Windows 95 and 98, for example, are standardized on the Intel microprocessor container. Who will prevail in this creative tension scenario? We believe that the first in the race to build up scale (in terms of customer base) will prevail.

It is important to keep in mind, however, that digitization for the sake of digitization does not automatically create value for the consumer. Here's a case in point: the Sony Bookman. This device was a bold attempt to add content (digital access to the text and graphics typically found in a book, magazine, or other printed product) to a container (a portable computer) in a truly innovative way. Yet, consumers quickly made it clear that they weren't interested in paying $900 to lug around a 2-pound device to read content that could more easily be stuck in book form into their briefcase or backpack. There was simply not enough value there.

However, a much more primitive combination of technology and printed material—namely, books on tape—has turned out to provide enormous value to consumers and has created a lucrative new publishing niche. The value is clear: The consumer can absorb the material of the book (or simply be entertained) while driving, walking, jogging, or engaging in any other kind of activity that would make traditional reading impossible. Audio books are not terribly sophisticated, technically speaking, but they score high in the container-plus-content value test because of their ability to help consumers leverage time more efficiently (yes, we're back to that again).

Action Ideas: Transforming Your Offering

"We can try to avoid making choices by doing nothing, but even that is a decision."

—*Gary Collins*

THUS FAR, WE HAVE DISCUSSED TWO NEW VALUE PROPOSITIONS CREATED BY THE DIGITAL economy: time value and content value. However, it is important to remember that conventional drivers of consumer value have not lost their importance. Consumers still care about price, quality, and brands. However, even these familiar ways of measuring value in the marketplace assume new meanings in the digital age. In this chapter, we'll review the more traditional value propositions that have held sway in the industrial economy and look at how they're being impacted by the digital economy. Then, we'll look at a number of different things you can do to transform your product offering.

Price

As companies begin reaping the benefits of new information technologies to streamline manufacturing, marketing, sales, and distribution operations, it is not unreasonable to expect that these savings be passed on to the consumer in the form of lower prices.

This may not happen immediately, however. Many companies, concerned that lower prices enabled by digital advances will cannibalize sales of their traditional products or services—remember Britannica's initial offering of a $1,000 CD-ROM?—will try to erect artificial barriers that prevent the true cost savings from reaching consumers. However, the fact is that more and more people are moving toward online purchasing and expecting lower and more competitive prices on the Internet. This will most likely become a significant mode of shopping in the near future. (Morgan Stanley projects that Internet retailing could reach $115 billion in sales as early as 2002.[1]) Conventional retail shopping will probably never go away entirely, because many people view the shopping experience as a social and recreational activity. However, given the future significance of online retailing, it is important to not be tied to a legacy pricing strategy tailored to conventional retail outlets.

Conventional pricing strategies are based on the limited availability of resources. For example, the price structure of telecommunication companies dates back to the days of copper wires, when calls were priced to discourage peak-time usage of a limited-capacity telephone system. Higher prices were charged to discourage nonessential telephone use during business hours; lower prices were charged during off hours to encourage people to consume this new service even when they didn't have an urgent need. As digital technologies such as fiber-optic cable arrived, communications bandwidth increased enormously, and so, pricing strategies changed.

With resource availability no longer the most significant constraint, pricing strategies in the telecom industry must be driven by the new arbiters of consumer value, such as data transmission speed, circuit availability, simultaneous voice and data transmission capability—in other words, the increased choices in *content* in the telecommunication offering must drive future pricing strategies.

Some businesses, however, manage to charge higher-than-market prices even when resources aren't constrained. Typically, we see price insensitivity (that is, people continue buying a product or service even when it is priced unreasonably higher than competing products) when the following *information access* problems are present (assuming that there are no external or artificial barriers to competition, such as regulations or legislation):

- *Lack of awareness.* The lack of information about competing products or services results in consumers accepting higher-priced products than they need to.

- *Inconvenience factor.* Even if the information about other options is available in some form, it is too difficult to access and analyze.

These information-related aspects of price insensitivity are already disappearing, thanks to the digital era. With the vast resources of the Internet at their fingertips, today's consumers are much better informed, and much less likely to pay more than they should for products and services. Among other things, the Internet allows the wired consumer to:

- Perform sophisticated searches to find information on whatever product or service they're seeking to buy.

- Compare product features and pricing across a broad range of manufacturers, distributors, retailers, and online vendors.

- Share information about a particular product, service, manufacturer, or retailer with other informed consumers via online discussion forums.

- Employ any of the ever-growing army of third-party agents now online, many of them specialists in a particular product area, who will search through proprietary and public databases on the consumers' behalf to get the best possible value.

In short, today's widespread availability of information is driving the economy toward a vastly more efficient pricing market.

Perhaps more interestingly, the onus of *supplying comparative information* has been shifted. Competitors no longer shoulder the entire burden of getting their product information, both specifications and prices, to consumers; other businesses are springing up to do precisely that. Information has become a product itself.

For example, digital pioneer Shopper.com gives buyers immediate price comparisons between different (and competing) merchants. Comparenet also offers shoppers full product descriptions, reviews, and price comparisons for more than 90,000 products.[2] Thus, with information widely available, companies will need to find other ways of differentiating their product. They might add extra features (content), or provide free upgrades or more liberal warranties.

Of course, for unique patented products or copyrighted materials, prices will not be significantly affected by this free flow of data (because there is no competing product to get information about). The only caveat to this argument is that an informed consumer can use the Internet to educate himself or herself on the difference between the unique offering and similar products or services, and perhaps decide that the difference is not worth the price premium. In such cases, the value of the patent could visibly decline. (For products or services that are purely digital in nature, patents and copyrights are much harder to define and protect. Thus, in the digital age, typical barriers to entering a given market niche will erode.)

This free flow of information will also encourage increased consumer demand for products customized to his or her individual requirements. As we've seen, the conventional mass production–mass marketing paradigm will no longer suffice for the discerning needs of the consumer in the digital marketplace. In the past, vendors were able to bundle multiple products and services together in an attempt to hide the real costs of the various components.

A classic example of this could be found in the early days of the cellular phone industry. Confusing "packages," each of which contain so many minutes of peak time usage, so many minutes of off-peak time usage, as well as variations on voice mail, call waiting, and caller ID features are bundled into various plans, each with a different monthly fee. The consumer was forced to choose one of these packages, and it was notoriously unclear how the individual components of a package contributed to its overall cost. (Eventually, of course, competing cellular phone companies hit on the bright idea of offering simplicity, as in flat rates, as a way of achieving competitive advantage—and it worked.)

Hiding component or individual prices is going to be increasingly difficult, given the fact that competitors will be ready to jump in and expose such information inequalities. True, consumers' demand for customization will result in numerous—and complex—product configurations and resulting prices. Don't underestimate the difficulty of comparing and contrasting these myriad configurations. It's not trivial. (Just try ordering a new computer to be custom-assembled from Dell, and compare it pricewise with a new computer to be custom-built by Gateway.) It's tricky business. Ultimately, however—consumers will agree—it is infinitely worth it, given that it will result in greater customization as well as ensure competitive prices.

Here's an interesting question, however: Will online manufacturers and retailers be able to determine from their vast reservoirs of consumer data how to vary their prices for a given product or service *by each individual consumer* based on their estimates of that consumer's price sensitivity? The answer is, of course, yes. Today, companies can tap into information databases ranging from point-of-sale capturing of a shopping list, to credit card purchase information, to tracking of cable channel viewing.

Look at Tesco PLC, one of the largest supermarkets in the United Kingdom. Tesco's shoppers are encouraged to sign up for and use a "Clubcard," a digitized loyalty card that gives them access to special deals and promotions, and which in turn allows Tesco to capture their spending behavior in great detail. It then uses that information to determine future sales, coupon mailings, and customized promotions—whatever it takes to continue bringing price-sensitive shoppers into the store.

Consumers will be enticed by promised cost savings to divulge intimate information about their buying behavior, which will then be used to sell them more products.

Quality

The overall quality of a product or service has always been an important factor for customers making buying decisions. As technology has improved over the decades (technology as used in both the design and manufacturing stages of creating a product or service), so generally has quality improved. Thus, in the digital economy, quality will become more of an expectation and less of a differentiating factor in consumer purchases.

To fulfill customer expectations of quality, companies will have to make sure that their design-to-manufacture processes are on par with industry-best practices. If not, they will see how very quickly their reputation flounders because consumers in the digital age will have easy access to information about quality problems or defects through the increasingly common use of e-mail, UseNet forums, and other communications technologies.

Branding

Yes, along with price and quality, traditional branding has a place in the digital economy—a very important place.

Historically, a brand comprised the core identity of a product, service, or organization. A brand can be represented by a symbol (the *Good Housekeeping* seal), a name (Disney), a motto ("with a name like Smuckers it has to be good"), or all of the above. In all cases, however, it works as a kind of shorthand, communicating a specific message about value, quality, or general functional or emotional attributes to the market at large.

Let's look at two classic American brands: the motto of Maxwell House coffee ("Good to the last drop") and the battle cry of John Deere agricultural and earthmoving equipment ("Nothing runs like a Deere"). Both send clear messages of quality and reliability to the market.

However, the communication of functional benefits such as these represents just one of the four ways that a brand offers value to a potential customer. The remaining three include the *relative price* benefit, or perceived value, of the product or service; the *self-expressive* benefit, or way in which the product or service helps the consumer express himself or herself; and, perhaps most important, the *emotional satisfaction* benefit that the consumer of the product or service will receive.

First, a brand may be thought of as an experience that its maker shares with consumers. How consumers buy a branded product, learn about its features, and use it gradually determines its value to *them*. Second, a brand caters to people's need for self-expression. Nike built its brand success on a promise of high-quality athletic gear *plus* a "Just do it" attitude that certain consumers enjoyed identifying with. The same principle applies to designer clothes brands, such as Calvin Klein or Gap, which helped consumers express themselves in different ways.

Finally, never underestimate the importance of delivering emotional satisfaction, however illogical, to the consumers of your product or service. Starbucks earned its brand success by providing, in addition to a pleasant ambiance and high-quality coffee, its customers with the emotional satisfaction of spending time in an eclectic and happening place.

As illustrated in Figure 4.1, the self-expressive benefits provided by brands tend to be the images that consumers wish to project *outwardly*. (I'm young, hip, and athletic—and I want everyone to know it.) The emotional benefits provided by brands are feelings that consumers savor *inwardly*. (I feel important and intelligent to be drinking my coffee in this place.)

FIGURE 4.1
The elements of brand value.

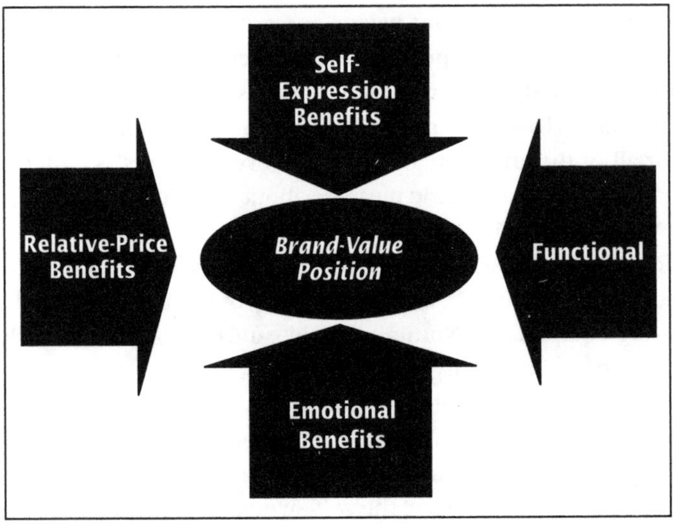

How Information Flow Can Affect Branding in the Digital Economy

In the industrial economy, a brand served to communicate *quality*, whether perceived or real, as well as *information* about the product. Most of the time, the lack of easily accessible information caused consumers to attach notions of *perceived* quality and *perceived* value to different brands, notions driven primarily by advertising, shelf prominence, and often price (many market research studies famously demonstrated that consumers were suspicious of the quality of products priced too low).

However, in the digital economy today's informed consumer gets information on quality, features, and price from trusted third-party providers, whose motivations are generally aligned with the consumer. Advertising campaigns can no longer be used effectively to fool or mislead the consumer. Brands that have relied on informational inefficiencies to communicate value will inevitably suffer a decline in their brand equity.

This isn't to say that brands can't project the image of quality, but that they will need to do so in an open, honest, and informational way. For example, in the past a consumer might have bought a digital camera by relying on word-of-mouth sources, by traveling to store after store, or by browsing through photography journals and viewing advertisements of the product. Today, using the Internet, the potential buyer might visit a specialized discussion forum (e.g., rec.photo.digital, www.dcforum.com) to see what he can learn from other buyers' experiences. He might log onto a consumer magazine site to read in-depth reviews. Then he might visit an online comparison tool (e.g., www.activebuyersguide.com) to do a point-by-point feature and price comparison. He may supplement all this information by visiting the suppliers' web sites, gathering information on such things as the price and availability of after-sales support, product availability, and ease of purchase.

In short, companies can no longer depend on using a brand to falsely sustain the appearance of value or quality—not when the consumer is well informed. In addition, the two "softer" aspects of brand value, self-expression and emotional satisfaction, will become increasingly important and will not be sustainable if the brand cannot offer consumers the basic benefits of function and value.

The primary value of a brand name, then, is entirely based on the consumer's perception of that brand built by the information they obtain, both from the seller and from third-party resources. As digital technology dramatically changes the way consumer perceptions evolve, established brands may well be at risk (see Figure 4.2).

FIGURE 4.2
Understanding brand value.

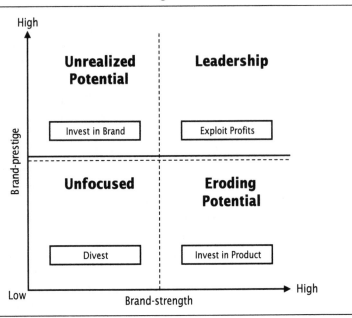

Thus many products will be able to retain brand equity despite advances in information technology. For example, the fashion industry thrives on brand names. Players like Versace and Ralph Lauren extract significant premiums for their merchandise, and even get customers to provide free advertising by wearing the company logo on their clothing. In fact, the power of the Ralph Lauren brand is so high that they were able to leverage it in diverse offerings such as paint—as it turned out, customers attributed the same high quality (and sense of style) to the paint as they did to the clothing.

Similarly, Swatch and Daimler-Benz collaborated on the design of the Smart Car (a trendy small car targeted at the European market) by leveraging Swatch's reputation for youthful trendiness with Daimler-Benz's reputation for quality engineering. Not surprisingly, the Smart Car turned out to be popular with young, quality- and appearance-conscious consumers.

In summary, increased consumer access to price and quality information will not necessarily have as great an impact on industries that place a higher priority on the two "softer" aspects of brand value: self-expression and emotional satisfaction.

Other Risks to Conventional Branding Strategies

In addition to the much greater access to competitive information, there are other forces unleashed by the digital economy that will threaten the effectiveness of conventional branding strategies (see Figure 4.3). These include:

- Needing to negotiate with a powerful, truly networked consumer community
- Losing control of the brand through excessive interaction with consumers
- Increasing fragmentation of traditional distribution channels
- Vanishing price premiums for branded products and services

Networked Community Power

As the digital economy continues to develop, we will increasingly see the emergence of *networked communities* that will come together, realize their buying strength, and negotiate with businesses to reduce prices paid for products and services.

FIGURE 4.3
Brands at risk in the digital economy.

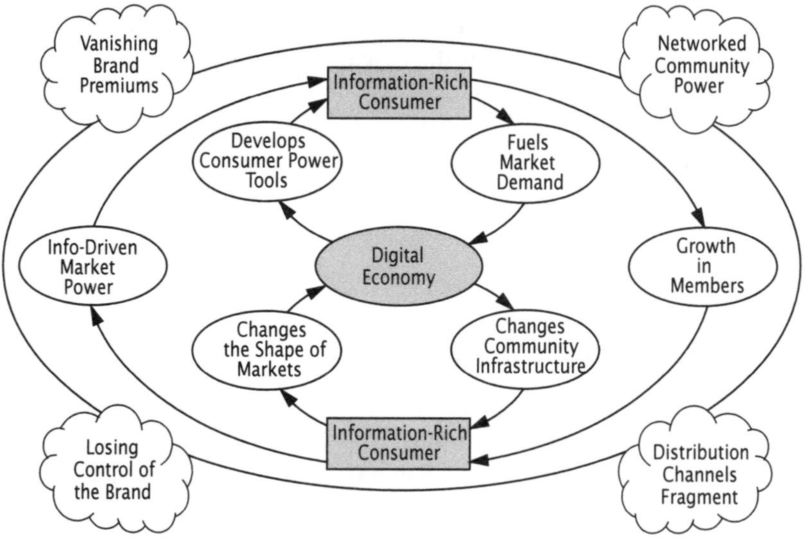

Members in a networked community have to abide by its rules or face repercussions. Wall Street is a good example of a self-regulating networked community. Wall Street routinely penalizes companies for less than forthright disclosures. Companies that miss their self-declared earnings targets are punished by drops in share price. Companies guilty of overstating sales or understating the impact of competitive offerings are also punished by Wall Street analysts. In fact, the entire Wall Street community is geared to see through the smoke screen often put up by corporate spin doctors who attempt to control or influence market perception.

Networked communities based around specific product or service offerings will increasingly have the ability to dramatically change the balance of power that currently exists between consumers, distributors, and manufacturers. Retailers, once brand-manufacturer *sales* agents, will become consumer *purchasing* agents.

For example, the proliferation of Usenet newsgroups, each with its own dedicated following, is a significant shaper of online public opinion and a powerful consolidator or destroyer (as the case may be) of demand for a particular product or service. Web sites such as www.netmarket.com also provide consolidation services for consumers, using their audiences to wield power over suppliers.

Many such newsgroups focus on a particular product or product category (for example, comp.sys.mac.digest is for Macintosh users), and they are highly influential among the customer base. (Sun Microsystems recently catered to the popularity of such groups by introducing a software package called Sun™ Community Server™ that enables the easy development of online electronic communities.[3])

Corporations are fully aware of the potentially huge influence that electronic communities can wield. In an effort to exert some influence over this phenomenon, companies are trying to create their own online communities—communities they can monitor closely—on their corporate web sites or sponsored web sites.

Losing Control of the Brand

The rise of networked communities presents a real threat to branding. Traditionally, brand image is created through one-way communication of advertising, sales promotions, and direct marketing—a communication path that had no provision for interacting directly with the consumer.

All that is now up for grabs, thanks to the two-way communication enabled by the Web.

Networked communities accelerate and amplify communication between consumers. The familiar adage, "One dissatisfied customer tells 10 other people," is amplified to "One dissatisfied customer can tell *100,000* people," in a networked community, as Intel Corporation learned to its chagrin. In November 1994, a defect that Intel called "a minor bug" in millions of its flagship Pentium microprocessors grew into a public relations debacle. The defect caused computers to give wrong answers in certain complex division problems involving the chip's floating-point processor. Downplaying user concerns, the firm said, "Statistically, the average person might see this problem once every 27,000 years." This explanation didn't sit well with researchers at Southern California's Jet Propulsion Laboratory and at many other scientific centers. One publication reported, "The issue attracted wider publicity after scientists and engineers began trading scores of angry messages in discussion groups on the Internet collection of computer networks."[4] Eventually, Intel agreed to replace the defective Pentium chips at no charge to consumers.

About building brands on the Web, author and digital-economy columnist David Kline says, "Branding on-line is far more challenging than in the offline world. That's because a good brand image depends not just upon your public relations staff, but also upon the experience of thousands or even millions of people when they encounter you on the Net."[5]

Companies can also make the interactive aspect of the Web work for them in creating brand equity. Take a look at what Garden Escape, an Internet-based gardening company, has successfully done. Its web site offers potential gardeners a seemingly endless array of products and services—a selection of 10,000 seeds, perennials, roses, and other gardening products from around the world—but that's not all. Cognizant of the power of the networked community, Garden Escape has created online magazines, electronic discussion forums and posts daily gardening tips that it encourages customers to respond to. The firm also provides free software tools for designing gardens (for serious gardeners only) and a toll-free hotline number for anyone with a question about anything at the site. All of this has contributed to significant generation of brand equity and loyalty among the online gardening community.[6]

Fragmented Distribution Channels

Many retailers still swear by an ancient axiom, "The three most important factors in retail success are location, location, and location." However, this axiom no longer directly applies in the digital economy: Globalization has transformed "location" forever from being a *physical* location to a combination of a *physical and cyberspace* location. As current distribution channels fragment and change, the most serious risk that traditional retailers take is letting new entrants define the rules of the game.

Yet, this is exactly what seems to be happening. Why? It is because successful retailers have invested years learning to play the physical location game. It remains the center of competitive dynamics in their business models, and successful players like the existing rules.

Sooner or later, though, something has to give. It's the same old story of Amazon.com versus Barnes and Noble, Blockbuster versus reel.com, and now, grocery delivery services such as Peapod and Streamline versus your neighborhood Ralph's or Safeway or Piggly Wiggly.

Peapod, Inc., and Streamline, Inc., are two examples of online stores that offer consumer-direct grocery shopping services, but they use slightly different models. Peapod supplies groceries to its customers upon request. Customers submit an electronic order when they are ready for groceries. Streamline, on the other hand, uses a "replenishment" model, wherein scheduled deliveries of groceries are sent as needed to the consumer's home in a special "Streamline Box," which allows for unattended delivery. Both of these models are threatening the conventional paradigm that consumers will shop for groceries at a retail store that is close to their homes.[7]

In an interview, Streamline, Inc., founder Tim DeMello commented on the future of grocery stores: "If you look at . . . current Streamline consumer[s], we're getting 80 percent of their grocery dollars. The store still gives them some sensory experience of food, and I suppose that's of value. But if you take 80 percent of those consumer dollars away, what's left for the physical store?"[8]

Vanishing Brand Premiums

Few consumers today will pay premium prices for branded products that lack clearly demonstrable value. After all, online shopping allows them to perform rapid comparisons of price, quality, and features. Sophisticated third-party search tools let digital shoppers compare hundreds of product features at thousands of locations worldwide. Thus, brands that fail to deliver value beyond top-of-mind brand recognition from past glory days can expect to wither on the virtual vine. Of course, consumers will continue to view some brands as social symbols and will continue to derive emotional satisfaction from certain products that can't be explained by feature or price comparisons. Still, brand managers set in their ways should not be complacent that they will escape unscathed. *Once it affects a few of your customers, you'll begin to take notice.*

A Call to Arms

As we've seen, the information revolution has created consumers with new demands and different priorities. They also have greatly enhanced expectations of the various businesses—including yours—that provide them with products and services. To adequately address these and other changes, you must begin transforming your consumer offerings. A diagnostic tool is provided in Appendix A to assist companies in determining how far along the path to digital compliance they currently are; the rest of this chapter provides an executive overview of actions that should be initiated immediately to ensure success in the digital economy.

Create a Strong Link to the Consumer by Streamlining Product Development Cycles

Although in the past companies have used information technology to speed up various business processes (such as manufacturing cycle time or order-to-delivery time) in the value chain, these efforts have generally focused on reducing costs or achieving some other competitive advantage. In the digital economy, however, all value chains must lead to the consumer, and a streamlined product development process is of prime importance.

Why is this particular business cycle so critical? What consumers want at any given moment is the key to success in the digital age. Consumers can be fickle. Companies must be able to quickly react to the latest market trends, and they must be able to incorporate changes into their product up until the last possible moment before shipping it to the customer.

For example, since the early 1980s, the automobile industry has used information technology to reduce the amount of time required to move a new car design from concept to production. Chrysler Corp., in particular, has managed to quickly produce automobiles that appeal to niche markets previously underserved by the "Big Three" automakers. By responding immediately to what consumers were saying, Chrysler quickly brought the Dodge Viper and the Plymouth Prowler to market, subsequently capturing loyal customers for subsequent models of those designs.

Likewise, when Netscape was developing its Navigator browser, it rolled out several Beta versions of the product in quick succession to get as much user feedback—and identify as many bugs—as possible before the final version was released. All of the customer comments were funneled back to the design team, who incorporated this critical information into their next Beta version, and so forth.

At the same time, Netscape kept a close eye on competitive offerings—especially Beta versions of Microsoft's Explorer product, which was under development at the same time—to make sure Navigator's features would be competitive. Designers went through innumerable design-build-test cycles until the very day Navigator officially shipped. (This approach is currently used in most new software development.) As new features, bug fixes, and customer-requested enhancements were developed, Netscape immediately released them for customers to download via the World Wide Web.

To streamline your product development cycle, you must do the following things:

Set up processes that continually capture up-to-the-minute market information—and then make sure that information is used. Begin by making *sure* you have multiple ways of getting feedback from your customers. For starters, set up web sites and electronic forums, but don't stop there. Organize seminars, issue press releases, establish telephone hot lines, and so on—whatever it takes to make sure you're hearing what your customers are saying.

Also—this is critical—don't forget to *give* this information to the relevant people on your product design and development teams so they can act upon it.

Similarly, you must continually monitor what competitors (traditional and nontraditional) are doing. Because emerging technologies are destroying traditional barriers to entry, you should make sure you keep your eye on potential (as well as existing) competitors. A critical mistake made by *Encyclopedia Britannica,* for example, was not recognizing that a software company, Microsoft, was turning into its most formidable adversary.

Constantly evaluate new and emerging technologies. You must also establish internal processes that monitor new and emerging technologies. Set up ways of assessing how they could impact your ability to get products to market more quickly. You should also be on alert for new technologies that can be used to satisfy previously unfulfilled customer needs. For example, in 1915, David Sarnoff conceived the notion of using radio technology to broadcast news, music, and sports. Prior to this, the radio was viewed solely as a means to establish point-to-point communication.

Attain the "Perfect" Degree of Consumer Interaction (None at All)

Companies in the digital economy are in a dilemma: They need to use as little of the consumer's time as possible when delivering their product or service; however, they need to somehow establish a tighter relationship to that same consumer. These two directives are at odds and can create conflicting strategies. After all, eliminating customer interaction should be the goal of all companies that truly understand the time-value proposition. Yet, as mentioned previously, this lack of customer interaction can lead to a degradation of customer loyalty if not managed properly. To offset automatic execution and maintain top-of-mind presence with the customer, companies must do the following:

- Leverage whatever customer interactions you *do* have. If a customer only spends 10 seconds per month placing an order or inquiring about a bill, use that time in the best possible way. For example, have the customer profile brought up on screen automatically when the consumer dials from home.

- Provide company information that customers may use or discard at their own discretion. For example, send an occasional e-mail about a promotion rather than making an intrusive dinner-hour telemarketing call. Amazon.com periodically sends out e-mail to customers suggesting new books or CDs they might be interested in based on their prior purchases. Most oil-change service businesses place an unobtrusive sticker with an estimate of when the next oil change will be due for the driver to use however he or she pleases.

- Effectively use third-party sources, such as networked communities, trade publications, and even traditional advertising, as vehicles to communicate your time-value proposition to current and future customers.

- Tailor the degree of interaction based on customer preference. For example, Streamline delivers groceries to customers using a replenishment model (items are automatically delivered when needed), whereas Peapod uses a requisition model (customers must place an order). Some customers are "high-touch"; others require (or desire) much less contact.

Look for Mix-and-Match Opportunities with Other Products and Services

Existing products can be creatively combined with other products or services to create entirely new offerings. As discussed in the previous chapter, separating a product or service into its content and container components can provide insight into other opportunities. For example, electric utilities have combined traditional mechanical meters with software controllers to provide intelligent power management capabilities to both commercial and residential customers. Pharmaceutical companies in the United States recently won the legal right to advertise uses of their products beyond those for which the Food and Drug Administration has granted approval—and many times these off-label applications require combining one drug with others. Sun Microsystems built its high-end workstation empire largely by using existing off-the-shelf technologies manufactured by existing computer makers, but put together in ways not previously contemplated.

Many other large companies in the electronics industry are collaborating to create technical innovations not possible if they tried to work alone. For example, Texas Instruments and Synopsys have entered into a collaborative agreement to develop a system-on-a-chip (SOC) design methodology that promises to create new digital products of exceptional speed and functionality; Texas Instruments has also formed an alliance with Hitachi to make micromirror components for high-definition televisions (HDTV); Cadence Design systems has launched an industrywide initiative that brings together system vendors, semiconductor companies, and software vendors to establish a new methodology for hardware/software codesign.[9]

The full ramifications of this type of creative collaboration, in which each organization focuses on what it does best and relies on alliances to bring an integrated offering to market, is discussed more completely in Part Four, "Intelligent Organizations."

Offer Customizable Products Based on Standard Components

If you want to pursue a mass customization strategy, you must first break down your consumer offerings (whether products or services) into the smallest possible units that can be mass-produced. You must then figure out the most efficient way to put those pieces together in combinations that meet the individual needs of your target customers.

How can you do this? It can be done through aggressive use of information technology—and the separation of the container and content portions of your existing products and services.

Indeed, many products are already manufactured in lots of one based on detailed buyer specifications in mass production facilities. For example, Dell, Gateway, and—by necessity—other personal computer manufacturers now offer consumers the ability to create custom computers from a selection of standard components. (Of course, these manufacturers also offer standard configurations particularly targeted to first-time computer buyers who feel unable to make correct choices on their own.)

It may be more cost-effective to reach different segments by offering just one base product, but "enabling" various features based on what the customer is willing to pay for. Microsoft Windows NT BackOffice is given to consumers on a CD-ROM that contains the entire suite of software applications. The purchaser is given digital "keys" that unlock only those BackOffice applications for which he or she paid. Likewise, Intel's Celeron microprocessor is just a "crippled" Pentium in which the chip's memory cache feature has been disabled, and which Intel sells at a lower price (even though the cost of manufacturing the chip is the same whether it ends up as a Pentium or a Celeron).

Add Additional Content to Your Existing Offerings Whenever Possible

Figure out ways to enhance the value of your consumer offering by embedding additional "content" into it. If you do this successfully, you will give the consumer the opportunity to move ahead without putting his or her current investment at risk. (Any truly new product or service will result in switching costs—remember that it took years to move consumers from records to tapes to CDs, largely because the switch required the purchase of a major new piece of equipment, the CD player.) When scientists and engineers conceived the idea of creating the Internet, they developed it as complementing (read: adding value) to the entire installed base of computers in the world. Years later, Internet browsers helped drive the explosive popularity of the Web because they added additional content to existing products.

Mobil Speedpass altered the entire structure of the gas retailing value chain by inserting a new intermediary (Mobil) into the financial transaction flow. Before Speedpass, Mobil had limited access to customer information, which hampered its efforts to develop an effective data-based marketing program. However, the rich stores of consumer information (added content which improves the consumer experience *and* improves Mobil's understanding of their consumers) created by the financial transaction aspects of the Speedpass system now provide Mobil with the information link necessary to develop and manage customer loyalty. Thus, Mobil Speedpass not only brought in new business and increased revenue, but also enabled the company to develop effective customer retention programs.

Align the Interests of All Container or Content Providers That Affect Your Consumer Offering

As previously discussed, the providers of the various content and container products often have competing business interests. When this happens, the consumer often takes the fall.

Consumers still remember the Betamax-VHS wars and (understandably) fear getting stuck with other "losing" product or technology standards. By the end of 1998, the new DVD-ROM disk drive began appearing in personal computers and home theater units. At approximately the same time, numerous competing "standards" emerged: one for recordable CD-ROMs, one for recordable DVD; and others for read-only DVD. The net result: Confused consumers are taking a wait-and-see attitude.

A similar battle is being waged between the Ericsson camp and the Qualcomm camp over the next generation of wireless communications protocol standards. Until these types of disputes can be settled, the digital telecom consumer will wait on the sidelines and stick with proven technologies and standards. (Contrast this with the situation in Europe, where GSM has been set as the mandated standard. Because consumers aren't faced with the risk of choosing the wrong product, the cellular phone penetration is dramatically higher than in the United States.)

Companies must play their part in supporting industry efforts to establish standards wherever possible. When such cooperation is not forthcoming, they must go with a flexible strategy. For example, multiple competing standards for digital television broadcasts currently exist. Television manufacturers must make the difficult choice of either betting the farm on the standard they believe is most likely to prevail, or of designing next-generation television sets that will be able to conform to a variety of standards.

Panasonic's response to this? To "unbundle" the television set into two components: a high-resolution monitor that will work no matter which standard wins, and a variety of receivers, one for each contending standard. In this way, Panasonic can participate in the birth of the potentially lucrative digital television market while hedging its bets on which standard is likely to emerge as dominant (this options-based strategy is discussed further in Chapter 9).

Don't Be Shy about Testing New Waters

Don't be wedded to your traditional ways of doing business. All too often, companies let long-standing infrastructure and outdated organizational models prevent them from moving on. The current dilemma that many manufacturers face: whether they can risk alienating current distribution partners (wholesale and retail alike) by selling directly to consumers. *Encyclopedia Britannica* had the same dilemma: Dump the salesforce or wither into bankruptcy. They chose to change and survive. Will you?

When American Airlines introduced its online ticketing program, it knew it could infuriate the travel agent community—yet, it proceeded. American recognized the need to explore alternative distribution channels, and not be tied to existing business processes. Online ticketing is now considered by most airlines as an essential way of doing business, and—surprise!—it has not eliminated consumers' use of travel agents for many of their travel needs. In fact, in responding to this challenge, travel agents have developed new services to further aid the customer. This is another example of the consumer winning in the digital economy.

Reposition Your Brand as Providing a Unique Solution to Real Consumer Needs

The digital economy accelerates the discovery and branding of new market space—as long as the brand comes to stand for a real solution to a real customer need. In April 1994, two former students—who had helped the University of Illinois develop an Internet navigating and browsing tool called Mosaic—formed Netscape Communications, Inc., to make the same technology available for surfing a burgeoning World Wide Web. Netscape quickly became the dominant link to the Internet well before Microsoft and others began pushing their own browsers and related technology. Netscape managed to grab this head start on Microsoft Corp. and others by hitting the market in December of 1994 using the Internet as its primary distribution channel (Microsoft wouldn't release Internet Explorer until it shipped Windows 95 nine months later). The result was that the newly christened Netscape Navigator achieved immediate brand recognition and managed to hold onto market leadership for three years.

Some other branding tips for the digital era:

- Consider branding new product-and-service combinations. For example, Streamline, Inc., combines online home shopping and grocery delivery with a dry cleaning and videotape rental delivery service. Not bad for a single phone call.
- Create networked communities of loyal customers by using your brand image as the binding force holding the community together.

- Foster the development of online forums by contributing advertising resources *and* employee time to facilitate conversations about your branded products and services. Become an active citizen of relevant networked communities.

Clearly Communicate the Value You Offer to Consumers

In the Industrial Age, the comparative price-performance ratios of what should have been competitive products or services varied greatly. Companies employed advertising and other public relations activities to create perceptions about value in the market—perceptions that may not have been based on fact.

However, in the emerging digital market, largely as a result of the vast amounts of information readily available to consumers, we see a much narrower spectrum of price-performance variability. (The capability that businesses now have to create mass-customized products that better fit individual consumers' requirements is also a factor here.) As new technologies emerge, the performance-to-price ratios of entire industries will likewise improve. Figure 4.4 illustrates the changes in price-performance ratios of the digital economy, with the boundary of the points representing the "technology frontier."

Let's look at how value can be successfully communicated to consumers in the digital marketplace.

FIGURE 4.4
Price performance change in the digital economy.

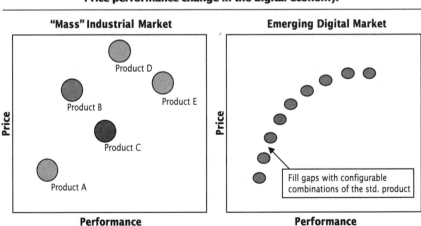

Need recognition. The consumer must recognize that he or she has a need that can probably be satisfied through purchasing a particular product or service.

Information search. The consumer begins searching for a product or service that satisfies this need. (Information on your offering must permeate all likely sources to ensure that your product is found whenever, wherever, and however your potential customer begins searching.)

Evaluation. The consumer evaluates and compares all offerings that promise to satisfy his or her need. In the past, these measures were primarily price, quality, or brand. Today's consumer will likely include time and content as primary measures of value.

Purchase. The consumer buys the best offering. (Here, the consumer will greatly appreciate such things as convenience and availability. In fact, ease of purchase figures highly in many consumers' final decisions.)

Use/experience. Keep in mind that consumers are constantly evaluating prior purchases with a view to future spending decisions. A positive experience with the product or service (as well as quick and convenient after-market support) will provide the consumer with a reason to come back—despite the existence of numerous competing products and services.

Obviously, effective communication of the value of an offering to the market is mandatory for success. Mobil took a calculated risk in allocating an entire year's marketing and promotion budget to communicate the value of Mobil Speedpass to their customers. The message was based on the added convenience to the consumer, in terms of the speed and ease of using the Speedpass. The company also stimulated the customers' curiosity by handing out necessary transponders free of charge. This strategy worked—customers were eager to see how "smart" these transponders were, and the free device was a powerful incentive to try the Mobil Speedpass.

Set Consumer Prices Based on the Value You Offer— Not on Your Costs

In the digital economy, knowledgeable consumers expect to pay for a product or service based on the value that they derive from it. Yet, most pricing strategies have traditionally been based on cost. (Grocery stores charge consumers the wholesale cost of a product plus a markup to cover its overhead and generate a profit.) Still, prices based on cost recovery or measures of acceptable profit may be out of touch with the digital marketplace. A London restaurant recently abolished the prices on its menu in favor of a "value-based" pricing policy in which patrons paid based on how much they thought they should pay (the perceived value). Astonishingly, the result has been a net increase in revenue. Customers have expressed comfort at knowing that if they have a rotten meal, they will pay an appropriate price; if they have a great meal, they are happy to pay accordingly. Plus, here's a bonus: Pricing strategies that allow customers to pay based on the value they receive inevitably result in increased customer loyalty.

America Online has been roundly criticized for treating its customer base as a captive audience to which it can flash advertising deals of all kinds—and they seem to be of widely varying quality—through pop-up messages that appear when a user logs on. It is apparent that AOL realizes significant advertising revenues from these advertisements; alternatively, AOL has also witnessed massive customer defections as former members quit in favor of Internet service providers that won't subject them to such intrusions. If AOL, however, were to change to a more "value-based" model and pool the demand in their membership to obtain volume price breaks and use part of those advertising revenues to reduce the consumer's monthly fees, the consumer would be much less likely to abandon the service. This pricing model is now used by some companies who give away PCs to consumers who are willing to sacrifice a portion of their screen for advertisements. Millions of consumers have signed up for these free PCs.

Seek (or Create) the Most Efficient Market Possible

So-called efficient markets have existed for stocks, bonds, and other financial instruments for decades. Now, we're seeing the emergence of efficient markets for a much broader range of products and services.

Many companies shy away from efficient markets as places that erode margins and commoditize products. Although there is an element of truth to this belief, companies must nevertheless acknowledge that all markets will constantly gravitate toward an efficient state (that's what information technology does), and that knowing how to be a player in these efficient markets will be a key requirement for success in the digital economy.

Participating in an efficient marketplace in which price is established based on supply and demand—and in which information is freely exchanged to allow consumers to understand the true value of a product or service—is the way of the future.

A new category of business marketplaces are being born in which buyers and sellers meet one another and make deals. FreeMarkets On-line of Pittsburgh, Pennsylvania, acts as an intermediary in new markets by helping its clients (typically, equipment manufacturers) develop rigorous specifications for supplies or components it needs, and then inviting qualified suppliers to participate in an online auction to win the business. The result is a savings of 10 percent to 15 percent on raw materials for the buyer—and very often a brand new (and potentially repeat) customer for the seller.

Conclusion

Today's consumer differs radically from the consumers found in previous economic eras. In today's rapid-paced world, work and personal responsibilities have increased. There's an endemic lack of time, and pressure is exerted from all quarters (from managers, spouses, children, and colleagues) to get *more* things done *faster.* The result is a market demand for faster and smarter products and services.

Traditional ways to appeal to consumers—offering better prices, higher-quality goods and services, or creating a strong brand image—are being challenged by two new measures of value: time and content.

Companies must proactively retool if they want to incorporate these new "value propositions" into their product and service portfolios. Specifically, they will need to create new products that mix traditional container and content offerings, and which offer consumers the most valuable commodity of all: additional time.

Pricing and branding strategies also need to evolve with the changing market. Companies can no longer rely on market inefficiencies or on branding based on false appearances; consumers increasingly possess sufficient information tools to seek out all relevant facts. In addition, brand and marketing managers need to understand that the rise of networked communities and the prolific information sharing between consumers could potentially apply downward pressure on brand equity; branding strategies in the digital age must take these new determinants of value into consideration or they will fail.

PART
THREE

Intelligent Markets

5

New Sources of Value in the Digital Marketplace

> "This 'telephone' has too many shortcomings to be seriously considered as a means of communication. The device is inherently of no value to us."
>
> —*Western Union internal memo, 1876*

AS WE'VE EXPLAINED IN PREVIOUS CHAPTERS, THE DIGITAL ECONOMY IS DIFFERENT BECAUSE it is a *networked* economy. That is, the businesses that hope to successfully compete in it must do so through collaboration, alliances, and constant communication with other businesses as well as with customers.

Gone are the days when companies could thrive by raising barriers against competition. (To paraphrase this a bit more poetically: No company can afford to be an island anymore.) Also gone are the days when vertical control of all aspects of a market's supply chain was considered the *über*-strategy—providing certain evidence that a business had achieved dominance within its industry niche. No longer can a company push standard products through a supply chain, forcing consumers to adapt to whatever it chooses to deliver to them.

As we previously explained, the digital economy has created a new breed of empowered consumers. In Part Two, we discussed how to create intelligent offerings to satisfy this intelligent customer.

This part, "Intelligent Markets," completes the next piece of the puzzle. Executives trying to formulate strategies appropriate for the digital economy must first understand the structure of—and the relationships between—participants in this dramatically new kind of market.

Chapters 5 through 7 put forth what we believe is the winning inter-enterprise business model for the digital economy. We call it the Digital Value Network, or DVN. We explain the importance of a DVN by illustrating how the traditional supply chain has evolved into a *value network* and how digital technology has advanced and enhanced this value network. We then describe the various components of a DVN, and challenge senior executives reading this book not only to identify their company's place in it, but also to take decisive steps in jump-starting the construction and development of a DVN within their own particular market niche.

After all, if *you* don't do it, someone else certainly will—and, subsequently reap the lucrative benefits of being first to adapt to the demands of the digital economy.

Evolution of the Traditional Supply Chain

Until fairly recently, businesses were focused on *physical* ways of generating value. The profitability of a market offering depended on cost (those materials and related activities that caused a firm to incur expenses when creating the product or service) and product differentiation (the materials and related activities that gave the product or service its unique characteristics compared with other offerings on the market).

In the nineteenth century, cost containment and product differentiation were the primary ways to enhance the value of a company. By the early twentieth century, physical efficiency—whether through using machines or other technical advances, or through figuring out more productive ways of leveraging human labor—became the focus of management. (The large-scale implementation of the assembly line by the Ford Motor Company was one of the first examples of increasing value through mechanical means; other firms made similar advancements in physical efficiency through time-and-motion studies that attempted to gain higher levels of productivity from employees.) In the decades since these pioneering efforts, the market became so efficient that increasingly there has been limited remaining value to be derived by exploiting the physical aspects of getting products and services to the end retailer.

In search of other ways to increase profitability, managers in the late 1950s began paying attention to the nonphysical elements of what was by now being called the *supply chain*. Because of advances in data processing and the ability to process large amounts of data into usable information, companies began applying statistical and mathematical methods to their operations, research and development, marketing, managerial, and other decision-making processes.

By 1958, the cost-benefit ratio of technology had shifted enough to use computers, rather than human beings, for some of the lower-level functions of information processing. For example, simple accounting/general ledger programs were created to manage financial information and to comply with federal regulations for financial statement reporting. Humans were no longer required to manually keep track of every transaction in physical ledgers. As the cost of information-processing technology continued to decline, the benefits of this "virtual" (that is, nonphysical) aspect of enhancing market value became more apparent. With this came the first glimpse of what was to become the digital economy.

This virtual element was initially characterized by a continuous increase in service sector employment (illustrated by U.S. Bureau of Labor Statistics numbers depicted in Figure 5.1) as companies began to apply digital technology to back-office processes, such as accounts receivable and payroll.

FIGURE 5.1
U.S. employment by occupation (percent of total).

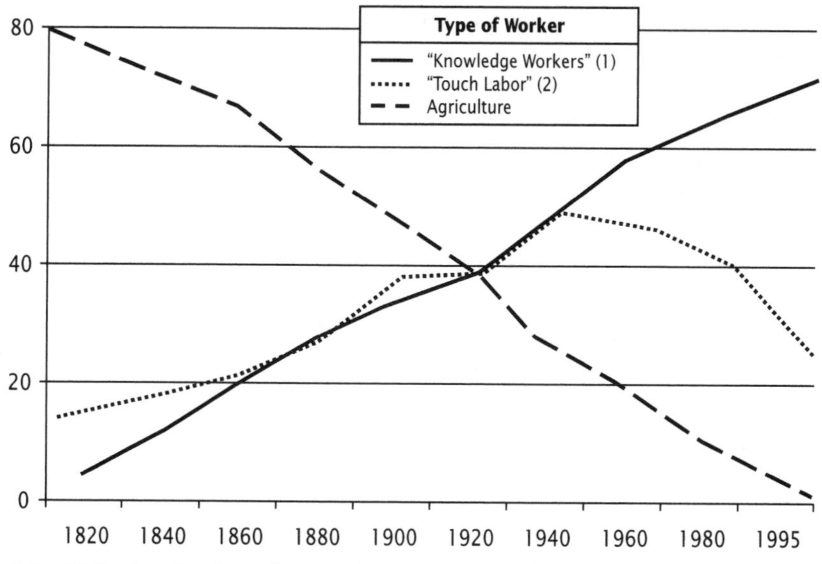

Note: (1) Consists of service workers, including positions such as finance, marketing, etc. in
industrial companies.
(2) Consists of physical workers in industrial firms.

Source: U.S. Bureau of Labor Statistics.

At first, the relative lack of sophistication of these early computer systems allowed only for the most basic automation of repetitive clerical functions.

By the 1980s, however, development of more sophisticated IT systems allowed managers to achieve competitive advantages in two ways. First, they were able to speed up processes by which internal business activities were completed. For example, information systems were used to enable materials requirement planning (MRP) systems, which automated the production process and were also used to implement activity-based costing (ABC) systems with automatic data collection, instead of time-and-motion studies which allocated overhead cost more appropriately. Second, they were able to more efficiently link the various external elements of the supply chain. This occurred through the use of EDI instead of paper orders and electronic funds transfer instead of checks, which facilitated the exchange of information.

As a result, companies were able to speed new products to market in a much timelier fashion; increase the number of inventory turns per quarter; reduce the need for warehouse space; and dramatically strengthen other aspects of the supply chain—concurrently improving overall profits and shareholder value across the supply chain.

For example, early implementers of large-scale customer and inventory databases realized tremendous efficiencies in existing sales and distribution processes; CAD/CAM systems and collaborative or workgroup tools further reduced cycle times for getting products to market.

By the early 1990s, computer technology had evolved to the point at which it became possible to electronically link businesses both within the traditional supply chain realm and outside the supply chain. For example, businesses were no longer just linking with suppliers and customers, but were linking with other companies for business functionality such as marketing and market research firms for information and expertise, universities for technical research, even IT value-added resellers for IT equipment sales and support. This integration of individual companies, each with its own links to suppliers, customers, and other value-adding business partners, became a highly interactive, information-rich *digital value chain*. In the digital value chain, the components of the chain can be examined for their value-added contribution to the *finished product or service*. This is in opposition to the traditional supply chain in which value contribution was limited to the immediate link in the supply chain, not by its tangible, identifiable contribution to the finished product.

Today, companies continue to find new ways to use information systems to compete and thrive in the nascent digital economy. No longer do supply chains require the same physical participants to add value to a product. Modern businesses realize that IT systems can replace entire physical segments of supply chains with virtual links. Traditional warehouses and distributors are enhancing their value proposition to the end consumer because they are realizing that the store-and-forward approach to supplying customers with physical products is rapidly becoming obsolete.

The resulting interactivity has created interdependencies among all participants, established new forms of competitive advantages, and, perhaps most important, opened the door to all kinds of new business opportunities.

A CASE IN POINT

Boise Cascade, an intermediary in the office-supply industry, realized early on that its days would be numbered if the company didn't rethink its business model. A $2-billion company, Boise Cascade traditionally acted as the middleman between more than 100 manufacturers of office products and the 17,000-plus end customers of those products. By the mid-1990s, Boise Cascade correctly recognized that the Internet had the potential to greatly diminish, or even eliminate entirely, the value it provided to both manufacturers and consumers within the existing supply chain.

Boise decided to grab the bull by its horns. In January 1998, the company opened a web site and invited customers to submit product orders electronically, rather than depending on traditional phone or fax methods. Boise expected that perhaps 1 percent to 2 percent of its customers would be interested. To its surprise, some 10 percent signed on by the end of 1998.

In the first six months after setting up its web site, Boise realized a saving of more than $1 million on an investment of just a few hundred thousand dollars, largely because of the time it saved sales representatives. Perhaps more important, these customers now saw Boise as an easy company to order products from, further securing their position as a vendor. Previously, more than 80 percent of existing customers used error-prone and time-consuming telephone calls or faxes to place orders. (The remaining 20 percent used proprietary electronic data interchange, or EDI, transmissions over private networks.) The Internet provided both kinds of customers with a secure, 24-hour-a-day, seven-days-a-week communication channel that was both more efficient and more cost-effective. The strategy seems to have effectively established Boise Cascade's place in the emerging digital economy.[1]

The example of Boise Cascade illustrates how smart companies are realizing that there are new value drivers in the emerging value chain, requiring them to formulate new strategies proactively to take advantage—and avoid potential pitfalls—of the opportunities created by the digital marketplace.

The Coming of Age of the Digital Value Chain

In his book, *Value Migration,* Adrian Slywotzky observes that "it is widely acknowledged that products go through cycles, from growth through obsolescence." However, he points out that it is less obvious but no less true that *business models* experience similar cycles and that they, too, are subject to what Slywotzky calls "economic obsolescence." In such cases, he writes, "value leaves economically obsolete business designs and flows to new business designs that more effectively create value for the customer and capture value for the producer."[2]

As indicated by Figure 5.2, the traditional supply chain process that most executives are familiar with is terribly dysfunctional. Fundamentally a "push-driven" system, it is replete with excessive physical movement, including repetitive product transportation, storage, and handling activities. Furthermore, it carries significant administrative, transactional, and financial costs that do not add any significant value to the end consumer. A major computer manufacturer once admitted to us that some of the components used in his computers had traveled 250,000 miles before they reached the end consumer!

Here's a stunning fact: Companies who participate in digital value chains that extend communication (and collaboration) beyond any two adjoining links create 65 percent more shareholder wealth for each dollar of earnings than those still operating in the traditional supply chain mode.[3] Perhaps most significantly, such companies are not merely focusing on increasing operational efficiency, reducing inventories, or shrinking manufacturing and delivery cycle times. Rather, they are concentrating their efforts on such things as *pipeline velocity.* [Pipeline velocity is characterized by the following factors: near-zero lead times, actual demand response instead of forecasting, zero-tolerance delivery schedules, synchronization of flow with true customer

FIGURE 5.2
Traditional supply chain.

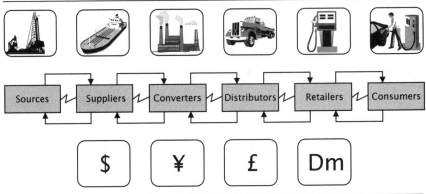

demand, removal of lot sizing, and absolute local (even on-the-spot) control to ensure immediate response to changes. These things occur throughout the entire supply chain.] In addition to pipeline velocity, these companies are also concentrating their efforts on quality, cash flow, and most important, IT-enabled flow of information to all members of the value chain. This is illustrated in Figure 5.3.

A CASE IN POINT

Wal-Mart's replacement of a traditional physical supply chain process with one based on notions of virtual (that is, informational) value has provided it with competitive advantages that most other retailers would die for. Conventional wisdom attributes Wal-Mart's success to a number of factors, including the innate business savvy of founder Sam Walton; the use of friendly greeters, who make customers feel welcome the minute they walk into any Wal-Mart store; the economies of scale that enable a how-low-can-you-go pricing strategy; and the obvious motivational benefits of making employees part-owners of the business.

However, one of the key reasons for Wal-Mart's success is the way the company uses information technology to replenish inventories using a logistics technique known as *cross-docking*. Under this system, goods delivered by manufacturers to a Wal-Mart warehouse are instantly grouped with appropriate goods from other manufacturers and immediately rerouted to the individual retail stores that need those particular items. Wal-Mart has completely eliminated the need to process, store, and presort excess inventory at the warehouse.

FIGURE 5.3
Seamlessly integrated value chain.

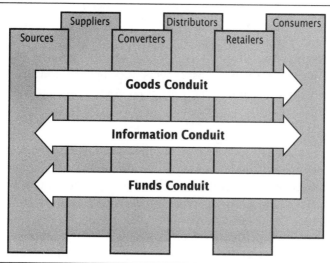

Forces Shaping the Digital Value Chain

It will be easier to understand these new digital value chain–based business models when you appreciate the forces making them not only possible, but necessary. We've identified three such forces, as outlined in the following.

Information and innovation. Because so many innovative new companies are springing up within the information technology sector, many otherwise savvy observers have reached the exceedingly wrong conclusion about where new wealth is being created. The *really* big story is that superior price/earnings ratios are not achieved by so-called technology companies, but by those companies that can rapidly translate customer insight into product and service innovations. (Tommy Hilfiger and Walt Disney are two prime examples of this.) True, most of these wealth-generating companies aggressively use information technology to bring their ideas to life. Their real focus, however, is on innovation, not the technology per se. Pixar uses technology extensively to create animated movies like *Toy Story,* but its focus is purely on innovation, not on technology.

Availability of capital. Capital has become more available in recent years due to expanding global markets, high retirement savings, low inflation, and attractive interest rates. In the traditional supply chain, the substantial investments required by the need for physically large manufacturing facilities and distribution centers represented major barriers to entry for would-be competitors. These barriers have been dismantled in recent years as a competitive global market has developed in contract manufacturing and logistics services. Through the vastly efficient information exchange made possible by technology, companies now successfully outsource many of these high-cost aspects of competing. Today, an entrepreneur with an idea can become a major competitor in a matter of months by contracting out capital-intensive manufacturing and distribution services.

Globalization. The globalization of capital flows is transforming the availability of capital. In addition to free trade in capital markets, a worldwide groundswell of deregulation—touching transportation, telecommunications, utilities, and financial services industries alike—has facilitated the globalization of business. One result of deregulation has been a reduction in the cost of services most directly affecting manufacturing, giving rise to new opportunities for the global sourcing of manufacturing services.

To summarize, in the digital economy, a company's value is not limited to the physical worth of its hard assets. Instead, its value is an aggregation of its physical and virtual elements—both hard and soft assets. The value of the virtual, or soft, elements (which extend or replace a physical environment with an environment in which goods and services exist as information), has come about largely because of dramatic advancements in IT. The following section highlights the growing importance of soft assets in the digital economy.

New Wealth from Soft Assets

New ideas and creative capacity are considered to be soft assets because they are not directly reflected on the balance sheet. These soft assets, however, are the primary creators of wealth in the digital economy. Global equity markets are becoming remarkably efficient in valuing firms that can transform soft, or information-based, assets into innovative new products, services, and business models.

Soft-asset companies. Terms like *soft, intangible,* or *information-based* are used to describe the dominant feature of companies in this category (including financial services, media, advertising, freight, wholesale, information services, software, and telecommunications networks). Although companies in the wholesale and freight segments have substantial investments in hard assets, their future role in the digital value chain will depend heavily on their ability to create and take advantage of information-based assets or content.

Hard-asset companies. This category includes manufacturers of consumer products, retailers, intermediate goods suppliers (including computer manufacturers), and raw materials suppliers (including the makers of computer chips.)

And the Winner Is. . . .

We traced the price/earning ratios of hard-asset versus soft-asset companies (the results are illustrated in Figure 5.4) and discovered that the P/E margin of difference between leading soft-asset and hard-asset companies has widened since 1991. Soft-asset companies are now generating 65 percent more shareholder wealth per dollar of earnings. (Of course, brands and other soft assets represent a large percentage of the value of consumer products companies and retailers. If it were possible to extract the value of soft assets

FIGURE 5.4
Price/earnings ratios for hard-asset versus soft-asset companies.
(*Note:* **Appendix B includes a more detailed description of this analysis.**)

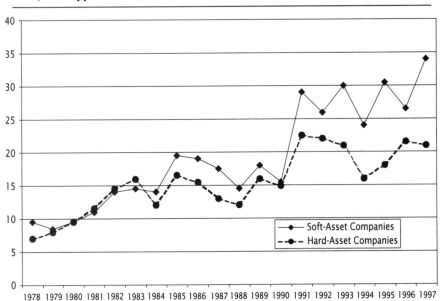

Source: A.T. Kearney analysis of price and earning data for publicly traded companies, based on data from the Institute for the Future and the U.S. Department of Commerce.[4]

from primarily hard-asset companies, we believe the gap between these two price/earnings lines would be even more dramatic and would demonstrate the increasingly rising value of soft assets in all companies.)

We believe that the superior P/E ratio exhibited by soft-asset companies is just one of the many indicators that reflect the consumer confidence in such companies and in their potential to create sustainable value.

Where Is Value Being Captured in Today's Value Chain?

In Figure 5.4, we used the U.S. Department of Commerce's Input/Output tables to examine where value is being produced in the digital marketplace in its current state of development. The Input/Output measure only includes the value actually added at a given stage in the value chain (see Appendix B for a description of each category in Figure 5.4).

Surprisingly, the value added by soft-asset companies totals $2.1 trillion compared with $2.8 trillion for the hard-asset companies (Figure 5.5). Let's put this in perspective: Approximately 43 percent of the total value of all goods and services created in today's economy is already being created by soft-asset companies. Compare this with approximately 37 percent in 1987 and 22 percent in 1957. Looking forward, according to U.S. Department of Commerce estimates, by 2017 some 60-plus percent of the gross product will originate from soft assets. The story is that if you're in a hard-asset-based industry, you'd better start looking for ways to incorporate soft assets (in the form of digital content perhaps?) into your customer value proposition.

The preceding exercise can be performed to see how well other countries around the globe are prepared for the digital economy.

For example, whereas the U.K. model resembles that of the United States, in China, the government owns most of the soft assets—and the technical infrastructure for a digital economy has yet to be created. When a government that controls national soft assets decides—as we believe most eventually will—to relinquish such control, look out for tremendous opportunities it will provide for companies worldwide.

FIGURE 5.5
Share of the $4.9 trillion U.S. virtual value chain (in billions of dollars).

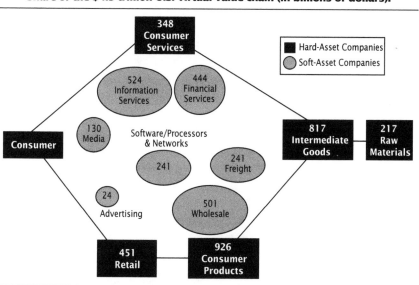

Source: Institute of the Future and U.S. Department of Commerce,
Gross Product Originating (GPO) by industry.

A CASE IN POINT

Shortly after the breakup of the Soviet Union, Latvia established The Latvian Research Network (LATNET) in 1992. Due to the limited resources and poor communications infrastructure in the country, LATNET searched for alternate ways to connect the numerous University of Latvia departments scattered around the capital city of Riga. The solution was to install a high-speed wireless LAN. Due to the country's relative lack of radio frequency licensing regulations, the low utilization of available bandwidths, and the recent availability of inexpensive and easy-to-use wireless LAN products, it was possible to develop a high-speed (2 Mbps) spread-spectrum wireless network that connected departments that were physically separated by as much as 28 miles. There are currently more than 30 sites that use these high-speed wireless links as an alternative to lower-speed leased telephone lines. Latvia and other countries are thus effectively using wireless technologies to completely leapfrog the networking roadblocks that U.S. companies face daily due to the installed base of copper wiring.

We expect that emerging markets may be able to skip evolutionary steps in the traditional supply chain development and move directly to the digital value chain model. Countries like Mexico, India, and Latvia are already bypassing infrastructure handicaps that presented significant barriers in the Industrial Age by investing in leading-edge information technology.

6

A New Business Model—The Digital Value Network

"Two are better than one; because they have a good reward for their labor. For if they fall, the one will lift up his fellow: but woe to him that is alone when he falleth; for he hath not another to help him up. Again, if two lie together, then they have heat: but how can one be warm alone? And if one prevail against him, two shall withstand him; and a threefold cord is not quickly broken."

—*The King James Bible, Ecclesiastes 4:9–12*

SINCE THE ADVENT OF MASS-MARKET RETAILING, MANUFACTURERS AND VENDORS HAVE MADE most of their customers' buying decisions. Companies choose what consumer needs they will meet, what markets they will serve, what product and service configurations they will offer, and what prices to charge.

Being a consumer in the industrial era has, thus, generally meant accepting limited choices and accepting compromise, often settling for the best available option, even if it isn't a perfect match.

As discussed in the previous chapters, one of the primary drivers of the digital economy is the rise of the empowered consumer. Consumer intelligence grows exponentially as more individuals interact as members of a community made possible through digital communications. We call it the "law of increasing knowledge," similar to the "law of increasing returns." As more consumers interact within a growing community, they attain more knowledge about the value-added aspect of products and services in the marketplace. Empowered by this knowledge, digital consumers have started making much more intelligent decisions about the products and services they buy.

As previously stated, we believe that consumers will increasingly demand additional simplicity, quality, customization, improved content, and especially time savings from market offerings. The DVN relies on this consumer-centric approach to business.

Don't be scared by the jargon. A digital value network (DVN) is really just a community of business partners and customers that is connected using information technology (IT). However, simply integrating your traditional supply chain by using IT doesn't a DVN make. The players in a DVN work together to maximize their combined value for the benefit of the end consumer.

Perhaps most important, a DVN is a much more dynamic entity than a traditional supply chain. The relationships within a DVN are fluid—forming, disintegrating, and reforming based on market dynamics and the whims of the consumer. Yesterday's supplier might be today's customer and tomorrow's competitor. Adam Brandenburger coined the term *co-opetition* to describe the win/win nature of these new business relationships in which elements of both cooperation and competition drive all players to produce everincreased value for their customers, consumers, and shareholders.[1] The one-for-all-and-all-for-one philosophy of the DVN is that the network will support the diverse business goals and decisions of all members (and, of course, all interested investors). A DVN has three components that work together to produce value for the end consumer.

First, DVNs are enabled by the tight electronic linkages found in *digital value chains*—highly efficient business relationships that allow for synchronous executing of business processes across the extended enterprise. These electronic links are often made possible through use of a standards-based technology platform that allows partners to execute a traditional business function in a digitally enhanced way. We call this a *digital function platform*, which forms the second building block.

And finally, there's a new form of business intermediary that supports DVNs: an *infomediary*. These new intermediaries provide a number of information-based functions that support the operation of the DVN and form the last piece of the DVN model.

The appeal of the DVN model is that it will produce superior market valuations for companies that embrace it because it replaces manually driven (or people-driven) processes with highly flexible, automated high-content information conduits. One need only look at Dell Computer to see the results. Investors are understandably excited, but hard work is still ahead before the theoretical promise can be turned into a sustainable operational reality.

The DVN model is an especially relevant one for larger organizations to consider. Why? Existing investments in physical assets, people, and ways of doing business, combined with a seemingly loyal customer base and existing product portfolio, are significant barriers to change. Thus, small start-up Davids lacking these constraints easily outmaneuver the Goliaths. Even large, established companies, however, can find ways to compete in the new electronic bazaar.

Components of a DVN

While the DVN model applies to both large and small companies, the individual components of the DVN model will affect different companies in different ways, depending on size, position within their industry, business strategy, and a variety of other factors.

The Digital Value Chain

As previously discussed, producers initially form a *digital value chain* to create a far more efficient, rapid, and flexible version of the traditional supply chain (remember pipeline velocity?). The digital value chain by necessity involves participants from a spectrum of separate businesses. One or more of these participants may take on the role of an *anchor,* much as a major retail establishment usually serves as the anchor in a shopping mall. The anchor in a digital value chain is the power player around which the digital value chain is organized and often optimized. For example, whereas a Nordstroms might be the anchor in a local shopping mall, Dell Computer is the anchor in a digital value chain for producing personal computers, workstations, and servers.

A particular business might assume the role of an anchor based upon a number of factors. It may be providing the major share of the value delivered to the consumer (as most people go to the mall for the major department stores, not the ancillary businesses), it may be the dominant supplier (Procter & Gamble controls the vast majority of the value chains through which its products flow), or it may be the owner of a product or service that cannot be duplicated by any other participant in the value chain (Wal-Mart owns the physical retail outlet and the brand recognition that draws the consumer to its stores). In some cases, the benevolent anchor works to maximize value to all the participants within the digital value chain, but more often the anchor is focused on maximizing its own profits.

Dell is a classic example of an anchor. Its particular digital value chain also includes component suppliers (such as hard drive manufacturers, monitor manufacturers, and the like), as well as R&D technology suppliers and after-sales support suppliers. As the anchor, Dell calls the shots, establishes the rules, decides on technologies, and in this instance, owns the consumer relationship.

Value chains and supply chains are relatively familiar concepts. It's the *digital* aspect of digital value chains that is providing exciting new ways to create value and minimize cost. Just look at the transformation of the automotive industry's traditional supply chain into a digital value chain. Traditional auto dealers incur big infrastructure costs to operate their businesses (leasing prime locations; maintaining large, expensive inventories; paying employee salaries and commissions; and so on)—costs that were automatically assumed to be permanently fixed overhead for doing business. Digital pioneers (like autobytel.com, CarPoint, and so forth) use the Internet to create a digital value chain that not only reduces the costs associated with the traditional supply chain (no physical lots, no physical inventories, for starters), but have also made the car buying experience more pleasant for the consumer (Figure 6.1).

Digital Function Platform

Combine multiple (two or more) digital value chains, and what do you get? You get a *digital function platform* (DFP). A DFP is simply a business service or technology platform that supports business processes across multiple value chains. Through a DFP, previously disconnected and autonomous value

FIGURE 6.1
Changing traditional supply chains into digital value chains.

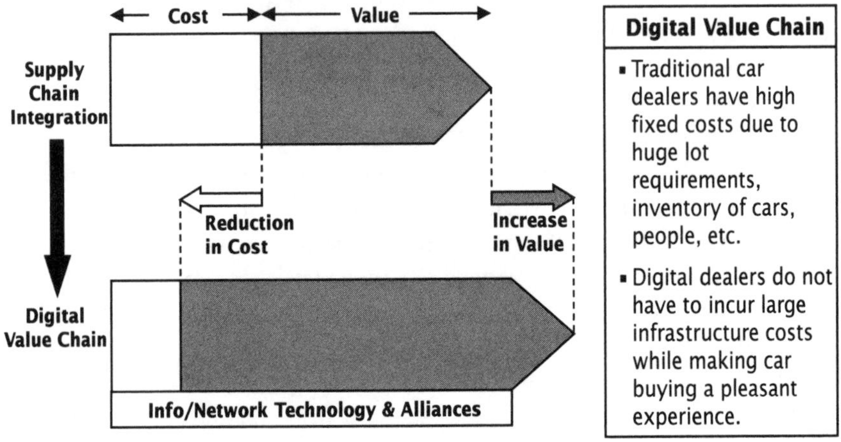

chains (for example, the tire value chain and the headlight value chain) are able to collaborate and combine their offerings (for example, create a car) more efficiently.

Digital function platforms can include a software package such as SAP or a turn-key business service such as Federal Express Powership. Under the hood, all DFPs are primarily digital in nature (and we don't mean using a fax machine); they can be applied across multiple value chains; and they provide a new way for those value chains to efficiently cooperate and create value for the consumer.

The concept of a DFP is somewhat theoretical. Although DFPs cannot be identified as underlying every product, or even every industry, the concept is no less useful to understand because as the digital economy progresses, these DFPs will play an ever increasing role in the marketplace. Because of this importance, we've chosen to name it to highlight the dramatic way these new digitized platforms are lubricating the gears of the digital economy, and subsequently enabling the creation of DVNs.

Things as basic as the floppy disk, or the set of ANSI EDI standards, can be considered DFPs. When you need to exchange documents with another company efficiently—even a company in another value chain that you've never dealt with before—the floppy disk provides a platform. In the not-too-distant past (prior to the PC), such an exchange was infinitely complicated because there was no global network and no standard file formats, disk formats, applications, and transmission alternatives.

Likewise, the standardization of communications protocols across the Internet enabled by ANSI EDI standards has resulted in immeasurable efficiency benefits for a broad number of people participating in innumerable value chains. At this level, the entire Internet can be considered the grand unified DFP for the digital economy.

Although a DFP can be as simple as a shared file format, it can also be a much more sophisticated set of products and services. More and more, we are seeing the creation of turnkey business services that are able to unite value chains to serve a variety of consumer industries. Consider a company that provides turnkey customer service for a personal computer manufacturer. The service uses the latest in call center technologies to handle calls and manage customer interaction. It connects to the manufacturer of the personal computers for the latest information on problems and solutions. It connects to the manufacturers of the PC components to tap into their databases of problems and solutions as well. It connects to the repair facilities of all of the value chain participants to facilitate the movement of products to and from repair depots, as well as the ordering and fulfillment of replacements.

Furthermore, the call center connects to the value chains of software providers and third-party warranty providers to support cross-selling opportunities. Also, the call center does this not only for the PC manufacturer and his value chain, but for an automobile manufacturer, and for a consumer electronics company. Thus, the basic customer support service is a true DFP—a platform for creating new value in the digital economy.

To take another example, electronic typesetting provides a DFP that existed even before the digital economy. Before the publishing industry fully embraced its current, largely digital, way of doing business, the benefits offered by advances in digital technology were confined to using electronic typesetting machines to reduce the cost of setting type by hand. (Most other aspects of the publishing business remained labor- and mechanically intensive until fairly recently.) Only later did the electronic typesetting DFPs become part of truly digital value chains, when the process of transferring analog information into digital form was complemented by digital formatting, cross-referencing, and printing activities subsequently adopted by myriad newspaper, magazine, research, book, and online publishing businesses.

The strength of a DFP lies in its cross-network integration, which allows it to take advantage of cross-industry opportunities. Figure 6.2 illustrates how, by employing horizontal business networks, a DFP reduces cost and increases value for all stakeholders.

FIGURE 6.2
Digital function platforms (DFPs)—joining value chains to create new value.

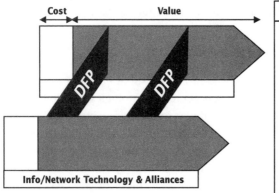

Cost Value	Digital Function Platform
DFP DFP	• All the appliances in a household could be connected through a DFP called "jini" (unveiled by Sun in January 1999). This common platform of communication enables appliances to work together to enhance value to the resident of the household.
Info/Network Technology & Alliances	• Another example is Microsoft's Windows OS.

BOTH FISH AND FOWL

Can a company play multiple roles within a DVN? The international shipping company DHL proves it can.

The company performs two very different roles, depending upon which value network we examine. For starters, DHL acts as a full-fledged DFP in relation to a host of value chains by providing electronic order taking, fulfillment, and delivery services to businesses ranging from consumer products distributors to law firms. In this role, they provide the actual digital platform that makes it possible for all these disparate value chains to operate smoothly.

On the other hand, as a primary shipper of books for the online bookseller Amazon.com, DHL is also simply a participant (albeit a valuable one) in a digital value chain. That is, DHL has not provided a distinctive digital platform for Amazon.com that creates new value by joining value chains, but it does participate efficiently in the flow of goods from the business to the consumer.

The New Middleman—The Infomediary

The word *infomediary* has been used to describe a wide range of companies and services in the digital economy. John Hagel and Marc Singer used the term in their book, *Net Worth,* to describe companies that collect and manage access to consumer information (more on that in Chapter 13).[2] Many firms are now emerging to provide these intermediary services between consumers and the companies that want access to their information—primarily over the Internet.

Others use the term "infomediary" more broadly, to describe a whole host of services around the collection and dissemination of all sorts of information (not just consumer information). We use the term here in the broader sense: to describe a variety of information-based intermediary services.

An infomediary service can involve the collection, dissemination, and control of a variety of types of information. It can also be any person or organization who *facilitates* the exchange of information between other parties, such as a company that matches buyers and sellers in an electronic market.

In broadening the definition, the line starts to blur between what is an infomediary and what is a DFP, and to a degree this confusion is deliberate. In fact, we want to emphasize that it isn't particularly important to identify precisely whether any given participant is a DFP, or a member of a digital value chain, or an infomediary. It's more important to understand how these various components enable DVNs, making these new networks possible. Therefore, a company can be an infomediary, they can supply a DFP, or they can simply be a participant in a digital value chain, or they can be all three depending on how you slice and dice it.

Much has been made of the recent trend toward disintermediation of traditional middlemen. As distribution channels have become flattened and companies have recognized the need to reach their customer directly rather than through third-party sales channels, many types of traditional intermediaries have been struggling. In the digital marketplace, however, there are a whole new set of services that must be provided to facilitate trade—services that previously were not possible or necessary. For example, the Internet would be of little use without search engines and portal sites like Yahoo! and Excite. What do we mean by new sets of services to facilitate trade? Simply, we mean that buyers and sellers still need to find each other, exchange information, and arrange for payment and delivery of goods and services. Companies still need to find customers, if not through brick-and-mortar retail outlets, then through online markets. Some products and services still need to be aggregated or combined before they create a compelling offering for the consumer. The consumer still needs to become educated on products and services in ways that producers may not be able to provide. Someone still needs to establish a price that the consumer is willing to pay while maximizing profits. If traditional middlemen are on the way out and the retail channel is being threatened by the Internet, who is going to provide these necessary functions? Intermediaries.

Let's look at some of the specific types of roles that infomediaries provide to enable the operation of a DVN.

- *Integrating services and needs.* The infomediary takes existing products and services and combines them to create a new offering that has a visibly higher value. For example, Add-a-Photo takes the electronic photo-uploading capabilities provided by PhotoNet and integrates them with American Greetings' electronic cards to create a service that allows users to personalize online greeting cards with the photos of their choice.

- *Aggregating services and needs.* By gathering suppliers and buyers to a single virtual space, the infomediary leverages volume transactions. Freight forwarders are a good example of companies that take shipments of goods from many sources and bundle them to make the shipments more economical.

- *Creating a floating price system based on supply and demand.* Buyers and sellers can therefore shop for, trade, auction off, or otherwise exchange products and payment in a dynamic online environment that reflects up-to-the-minute market conditions. Online auction houses like eBay are classic examples in this category. eBay facilitates an online auction so that individual buyers can bid on products from a broad range of sellers—products that span more than 1,000 categories, including collectibles, antiques, sports memorabilia, computers, toys, coins, stamps, music, pottery, glass, photography, electronics, jewelry, gemstones, and much more.

- *Managing the flow of products from the initial supplier to the final customer.* FastParts Trading Exchange, for example, facilitates transactions between multiple anonymous buyers and suppliers of electronic components. FastParts coordinates all trade fulfillment activities, from fund collection to shipping parts, generating revenue for itself through collecting a commission for each transaction completed.

- *Managing an ever-changing electronic affinity group made up of vendors, suppliers, and customers—the composition of which changes in response to customers' needs and preferences.* GE's Trading Process Network (TPN) accomplishes this task by accepting bids for anything from any supplier who chooses to participate via the Internet. Anyone can submit an RFQ, and any trading member can respond with his or her products or services. The openness of this process has resulted in prices 10 percent to 15 percent lower than in traditional bidding, because suppliers are not sure who else is involved in the actual bidding.[3]

- *Monitoring the performance of all members of a DVN.* By reporting on the performance of the various participants in the value network, and providing necessary data and analyses across all market activities, infomediaries make sure that all members are informed and understand the expectations the value network has of them.

- *Saving time for DVN members.* Infomediaries inform all participants in a value network of changes in price and availability of services in which they are likely to be interested. This function may also extend to gathering information from members about services they desire that do *not* currently exist within the DVN and finding a source of the service when sufficient demand is demonstrated. Take Travelocity, which started out as a one-stop information shop for price-conscious air travelers. The service now also provides information on hotel reservations, car rentals, vacations, and other travel-related products that an airline customer would conceivably be interested in. Furthermore, the site collects information on the types of services that consumers are looking for, which is valuable to these service providers and allows them to better serve their markets.

- *Managing operational functions that include warranty, exchange, charge-backs, returns, and general troubleshooting activities.* The role of the infomediary is not finished when an electronic sale is completed. Providing after-sales services is an essential aspect of a successful DVN transaction. Gateway, for instance, not only assembles computers for buyers, but also provide after-sales support, warranties, exchanges, and charge-backs by taking responsibility for managing the hundreds of suppliers providing them with the components that go into a single personal computer.

- *Developing new customers and markets.* Telia (see the sidebar entitled "Case in Point: Telia"), with its Vision 2001 service, acts as an infomediary by actively increasing market share for members of its DVN within the deregulated European telecommunications market.

Of course, infomediaries don't need to wear *all* these hats. Some infomediaries may elect to organize the demand side (or buyers of a product or service) within a DVN; others may elect to organize the supply side (or sellers) in the network. For example, Amazon.com and Computer ESP have chosen to focus on the needs of the buyers, whereas companies such as FastParts, NetMarket, and CUC International concentrate on helping the sellers in their market niches. Still another model brings together several specialized infomediaries under one umbrella. For example, the online service AOL is, in a sense, a superinfomediary, providing subscribers with a portal to a great many specialized infomediaries.

A CASE IN POINT: TELIA

When Sweden liberalized its telecommunications market in 1993, Telia, the largest telecommunications company, had a tough choice to make. Should it continue its rule of being a "pure" communications services provider, or should it change its service offering by becoming an infomediary through offering integrated solutions from many vendors?

In the midst of a new market in which commodity-like product offerings and steep competition for customers and profits prevailed, Telia created its Vision 2001 strategy. The goal: 15 percent of its total revenue in 2001 should come from entering new service areas. This vision is to be achieved in three ways: by further developing the network into an attractive platform for future advanced multimedia services; by adding value to the service offering as a mechanism for maintaining end customer contact; and by expanding geographically.

To achieve desired geographic growth, Telia is expanding throughout Scandinavia with operations in Finland, Norway, Denmark, the Baltic States, and other overseas markets. To develop its network capabilities, Telia is investing in new services, including broadband IP networks, Internet telephony, Digital TV, and mobile electronic commerce.

Telia gained valuable experience early in the digital economy through experiments it had previously made providing consumer Internet service, as well as organizing online communities for travelers, sports fans, and other people with specific interests. Coupling the knowledge gained from these early forays with its established successful telecommunications business models, Telia was uniquely positioned to deliver a new set of infomediary services to northern Europe.

The road to becoming an infomediary has not been without its difficulties, however. Telia launched a new business unit (Telia Tradebase) and developed a product package (Tradebase) together with several partners, which was launched in October 1996, but which failed. Tradebase offered a complete bundle of services for companies interested in electronic commerce, primarily those that sold products and services to the government. It incorporated an X.400 EDI network with software and support services to simplify and stream-line procurement functions. The original Tradebase business model resembled the business model of a software company, which is based on an initial invest-ment for the software development that is later recovered by the sales of soft-ware licenses. The software was installed at each client site and the network was used for communication purposes only. Telia was responsible for the development and deployment of the Tradebase software, the information ser-vices, and the coordination with its partners. The partners were responsible for conducting prestudies at prospective customers and installing the software, including integrating it with existing customer systems.

The market responded poorly to this offering for a number of reasons. First, the software licensing required under the Tradebase architecture was expen-sive and complicated to deploy. Second, government agencies and their sup-pliers weren't as enthusiastic about moving to electronic commerce as commercial organizations were—they required a more clearly articulated pay-back schedule. Third, and perhaps most important, Telia simply wasn't pre-pared organizationally to sell and service the Tradebase offering, which was, after all, radically different from its traditional telecommunications services.

After extensive analysis, Telia reorganized and consolidated its electronic commerce efforts in 1998 and revised its business model. This revised business model incorporates the key principles of the traditional business model of a telecommunications company: The new offerings are network-centric (no com-plex client site software installation), transaction-based (no large up-front investment for customers), and based on open technologies. The latter of these principles allows Telia to customize customer installations using industry-standard technologies. By using standard components and interfaces, Telia is able to partner with other hardware, software, and service providers to focus on its core value-adding products and services, while sourcing individual compo-nents externally.

Although Telia's original business model for Tradebase was unsatisfactory, the company entered the market early enough to learn from mistakes, and still have sufficient time to reassess, reorganize, and redistribute the product using a business model more appropriate to the digital economy. The revised business model allowed Telia to focus on its core competencies and to engage partners for other components of the model. As a result, Telia positioned itself as a leading solution provider and integrator in an emerging digital market.

Lessons Learned

The process that Telia went through in developing and deploying infomediary services provides other would-be infomediaries with several important lessons:

(Continued)

Enter early and learn from your mistakes. Telia entered the electronic commerce business as an early adapter. After it realized the pitfalls of its original approach, the company quickly analyzed problems and adjusted with solutions. The early start enabled Telia to gain valuable experience, without which it would not have understood how to compete successfully in the brave new telecom world of a deregulated market.

Align your business model to your core competencies. Telia entered the electronic commerce business with a business model not aligned to its core competencies. After Telia revised its approach to fit its overall business model, it was able to provide a sustainable market offering.

Focus on your competencies and supplement through partnerships. Telia realized quickly that it couldn't deploy a complete infomediary service spectrum on its own. It entered strategic, but nonexclusive partnerships and positioned itself as the solution provider and integrator. Furthermore, Telia stepped back from entering areas like professional services and content management that required different business models, instead choosing to find partners who could offer those capabilities more efficiently.

Bringing It All Together

A DVN, therefore, combines these elements: digital value chains, a DFP, related infomediaries, and of course, the consumer (see Figure 6.3). Together, these participants in the network act to benefit *all* members of the network in ways that previously would not have been possible. Although different DVNs will have varying numbers of individual components like infomediaries, DVNs will very likely have at least one of each element. Understanding the role you play in your DVN is vital for future success and sustainability—and is the focus of Chapter 7.

It's important, also, to understand that any of the digital components used to create a given DVN might also be used to create, or be a part of, *other* DVNs. For example, Amazon.com's DFP was built to help purchasers locate and select books; however, the online bookseller's chief value really had nothing to do with books, per se. If tomorrow there were no books to be sold, Amazon could take the same business model, apply it to some other kind of product, and still be successful, because the service it provides is based on information. A whole new DVN could be created in, for example, wine retailing, quite easily.

DELL USES NETWORKS TO HARVEST DIGITAL VALUE

Dell has used the Internet to integrate its supply chain into a digital value chain that links component and parts manufacturers all over the world. Customers enter orders via the company's Internet or Intranet sites. Dell transfers orders through its internal information system to its logistics partners, who are responsible for physically delivering the products. It also uses the system for

FIGURE 6.3
The digital value network (DVN).

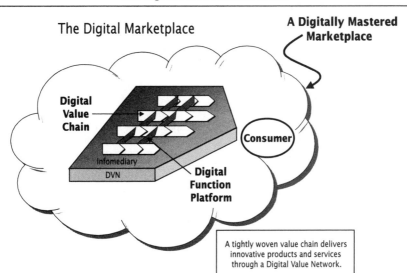

The Digital Marketplace

A Digitally Mastered Marketplace

Digital Value Chain

Infomediary

DVN

Digital Function Platform

Consumer

A tightly woven value chain delivers innovative products and services through a Digital Value Network.

just-in-time restocking of parts. Dell works with only a small select set of suppliers and forges very deep relationships with them. Suppliers' employees actually work in Dell's facilities to help design new products, solve manufacturing problems, and provide input to the customer support center.

Dell also uses a tightly coupled DFP to allow customers, in effect, to design their own computers. Buyers on its Internet site can select both the hardware and the software they want installed on a new computer. Corporate buyers can choose from among stored hardware and software combinations that conform to their company's standards. The software is downloaded onto the computer's hard disk while it is still on the production line, a service that saves corporate customers' IT staff hours of setup time when rolling out new computer systems. This Dell DFP thus provides customers with the ability to self-configure products—a service for which customers willingly pay a premium.

By keeping close track of customer preferences, Dell's build-to-order system also conveys up-to-the-minute data to its suppliers on type and quantities of parts needed. As a result, Dell carries virtually no raw goods inventory. This direct-sales model provides an even bigger competitive edge at times when advances in technology mean new computer models must be introduced. Traditionally, computer firms were stuck with warehouses full of out-of-date stock. Competitors still without integrated value chains are battered, whereas Dell escapes unscathed through its enhanced ability to respond rapidly to market change. In this way, Dell has effectively exchanged hard assets (inventory) into information assets. At a time when competing firms can have excess overstock of obsolete merchandise, Dell can cut prices on new products by 7 percent to 10 percent and still be profitable. Dell's electronic commerce system

(Continued)

moves inventory so quickly that the company frequently operates without using its own capital, because Dell receives full payment from customers before it pays suppliers.

Network-based business models such as Dell's, with their efficiencies and cost-saving advantages, provide a flow of information whose benefits go far beyond real-time decision making. Big cost efficiencies result when firms use digital networks to bypass bottlenecks in the supply chain. By selling directly to the end user, Dell eliminates much of the cost of warehousing, distribution, and retailing. Dell and members of its electronic supply chain reap cost benefits because the customer does most of the data entry, eliminating the need for the duplication of work by clerks in the various companies. Additionally, write-offs of excess inventory are rare, and capacity scheduling is greatly improved. Other less obvious benefits include cuts in cycle time for sales, manufacturing, and fulfillment operation; improved decision making; more efficient customer service; and higher product and service quality.

Dell provides its suppliers with sales forecasts so they can accurately meet demand, assuring its ability to fill the pipeline with products customers are eager to have. Dell's system allows its engineers to share technical information with suppliers for new designs, increasing speed to market and reliability of new products. Dell can do this kind of information sharing because suppliers have modified their information systems and their own business processes specifically to interface with Dell's.

True Digital Value Networks Begin to Evolve

To date, only a few companies have moved from possessing a traditional supply chain, to becoming part of a digital value chain, to the ultimate step of forming a DVN.

There is ample evidence to suggest that early forms of DVNs are emerging, most based upon early EDI private networks, but some are evolving by rallying around Internet-based infomediaries such as AOL and eBay. We believe, from some of these early attempts, that DVN pioneers can expect superior investment returns virtually every step of the way. However, these early experiences also suggest that commercial success does not necessarily start with copycat maneuvers.

Moreover, premature attempts to launch a DVN could, in fact, be a recipe for disaster—especially if the basic infrastructure requirements for success are not yet in place. Dell would never have evolved without the telephone, and Wal-Mart would not likely be what it is today without satellites. Companies must begin by thoroughly understanding the building blocks essential to success in basic digital communication and integration. Each step taken should improve the firm's ability to deliver value to its customers; each step must also pass a hard-headed test to make sure it helps the overall business. (There are many things that your customers would love, but which would send you to bankruptcy court.)

A successful DVN, therefore, must be carefully crafted by adopting an evolutionary strategy. Gain experience in the market, assemble allies, build relationships, and enhance your electronic business capabilities *in stages*. An evolutionary strategy, however, does not mean going slowly. It, in fact, requires a great deal of speed. A successful DVN requires bringing together many participating entities, each with its own mature set of capabilities, and doing so as quickly as possible.

Action Ideas: Beginning the DVN Journey

"There are many ways of going forward, but only one way of standing still."

—Franklin D. Roosevelt

DIGITAL VALUE NETWORKS CAN AFFECT EVERYTHING YOU DO—FROM PURCHASING BASIC supplies to determining how products and services will be advertised, merchandised, ordered, and delivered. Customers can be provided with easier access to producers and wholesalers. Producers or wholesalers can form electronic alliances with overnight delivery companies. Industry-specific networks can expand to serve multiple industries. Global firms can electronically (and seamlessly) integrate suppliers and factories worldwide. With all of these possibilities, where should you begin? We suggest a three-step approach. First, focus on the most promising initial initiatives (the low-hanging fruit, if you will). Second, understand those actions you can take that facilitate a smooth entry into the new digital age. Finally, be armed with an awareness of the potential pitfalls. There are a lot of them.

Focus on the Most Promising Initial Initiatives

A digital value network (DVN) isn't created overnight, and you can't put the business on hold while you fill the whiteboards with your "master plan." Moving from business as usual to a DVN can and must be done in a way that supports and enhances your current business model while moving you incrementally in the right direction.

Tailor the First Application to Address Whatever Is Currently Driving Your Industry

One of the most fundamental building blocks of DVNs is electronic commerce. Therefore, the first step in building a DVN—or becoming a part of one—is to move into electronic commerce by designing a customized entry strategy based on your particular industry. For example:

- Manufacturers should begin by setting up a *digital value chain* that, in the short term, will help reduce costs and improve efficiencies. In the long term, of course, you should continue adding capabilities that enhance the value you offer to your partner companies in the value chain. This is a starting point, from which the goal should be to grow into a true DVN. One major chemical company is in the process of doing this by implementing a system in which storage capacity levels are rapidly communicated via satellite to headquarters. This sets up a replenishment schedule, and then electronically sends the information to a trucking company, which ties the information into a routing schedule letting the trucks know where to go and when. The company's ultimate goal is to extend from this starting point into a DVN capable of interacting with customers, suppliers, and technical experts around the globe.

- Traditional wholesalers, distributors, and retailers need to begin by staving off the risk of disintermediation (being eliminated). Specifically, they can protect their positions in existing supply chains and value chains by setting up a *digital function platform* (DFP) that leverages the business's value-adding capabilities and anchors the business in multiple value chains. For example, automotive dealerships could leverage their position as parts distributors by offering more products and services to repair shops, end consumers, and after-market automotive performance stores that complement their existing product and service portfolio. After successfully building this initial DFP, an ambitious organization could grow into a true DVN with links to manufacturers and designers, providing an enhanced ability to develop customized products. By initially setting up the DFP that conforms most closely to today's business environment, companies increase the likelihood of success, and position themselves for future growth.

A leader in the aerospace industry did this very thing. By developing an electronic sensing device for airplanes, GE can diagnose problems while a plane is in flight and communicate them back to its maintenance center, which then makes sure the appropriate parts and technicians are standing by when the plane lands. "Power-by-the-hour" contracts for airplane maintenance have been around for more than a decade, but not until sensors were put directly on the engines—and maintenance needs that could be more precisely predicted—could GE profitably sell full-service contracts. Now, however, GE is privy to an information flow it can use to do everything from schedule technicians, to order parts from suppliers, to improve its manufacturing capability by knowing which parts fail most often and for what reason.

- Current intermediaries must concentrate on initiating *infomediary services* associated with their current offerings, customers, and brands. The goal is to exploit the value of existing activities by extending them to this new digital realm. Care must be taken, however, to ensure that the necessary digital function platforms are in place. For example, EDS and InterWorld are developing an infomediary service for the Hong Kong Harbor that will facilitate data sharing among all shippers, exporters, and manufacturers who use the harbor—a potential market of 230,000 companies. As the system evolves, these companies will become electronically (and strategically) linked to other essential services, such as ground support.

Fund Early Efforts with Money Saved through Increased Efficiency

Cost saving is, initially, one of the most compelling reasons for introducing a DVN, although it will easily be dwarfed by the long-term value-adding aspects that DVNs provide. Money saved by electronically linking business partners together provides a company with extra resources to accelerate growth. Early benefits that can be reaped include eliminating duplicate activities, like entering the same data for each company's books, thus streamlining accounts receivable and payable departments.

A company can realize particularly big cost savings when it manages to eliminate a complete step or two in the traditional supply chain. For instance, allowing customers to go online to place and track product orders in real time not only improves customer service but also cuts labor costs. This concept is best exemplified by Federal Express, the world's largest express transportation company. FedEx customers go online to fill out shipment information, print their own bar-coded label using a laser printer, and either choose the nearest drop-off location or request a FedEx courier pickup. About 60 percent of the company's transactions are now performed this way. The result? FedEx processes more requests with fewer employees—and dramatically less expense. The labor associated with tracking these packages is passed directly on to the consumer; FedEx has thus simultaneously improved customer support and increased customer loyalty in a fiercely competitive market.

Sara Lee uses electronic commerce to make its knit-products division much more efficient. It links all functions from design, to engineering, pricing, and manufacturing through a central database. The company sends all new designs, as well as changes to existing products, to supply chain participants through e-mail. It records who has approved or denied change requests automatically, and lets everyone in the chain know the status of a particular project at all times.

Cutting fixed, or overhead, costs can lead to top-line results as well. An example is inventory reduction. Digital value networks promise to cut inventory levels by 80 percent to 90 percent over the next decade.[1] Reduced inventory, however, is less than half the story. In a digital network, schedulers get enough information in a timely fashion to more easily make scheduling changes when new demand arises, filling up incremental capacity that would otherwise go unused. As capacity utilization increases, companies can make existing plants more productive, thus reducing the need to build new manufacturing facilities. In some cases, this may provide the opportunity to divest unneeded capacity, staffing existing plants with the additional labor to handle the increased demand, or reducing the size of the workforce.

Another hefty overhead expense, billing your value chain partners for goods or services provided, can be virtually eliminated in a DVN. Business partners of the future will agree that everyone gets paid simultaneously—at the point when the end customer buys the product or service in question. Each partner will be immediately credited with *their share* of the sale. Because inventory levels have already been cut to a fraction of their previous level, every partner experiences improved cash flow.

Even more basic costs can be slashed, because geographic location is no longer an issue when sourcing raw materials. With an effective online purchasing program, firms can easily find the best and cheapest suppliers for their needs, wherever they happen to be located around the world. Japan Airlines, for example, sources supplies worldwide through its web site, thus freeing the carrier from ties to more expensive local suppliers. General Electric uses its online procurement system to conduct commercial contract negotiations with thousands of suppliers. GE wants to draw in even more suppliers as well as customers to create a vast electronic clearinghouse in which hundreds of thousands of firms can exchange trillions of dollars of industrial inputs—with GE running the show, of course. (The goal is to emulate the SABRE airline reservation system, only for airline parts, not passenger seats; because although American Airlines developed SABRE to gain an advantage with travelers over other airlines, it soon found it could make more money if its competitors also used the system.[2])

Develop New Ways to Collect and Exploit Customer Information

The ability to more closely track customer preferences is one of the most obvious advantages of being part of a DVN. When consumers communicate their needs directly to you, you can speed development of new products with these "most wanted" features to market. In effect, goods that the best customers want to buy get to market first, thus conferring a competitive advantage to the firm that communicates effectively with its most knowledgeable—and often its most profitable—customers.

Furthermore, companies can respond to hypothetical situations. You can figure out, from the electronic data, what should have been in the 30 percent of orders that were not filled correctly.

Companies can also electronically share market trend information with their suppliers. At GM, engineers share technical information online with suppliers for new designs, increasing speed to market and reliability of new products. Nabisco is setting up Internet pilots (using Manugistics software) with large retailers such as Wal-Mart and Wegmans to collaborate on forecasting consumer demand. The program is expected to reduce cycle time, cut inventory costs, and ensure that customers never leave a store empty-handed due to stock outs.

A key feature of a DVN is customizing the network to serve both the replenishment and impulse buying needs of customers. A prescription drug is one product category for which replenishment strategies are already being developed. Elderly patients often cannot go to the pharmacy to refill prescriptions. An automatic replenishment schedule assures the physician and the patient that a supply of vital medications is always on hand. One pharmaceutical company is experimenting with "smart prescriptions." The prescription container rests in a cradle that has modem access to an automatic replenishment service. Each time the patient takes a dose, a message is logged so a prescription refill is created in a timely manner.

Finally, customer information from one line of business can be invaluable for cross-selling other products that you also manufacture. Cross-use occurs frequently in traditional venues such as supermarkets, where snacks are placed next to the drink cooler, knowing that potato chip nibblers will want to quench their thirst and beer drinkers will crave pretzels. In the digital economy, cross-selling can be customized. Search for a book on Amazon.com, and you will also be given the titles of books that other customers bought when they purchased the same book, as well as other books by the same author. These additional titles spark a customer's interest, leading to even more sales.

DELL'S EVOLUTION TOWARD A DIGITAL VALUE NETWORK

At Dell, the digital value chain has evolved from an ancillary support activity into a system that drives the entire business. The next step, creating a DVN, promises even greater benefits for participating firms. Dell, however, has a successful business model that delivers results today. Should Dell be moving toward a DVN?

To answer this question, we must first analyze the current situation, as well as the steps required to turn a value chain into a DVN: first, the development of infomediary services; and second, taking the current members of the value chain and forging them into a true *community* in which every participant contributes to the profitability of every other participant.

Infomediary Services Are Partially Developed
The value of the current information services provided to suppliers and corporate customers cannot currently be separated from the tangible Dell products. They are currently useful only to Dell's suppliers, and only when used by members of the value chain when producing Dell products. As a result, the information Dell gathers and shares does not represent a stand-alone product that could sustain a separate business enterprise in the same way that data supplied by a firm like Dun & Bradstreet does. To turn Dell's information into the raw material for a viable, stand-alone infomediary services business, two things would need to happen.

First, the information must be made available for use in non-Dell products. To the extent that Dell customers constitute a representative sample of the more sophisticated segment of personal computer buyers, this could probably be done now. Doing so, however, would lessen one piece of Dell's competitive advantage—knowing the latest trends in consumer demand. It is, therefore, not in Dell's commercial interest to spread this intelligence, unless those competitors manage first in some other way to lessen the impact that the proprietary information currently contributes to Dell's product cycle and inventory reduction advantages.

Second, the information collected would have to be broader in scope than that which Dell currently gathers. This potential change has two aspects, because broader information would also benefit Dell. Suppose that every

(Continued)

feature newly announced by component suppliers was made available in the configuration choices offered on Dell's web site. If the web site operated as a configuration consultant (an intelligent configurator that understood when a combination was not valid, and could suggest alternatives), Dell would have an infomediary service that could advise PC shoppers on the implications of various choices and allow them to define their computer from the chip level on up. Dell could also use this information to tell suppliers which component combinations were most attractive to customers. This intelligent service would vastly increase the value of the information collected by Dell—but it would also change the buyers' reason for visiting the site. If Dell was not prepared to sell every newly announced component, it would not be in Dell's interest to point out capabilities that might cost them sales (oh, you don't have it? I'll go to Gateway). Furthermore, by visibly failing to support everything touted as the latest and greatest, Dell could destroy its image as a technological leader. If, however, competitors develop tailored ordering that matches Dell's current capabilities, Dell would have little to lose by moving in this direction (and, in fact, it may be the only way to maintain a competitive advantage).

The strength of the Dell brand would probably make an infomediary service business not only feasible, but highly profitable. It would also, however, alter their current competitive advantage. Harvesting the potential value generated by an infomediary would require a dramatic shift in focus in their current way of doing business. This type of change is a strategic business decision requiring careful analysis and consideration at the executive level.

Creating a True Community
People who order through Dell realize value, but that value is a result of the actual purchase transaction, not necessarily from the information Dell provides. There is little value derived from the number of customers using the site (beyond the traditional side-effect of scale economies because there is no provision for creating content based upon the collective transactions). As a result, the mechanisms are not in place to create the true community atmosphere, which would act to trigger increasing returns to scale.

Should Dell Push toward a DVN?
We believe that Dell is already proving the validity and value of the DVN concept. Dell has already created exceptional value by bringing together the value chains of multiple component manufacturers into a value-added product to the end consumer—customized personal computers. Dell is acting as the anchor in the network of suppliers. Dell's value in its network is its capability to efficiently connect all the component suppliers in a tightly knit DVN.

The next step in Dell's evolution would occur if multiple digital value chains converged via a DFP to produce multiple value-added services to the consumer. For example, Dell could proactively jump-start the creation of a DVN that would center around the Windows operating system. The multiple value chains would include those centered around computer peripherals (handheld devices, external storage, global positioning satellites, and so on) and software manufacturers (makers of antivirus or troubleshooting tools, for example). This ultimate DVN would provide a plethora of complementary services and devices to personal computer users.

Guidelines for Smooth Entry into the Digital Economy

Here are our guidelines for a smooth transition to becoming part of a successful DVN:

- Understand the potential power shift that a networked community can force on your industry. Keep in mind that it can tip in any direction: toward customers, electronic retailers, producers, or infomediaries.

- Construct initiatives with a clear understanding of how they will impact the *value* you offer to your customers.

- Build your network community as quickly as possible. When one person owned a fax machine, it was useless. As ownership grew, the fax machine's value increased exponentially. The same is true of any networked community. The addition of one node to the network adds more than one node's worth of value to that network.

- Align with players who are likely to be the most powerful in the digital economy. Form alliances with them quickly. Decide which members of the network you will represent—customers (buyers) or producers (sellers)? Base your decision on what the overall value the network will offer participants in the long term, not just on the basis of short-term profit.

- Determine how to enhance the value of the network community, particularly from the view of the customer, and share your vision of the potential value with other participants. Be a giver and not just a taker; withstand the temptation to extract power or profit from the community while trying to prevent others from doing the same.

- Make the network user friendly; make it easy to do business on it. Address customers' ultimate needs, and be prepared to change current processes as often as is necessary to suit them.

- Make trust a critical asset. Install monitoring and security systems, set standards for control of data, and appoint an ombudsman to handle complaints. In this way the network will be perceived as a trustworthy place on which to conduct business.

- Use the network to make your brand name synonymous with the generic product or service—as FedEx and Xerox have done.

- Think big—globally, to be exact.

- Experiment and continuously innovate; speed of innovation is critical. Empower your employees and give them a mandate to experiment and try new ideas.

- Act now, but have an innovative plan B—and C, and D. Don't wait to take action until it's catch-up time.

Be Aware of These Trouble Spots

Of course, we don't mean to imply that shifting to a DVN strategy will necessarily be all smooth sailing. Following is an overview of some of the major potential roadblocks.

Technology indecision. Failure to properly understand technology needs is serious, but analysis paralysis (endless debates over the perfect solution) can be fatal. A web site and the right electronic business infrastructure are critical enabling technologies, but other technology decisions can be harder to make. Corporate leaders can squander their chances to acquire the truly attractive virtual property of relationships with customers and suppliers if they become stalled over technology issues.

Lack of compatibility. Business-to-business networks work only if suppliers and buyers are willing and able to conduct business electronically through open networking standards. Unless the initiator of a digital value chain has enough power and influence (usually the result of controlling an overwhelming proportion of market share) to force participants to use a proprietary system, it's best to stick with industry standards. In the case of Dell, suppliers modified their information systems to the computer maker's standard. However, most businesses will resist such pressure—so the technology you use should be readily available throughout your particular market niche.

Lack of access. Major Japanese electronics companies obtain about 70 percent of components through the EDI system created by the Electronics Industry Association of Japan. Japanese companies, however, use only a small part of the capability of the network—the part made for order placement and invoicing—preferring to negotiate terms and conditions via telephone or personal meetings. This is a cultural preference. For example, Japanese electrical engineers do not use the network for exchanging technical information with their peers for the simple reason that most professionals lack access to the system. The point is that no matter how sophisticated the technology you put into place to enable electronic communication, it's only good if participants agree to actually *use* it.

Stranded assets. Many capital-intensive firms may continue to focus on improving their asset utilization, missing significant future opportunities in the process. Successful firms will continuously reevaluate the competitive value their hard assets produce, and be ready to invest, redirect, or divest of these assets as the market changes. Many Internet start-up firms, for example, have been successful because they do not have a significant capital investment to manage and are better able to focus on the future. The challenge for older, more conventional corporations is to determine how to maximize the return on the existing investments while concurrently moving toward a DVN without being afraid to divest stranded assets.

Lack of standardized descriptions. In industries such as clothing or furniture manufacturing, in which differentiation has always been a problem, and rivalry has been intense, a single company is unlikely to have the market power to force a standardized electronic way of describing products onto the industry at large. In such cases, standards may be set by industry-wide cooperative boards, such as Hong Kong's CargoNet; government agencies; or independent, impartial standards bodies created by industry participants, such as the W3C (World Wide Web Consortium), IETF (Internet Engineering Task Force), AMA (American Medical Association), or ABA (American Bankers Association).

Customers make product decisions by sampling. In industries in which the product is complex or not standardized enough to be easily provided with some sort of quality "stamp" or "grade," customers are reluctant to buy without personally sampling the product. Textile buyers like to feel a fabric; wine merchants need to sip, sniff, and then hold the product up to the light. Products that are not commodities must, therefore, have a "sampling" strategy. Apparel Exchange, an online fabric auction firm, solves this problem by sending swatches of fabric to potential buyers by overnight courier. Lands' End, the sportswear merchant, also offers a swatch service to buyers via its web site, in addition to graphical representations and detailed descriptions within its web site.

Lessons for Modern Management

The first experiments in collaborative electronic commerce are already sending tremors of change through markets, forcing companies to rethink how their industries might be organized. Someday soon a DVN may even change the look of the all-important corporate strategy meeting. Instead of the senior executives of a firm sitting around a conference table and issuing dictums, key managers from dozens of different businesses could be participating in critical strategic decisions from offices, factories, and retail stores throughout the globe. Key business partners, suppliers, and customers will be involved, using two-way video or other electronic collaboration tools.

Those currently remaining on the sidelines of the digital era might do well to pay heed to an organization that launched transactions on a global scale more than 10 centuries ago. That's right—the Catholic Church. Its crusaders conquered the Holy Lands, attempting to subjugate the people, and insulate the Christian world from the influences of the Muslim faith. Meanwhile Christian merchants in Spain and Italy took a different track and began building communities of mutual interests with their Muslim neighbors. They even went so far as to convert to the Arabic numbering system—and subsequently grew rich trading in spices and textiles. The more flexible local merchants learned three lessons:

- Riches gained by exploring *terra nova* come from unexpected findings rather than from reaching anticipated goals.
- More can be learned from your trading partners than from adversaries.
- Venturesome traders can learn capabilities that set them apart from more indecisive rivals.

The idea is not to join the information superhighway merely because it is there; becoming a digital company should represent a means, not an end. However, those who want to remain masters of their fate in the pending digital economy must begin—immediately—to start building a DVN, or electronic community, in which each participant profits.

Today, most corporations point with pride to their Intranets, Extranets, and electronic data interchange (EDI) systems. Yet, these systems largely isolate the organization from its customers and all but a few chosen suppliers. Those who truly want to be masters of the digital economy will emphasize a digital *community,* in which all participants work with the new tools to learn and prosper together.

PART
FOUR

Intelligent
Organizations

The Evolution of Organizational Structures

"There is no security on this earth, there is only opportunity."
—*Douglas MacArthur*

BEGINNING IN THE LATE 1980S AND CONTINUING THROUGHOUT THIS DECADE, EXECUTIVES began realizing that traditional ways of doing business simply weren't working for them anymore. Early responses to what were obviously powerful economic changes included reengineering, downsizing, and outsourcing. As a direct result of this, many things that companies used to accomplish internally are now handled by business partners or subcontractors. Temporary workers, contractors, and consultants make up increasingly sizable percentages of many corporate workforces. The brick walls that formerly divided companies from the outside world (customers, suppliers, retailers, and so forth) have been permeated by numerous forms of electronic communication such as EDI and the Internet.

In this environment, the basic definition of what is and what is not a "company" has become murky, indeed. When you call a business, and the telephone is answered by a sprightly voice that says, "Thanks for calling XYZ Corporation!," you can no longer be sure if you've reached the company's physical facility, a subsidiary in another state, a local answering service, or a third-party call center on the other side of the country. When contacted by representatives of a business, you often have no idea where they are calling from (their office? their home office? their car?), or even whether they are full-time employees, part-time telecommuters, or contractors for the day.

Perhaps it doesn't matter, if the business in question still provides you, the customer, what you need in a timely fashion—but that's a big "if."

Today's corporate leaders must make tough decisions about the kind of value their company delivers to the marketplace. Correspondingly, they need to decide not only what they should do to enhance this value, but also what they should *not* do. In short, some things will be better left in the capable hands of partners, contractors, or even the open market.

As we discussed in Part Two, CEOs increasingly must focus on creating products and services using time and content as the new yardsticks of consumer value. Consumers, for the first time, have taken the front and center seats in the strategic ballpark, as shown in Figure 8.1.

Part Two outlined many ways to go about creating the new "intelligent" products and services that will be needed to ensure your company's success in the digital economy.

This chapter, as well as Chapters 9 and 10, goes a step further: helping you understand how to restructure your *organization* so it is capable of producing these products and services—when the customer wants them, where they want them, and how they want them.

FIGURE 8.1
The digital marketplace.

The Digital Marketplace

How do YOU Master this Marketplace?

Manufacturers
Suppliers
Service Providers
Business Partners
Your Company
Consumer
Distribution Channels
Networked Communities
Infomediaries
Aggregators
Intermediaries

Power has shifted toward consumers who demand "Intelligent" products that deliver new dimensions of value—*time and content*—in addition to the current dimensions of value—price and quality.

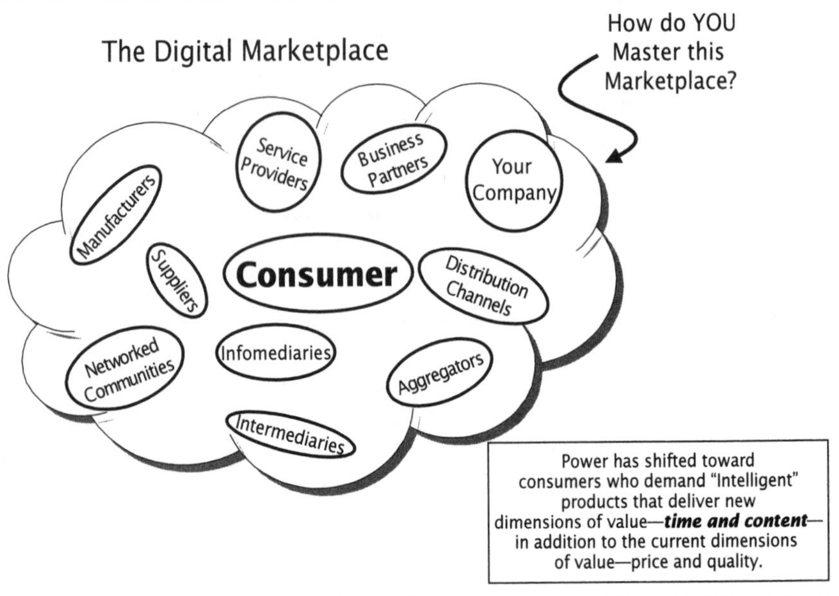

This organizational evolution is a necessary first step in mastering the digital marketplace, and is the only way to clear the metaphorical fog in the preceding diagram that symbolizes the chaos that many CEOs are now experiencing. However, without an understanding of the digital marketplace [digital value network (DVN)] in which this new organization will operate, and the type of products (intelligent products) it will produce, this discussion would be of limited use. Therefore, it is the third and final major topic that is covered, and at the end of Part Four, "Intelligent Organizations," you should have a complete picture of how to master the digital marketplace by transforming your offering, markets, and organization.

After reading Chapters 8, 9, and 10, you will carry away an in-depth knowledge of how information technology (IT) has already made obsolete traditional ways of thinking about the *cost* of exchanging goods, money, and information in the digital market. You will also understand why your company has to transform itself into a nimble and flexible value-based organization (VBO) to compete effectively given the new economic rules of the digital age.

The Evolution of the Corporation

Today's corporate structure has been shaped by many events over the past 40 years. The 1960s witnessed the rise of the conglomerate in the interest of diversification. (Interestingly enough, the practice of "conglomeration" is commonly accepted today as unnecessary, because stockholders prefer to achieve diversification through personally creating stock portfolios that more closely suit their individual risk-reward preferences.) Back then, however, CEOs were still using diversification as a way of reducing shareholder risk; in the process, however, they often lost focus. Specifically, by spreading themselves too thin across a broad range of activities unrelated to their core businesses, CEOs found themselves floundering even in those market niches they had previously dominated.

The 1970s witnessed the rebirth of the vertically integrated organization. Companies began aggressively expanding their size and reach within an industry in the hopes of achieving massive economies of scale as well as industry dominance. This, too, was a relatively short-lived strategy. During the 1980s and 1990s, the trend toward vertically integrated organizations declined as the synergies achieved turned out to be significantly smaller than the overhead costs of maintaining them.

Yet, although most companies eventually decided to carve out a smaller, more focused piece of the supply chain for themselves (rather than trying to own the entire chain), few could articulate why they own the particular piece they do, or what piece they will own tomorrow. Even fewer have any sense of the true value they provide to the eventual consumer.

The reason for this ignorance is that most businesses are still driven by traditional command-and-control organizational models that are ineffective because they simply cannot respond with the speed and decisiveness necessary to be competitive in the digital economy. Business in the digital economy means delivering best-in-class capabilities in conjunction with a network of business partners who bring their best-in-class capabilities together to deliver fast, comprehensive solutions to a demanding but constantly evolving market.

Traditional Organizational Design

To understand where the digital economy is taking the organizational model, let's take a look at where it's been. Traditional organizational theory holds that the structure of a company is the logical outcome of environmental, technological, and strategic factors.[1] The main purpose of such a structure is to create, coordinate, and control the synergy that makes the value of the whole greater than the sum of its parts.

Traditional theory further maintains that to fulfill its primary purpose, a company must be structured primarily in a hierarchical manner, with clearly defined authority and lines of communication, and with well-understood divisions of labor and responsibility. We want to stress that the following three goals remain valid for companies who wish to compete in the digital economy. However, the *way* they are fulfilled varies dramatically. These goals include the following:

- To facilitate information flows and decision making to meet the demands of customers, suppliers, and regulatory agencies
- To define with clarity the respective responsibilities of various individuals, teams, departments, and divisions
- To create the desired levels of integration and coordination among these entities[2]

Take note: Each of these goals is directly or indirectly related to the effective and efficient management of information.

In years past, so-called middle managers were responsible for this exchange of information. The primary role of middle management, in fact, was to consolidate and summarize information coming from below (operations) for the benefit of those above (senior managers), as well as to disseminate information generated at the top of the organizational structure.

As technology created new, more effective methods of managing information, the basic rules and conventions upon which every organization was founded began being questioned. As employees adopted e-mail, voice mail, and groupware, and as businesses adopted intranets, electronic commerce, virtual private networks, virtual network exchanges, and other methods of communication and collaboration, the ability of companies to meet each of the three goals more effectively using technological rather than human intermediaries significantly increased. This phenomenon can be witnessed by the disappearance of middle management over the last 10 years. As technology improves the organization's ability to communicate, the layers of management originally needed to perform these functions have evaporated.

It's important, however, for companies to go one step further. Technology can do more than enhance communication, integration, and decision making. If you hope to master the digital marketplace, your company must use technology to create value—real, tangible value that the customer recognizes and upon which he or she bases real purchasing decisions. (In the next chapter, we will present our own 12-step program for doing exactly this.)

Managerial Control versus Entrepreneurial Freedom

Traditionally, most organizations employed one of the following organizational structures: hierarchical, matrix, product-based, or geography-based. More recently, two other kinds of structures have evolved: horizontal and network-based. (For detailed descriptions of each, please see Appendix A.)

Each of the four traditional kinds of organizational structures (the first four listed previously) can effectively control large quantities of capital assets from the top. However, in the digital economy, opportunities have short shelf lives (a few months, if that), and the first company to enter a new market achieves significantly greater benefits than so-called early adopters of the past. Top-down control is no longer enough.

The digital economy requires an organization that can adapt much more quickly. The organization, therefore, must leverage the entrepreneurial capabilities of its employees if it hopes to adequately respond to short-shelf-life opportunities. To do so, it must provide employees with sufficient incentives and flexibility.

To understand why these things are important, keep in mind that the ultimate goal of any company is to create value. Value comes from employing the right people, equipped with the right tools in the right environment, enabled by the right technology, who can then create a product or service that consumers will want to buy. In the digital age, employees, not physical assets, become your most effective resource, because they create the intellectual assets from which your consumers will increasingly derive value. (See the discussion of "New Wealth from Soft Assets" in Chapter 5.) It is easy to see how important individual employee ability and entrepreneurial skill will become in the digital economy.

The four traditional kinds of organizational structures ensure that employees will act (and react) in a predictable and highly controlled fashion. This environment of checks and balances ensures the integrity of the system as a whole, and makes sure that tasks are completed correctly and on time. However, these coordination-and-control systems also create bureaucracies that impede the ability of employees to create and innovate. The problem magnifies as the number of employees involved in a particular task increases.

For example, the simple task of fulfilling a single customer service or support request may require the involvement of a customer service agent, a product engineer, a design engineer, and several engineering managers. Whether a functional, product, matrix, or geographical structure is in place, a chain of events needs to happen, involving each of the above employees in a more or less serial fashion to fulfill the request. This usually involves invoking the services of each employee by navigating the organizational structure and "throwing the problem over the wall"—that is, handing over responsibility to someone else once a particular employee's task is completed. Because the problem is handed off from person to person, a system of checks and balances is required to ensure that, overall, the desired result (fixing the customer's problem) has occurred.

The result is a lethargic business model that reacts predictably to most events—in which senior management is responsible for controlling the business by communicating through the established structure. This creates a system in which employees simply carry out orders and have no contact with or responsibility to actual customers. This insulation from the market made sense when the primary goal of the corporation—as established in the Industrial Age—was to minimize costs through routine performance of repetitive tasks.

However, those tasks are now almost uniformly automated, and yet companies are still organized around them. Such businesses are rapidly becoming stagnant and sluggish, and they are finding themselves abandoned by customers who long ago realized no one was listening to them.

Oh Brave New Networked World That Has Such Organizations in It

On the other hand, a business that transforms itself around a *network* organizational structure requires much fewer checks and balances because responsibility is not delegated. For example, when new challenges arise, a network organizational structure responds by forming a cross-functional team on the fly to address the need. This team can be composed of individuals of varying backgrounds and experience, and is usually led by a senior employee who owns the responsibility. Therefore, the responsibility is not delegated down through the ranks, but is assumed by a cross-functional subset of employees who team to attack the challenge, then disband when the challenge is overcome. When organized this way, employees solve any problem at hand in parallel fashion by pulling together skills from multiple disciplines. The costs of communicating within the cross-functional team can be reduced and eventually become insignificant.

The network structure is the only form that truly attempts to take advantage of the skills of entrepreneurial employees who are individually committed to creating new value. There *is* a drawback to the network organizational structure, however, in that it is myopic, focusing on internal capabilities instead of focusing outward. When teams form to attack challenges, they are created using skills internal to the organization.

The ideal organizational structure would use the network model, but would also take advantage of information technology to incorporate the skills and capabilities of other companies to meet customer needs.

By reaching outside the four walls of the business and taking advantage of the competencies of external businesses, companies can focus specifically on what they do best—their core competencies. They do only what they do best in response to market demand.

The traditional organizational structures, therefore, are fast becoming relics due to their inflexibility, lack of support for individual contribution, and primary focus on internal operations. A new organizational structure is necessary—one that leverages the network model for internal value-adding capabilities, and focuses on harnessing the competencies of external business partners for those functions for which it has no specific competence. We call this the *value-based organization* (VBO).

Introducing the Value-Based Organization

As we've previously explained, the new digital economy demands a new corporate organizational structure that pays strict attention to what customers want *now*. Running a business in the digital age without this sort of focus is like trying to drive a car by looking in the rear-view mirror. Your business may have delivered great products in the past, but without understanding what your customer wants today, you could be left without any market at all.

Thus, the necessity for the VBO: a modular and reconfigurable collection of individuals (and related skills) that can be used or set aside as the competitive situation demands.

CASE IN POINT

Some companies go well "outside the box" of standard market research methods to better understand consumer behavior and desires. For example, conventional wisdom has it that "white goods" (for example, washing machines, dishwashers, refrigerators) are all pretty much the same, and that consequently, price and color are the primary product differentiators. Maytag, using the science of ethnography, puts observers in the homes of consumers to understand what they really *do* with these products—and, correspondingly, what else they might want. By not believing what customers *said* they wanted in traditional telephone and print surveys, Maytag has created a continuous stream of winning products—including refrigerators whose shelves can be adjusted while loaded, dishwashers that not only clean but also sanitize, and a washing machine that can wash 10 king-size sheets at once while using significantly less water than conventional washing machines.

Once the customer's needs (and wants) are understood, a VBO performs only those functions that it does better than anyone else in the market. It relies on external business relationships for services that others perform better. Innovation is the main driver of business as it constantly pursues new market opportunities by creating new products and services. It continuously looks for more efficient partners for all noncritical activities and it seeks ways to take advantage of its true value-adding capabilities to expand its business further, capitalizing on opportunities in alternate markets and alternate industries.

The VBO, in short, reshapes and adapts itself to meet market demands in the shortest possible time, with the fewest possible resources. The result is a firm completely exposed to the market, able to respond to changing conditions in a flash, and in turn able to create the most value for its customers and shareholders alike.

Make New Friends

After making the customer their prime focus, the second thing value-based companies must learn is how to look *outward* for help serving that customer.

Traditional companies naturally focus internally when a need arises. They build additional capabilities as necessary—perhaps a new sales division to handle an emerging channel, or a new manufacturing division to produce a key product component. As such firms grow, their focus eventually centers around cost reduction and productivity improvements. Such firms only look outside company walls when there are obvious cost and efficiency advantages to be had. Only a too-good-to-be-true outsourcing contract that promises to slash distribution costs in half, for example, will be seized by a traditional company.

These companies, afraid to trust the information systems required to support outsourcing, have chosen to keep their bloated organizations intact instead of sharpening their focus and hiring others to perform ancillary functions such as human resources administration. Such organizations have lost sight of their main reasons to exist—to serve their customers and to increase the value of their shareholders' investments. If they are to become fast, flexible, and capable of creating new value, they must learn to take advantage of and to trust the information infrastructure.

On the other hand, the VBO, through its ability to look outwardly and into the market for needed capabilities, has a longer-term strategy: It builds an *interface* that allows it to access external resources quickly and cheaply whenever it needs to. Think of it as building a portable gangway that can be instantaneously extended in any direction, rather than constructing a 12-ton permanent bridge that can only link point A to point B.

Value-based organizations, in essence, resemble LEGO™-brand building blocks so popular with young children. They are based on modular units that can be pulled apart and put together in different configurations, based on the needs of the company and the demands of the market. With LEGOs, a child doesn't own one toy, but a potentially unending supply of toys that can be built with a combination of standard (low-value adding) and specialized (high-value adding) blocks.

The focus on combining your value-added competencies (VACs) with other companies to exploit market opportunities and create new value is already happening.

CASE IN POINT

You might think the core competency of the Swiss company that makes Swatch wristwatches . . . is watchmaking. It seems obvious. However, the company seems to take a broader view: that its ability to appeal to young people is a value-added competence in itself.

In a prototypically digital age move, Swatch teamed up with Mercedes-Benz to create the Smart Car, an inexpensive automobile that debuted in Europe in 1998. Besides its price and small size, the auto's distinguishing feature is an optional kit with a variety of brightly colored body panels that owners use to change the shape and color of the car at will, just as owners of the wrist-watches can change colors to match their mood and outfit. By identifying its real value-added competency (appealing to trend-conscious young consumers), Swatch successfully entered a brand new market in a very short time by combining its value-added competence with that of Mercedes-Benz.

Value-Added Competencies

You may have noticed that sometimes children will "borrow" LEGO pieces from friends or neighbors to create newer, cooler (read: higher value), and more innovative structures. The same is true with the VBO. By constantly monitoring and evaluating their internal portfolio of building blocks, they're careful to maintain ownership of only those blocks that allow them to deliver value. We call this their core competency. Onto this core competency they can plug and unplug additional functionality from other businesses as the need arises—through outsourcing, partnerships, joint ventures, and strategic alliances with firms possessing specific talents and capabilities.

Increasingly, value-based companies will use portfolio management techniques to measure the critical factors (costs, revenues, systems, and processes) of each organizational unit against the market. They will subsequently determine whether capabilities should be maintained internally (that is, whether it's a core competency) or whether it should be sourced externally.

A *value-added competency* (VAC) is what Gary Hamel and C. K. Prahalad describe in their book, *Competing for the Future*, as a *core competency,* with the stipulation that the competency in question must provide tangible, sustainable value to the consumer. (Hamel and Prahalad make a similar point in their book, but most discussions of core competencies omit this important distinction.)[3]

NEW TERMINOLOGY TO TAKE NOTE OF

The goal of the value-based organization (VBO) is to perform *only* those activities that support the company's value-added competencies, or VACs. Most companies have yet to distinguish those activities that directly support their VACs and those that are superfluous.

VAC. Those things the company does that directly provide value to the consumer with all of the following characteristics: These activities are unique (no other company does them quite the same way), extendable (not confined to a single individual, product, or group), and create value that the customer recognizes and associates directly with the company.

Non-VAC. Functions or processes that do *not* directly provide value to the consumer in one or more of the following areas: These functions are not unique, are not extendable, and/or do not create recognizable value from the customer's perspective. These functions are better left in the hands of more capable external business partners.

The term *non-VAC* does not imply that these activities fail to add value. All activities that companies perform probably add value in some form or another. The term is used to describe those activities that nevertheless fall outside of the realm of the firm's *true competencies*.

Hamel and Prahalad's definition of core competencies identifies three components: skill, technology, and capability. Each of these components is present in every VAC, and the strategic combination of these components creates true VACs.

In turn, each VAC must possess three characteristics. First, it must be unique—different from what others are doing and done better than anyone else. Second, the VAC must be extendable, transcending individual products and business units. For example, one of Cisco System's VACs is data transmission. This competence transcends most of their products and clearly differentiates them from other businesses. However, if Cisco identified switching technology for 155-Mbps ATM networks as their VAC, they would be incorrect because that is a specific technology that can be purchased, imitated, or replaced with more advanced technology. It may be a component of a VAC, but is not a VAC in and of itself. The ability to develop high-speed networks, on the other hand, would be a VAC.

The final characteristic of a VAC is that the three components must create value *as perceived by the consumer.* This is essential. A company may have the skill, technology, and capability to create a new product, but if the value that company adds to the product is not recognizable by the consumer, there is no VAC involved. Witness the demise of the OS/2 operating system from IBM, and the NetWare network operating system from Novell. These two products were at one point in time created from competencies that were unique and extendable, but they eventually failed to add value as perceived by the end consumer.

This last characteristic is the most overlooked characteristic of VACs, but is an absolutely critical driver of value in the VBO.

Value-added competencies are composed of many value-added activities and are embedded in the very fabric of the organization. Capabilities that revolve around a specific technology platform or a few talented employees are rarely VACs because they are not sustainable. If competitors can copy them, if employees can take them when they leave the company, or if they vanish if technologies change, they are not true VACs. Value-added competencies are sustainable over the long term if properly nurtured.

By no means are VACs easy to identify, however. Assessing the value of your various business activities is a difficult, and subjective, process. In addition, one company's low-value, noncore activity can be another's VAC. For example, most companies no longer directly employ the individuals who clean their office buildings or maintain their plants. That function is of relatively low value in the larger scheme of running a business and making a profit, but the vendor providing the cleaning or watering/plant maintenance service may not see things this way. For that business, it's probably their VAC.

The same principles that apply to identifying value within the activities of a VBO apply to identifying those members of a company's workforce who are truly necessary. The digital economy demands that CEOs shift their attention from managing fixed assets to managing intellectual capital resources. This shift is necessary because the value created in the digital economy is coming less from physical products and physical labor, and more from the knowledge and intellectual capital resources that employees provide.

Witness the labor market in Silicon Valley, in which employees switch jobs much more frequently than would previously have been considered wise (in terms of individual careers, that is). This fluid labor market is really a fluid *knowledge* market, because innovative companies are willing to pay hefty salaries to attract the best knowledge resources. This is how it should be. To achieve the most effective, flexible, and innovative VBO, the principles of economic value and VACs must be applied to every person in the organization. Each employee should be constantly evaluated based on the value they create and the skills they deliver.

Many companies erroneously believed they knew their VACs and the activities that supported them. For example, Barnes and Noble believed its VAC involved selling literature in a convenient and comfortable environment. Although this activity was certainly important, and could even be considered core, it was not as sustainable as Barnes and Noble believed. The goal of every company is, or should be, to create and sustain new value, and in creating new value companies must understand what their value-creating capabilities are. Companies that fail to identify the true value they provide in the market will likely be replaced swiftly and without time to adapt. For example, traditional bookstores such as Barnes and Noble still exist mainly because of nostalgia, inexpensive entertainment (reading books is a free activity if done inside the store), fancy coffee shops, and consumers' fear of using their credit cards to make online purchases. As customers lose this fear (and they will—remember how ATM machines were shunned when they first appeared), and as the attraction of nostalgia is replaced by a desire for increased discretionary time, traditional bookstores will have to create a more sustainable value proposition to survive. Barnes and Noble, along with every other major retail bookseller, is really in the business of selling prescreened published *information* to consumers *when* they want it, *where* they want it, for the *right price*. This is their VAC, and because most booksellers could not fully meet this need, other companies, like Amazon.com, have entered the market. (The fact that Amazon.com has been so successful is proof of what a bookseller's sustainable VAC must be.) This is not to say that physical bookstores are no longer needed, it is simply saying that they do not fully address the value of selling books and related goods. To Barnes and Noble's credit, it realized this quickly, and has since expanded into the online realm.

Companies have attempted to identify the true value they add to the marketplace by a number of different methodologies. The disciplines of economic value analysis (EVA™) and economic value creation (EVC) are widely practiced to assess the value of a company as a whole and, occasionally, to assess the value of individual products or product lines.

The problem is that these disciplines use purely financial accounting numbers as the basis for their analyses. They also attempt to measure value based on the amount of capital employed, making it difficult to determine the value of intangibles, such as customer loyalty or an exceedingly skilled and knowledgeable pool of employees. These disciplines also do not work well when attempting to determine the value of activities, such as an isolated business process or a single step within a process.

Therefore, we have created a new methodology for determining economic value created by an internal business unit, process, or step. (See the sidebar entitled "How to Identify the Value of an Internal Activity.")

HOW TO IDENTIFY THE VALUE OF AN INTERNAL ACTIVITY

Identify a direct (and serious) competitor for the activity (function or business process) in question. (Do this by asking yourself: Who would your business look to if forced to find an alternative source for it?) For example, to identify a serious alternative for payroll processing you would very likely consider ADP, a company who specializes in payroll processing. If individual branches or divisions of your company perform their own payroll processing, you may consider other divisions to be serious competitors for benchmarking purposes.

Estimate the cost your direct competitor pays (or charges) to perform the activity in question. Sum up raw materials, overhead, labor, and all other tangible or intangible expenses.

Appraise the quality of your competitor's version of the activity. What are the defect levels? Error rates? How loyal are customers? Include all other factors, tangible or intangible, that impact quality.

Identify all of the factors that distinguish your activity from the competitor's: higher/lower overhead costs, more/less direct labor, better/poorer safety, better/poorer reliability, higher/lower efficiency, shorter/longer cycle time, better/worse cost-effectiveness, faster/slower service.

Measure the value of each of these distinguishing factors through industry information, industry best practices, past experience, and so forth. The information obtained should be both qualitative (for example, degree of content, perceived performance advantages, styling, or reputation) and quantitative (for example, tangible time savings, defect rates, profit margins, industry reliability data). The value should be calculated and clearly stated based on incremental cost/benefit units.

Determine whether your activity adds or detracts value from your consumer offering, based on how well (and how cheaply) your competitor could do it.

Although identifying the value created by an internal activity or process is important, identifying the company's VACs is instrumental in building an organization capable of operating in the digital economy; however, it is not the only hurdle in becoming a VBO. These hurdles and the process of overcoming them will be discussed in the next chapter, but first, a discussion of the enablers of this radical new organizational structure is provided to solidify the foundation upon which the VBO is built.

Enablers of Value-Based Organizations

Value-added competencies, as discussed in the previous section, are the true value drivers of the VBO in the digital economy. They are not, however, the only factors. There are two key enablers of the VBO that cannot be overlooked. These are efficient markets and IT.

- *Efficient markets* provide the necessary business partners to perform many, if not all, of a VBO's noncore activities.

- *Information technology* (IT) drastically reduces the transaction costs of conducting business, allowing the outsourcing of non-VAC functionality.

Efficient markets exist and are developing for every conceivable good or service. It's only a matter of time before there are efficient markets for the vast majority of business capabilities. To utilize (and in some cases create) these efficient markets, IT is quickly dissolving the glue that holds traditional organizations together. Not only does IT automate routine business processes, but it provides a platform for revolutionary changes in the very way business processes are performed—and by whom they are performed.

The Emergence of Efficient Markets

An efficient market is an environment in which buyers and sellers can easily identify each other, exchange information about their wants and needs, agree to a price, and exchange goods and/or services and/or funds in a relatively fluid, relatively frictionless environment. In efficient markets, information, communication, funds transfer, and possibly even the goods and services themselves will be digital, rather than physical, commodities.

Digital value networks (DVNs), as discussed in Chapter 6, are a key enabler of efficient markets. Markets will never be perfectly efficient; there will only be degrees of efficiency. In the digital economy, however, the degree of efficiency for any given market is enhanced on a daily basis.

CASE IN POINT

The market for semiconductor product development is rapidly reaching a high level of efficiency. Companies of all kinds are forming partnerships in which their internal skills can be complemented with skills of other organizations to create new intelligent products. For example, such partnerships have produced system-on-a-chip (SOC) semiconductors, which are in turn used in a wide variety of applications to create new products. According to an article written by Lynda Kaye, Cadence Design Systems' director of international marketing, "many established semiconductor, systems, and electronic design automation (EDA) companies are discovering that a vertically integrated organization may be too cumbersome to address an ever increasing market demand, and partnerships are becoming more common. To remain competitive, many companies are revolutionizing their approach to the business of product development with two significant and closely related shifts: collaboration and focus on core competencies."

The same article cited a recent report by management consulting firm Harbor Research describing these new types of relationships: "Partnerships are the fastest, and in many respects the lowest-risk, means of adding more delivered value for customers. They are an integral part of every systems supplier's strategy."[4]

An often-used reason for mergers and acquisitions and for keeping non-core functions in-house is that markets remain immature over a fairly lengthy and fairly predictable length of time. This, however, is changing very quickly. The IT revolution has created a society that has immediate access to a world of information that was not available, and in many cases did not exist, 15 or 20 years ago. Today, information is available from virtually anywhere in the world through both public and private computer networks. This has thoroughly revolutionized the way in which people share information, drastically reducing the cost of sharing it.

However, the digital economy has not only increased the efficiency of existing markets, it has also created new markets for goods and services. New, more efficient markets emerging in a variety of industries are already putting extreme pressure on existing firms. Increasingly, existing players will be forced to reduce or even eliminate internal costs, to become more flexible, and to capitalize on their intellectual capital to simultaneously find markets for new products and new markets for existing products.

For example, warehousing and delivery companies are bringing previously unimagined new efficiencies to their offerings thanks to digital wireless technology. High-volume, low-cost overnight package delivery was simply not feasible until packages could be tracked using bar code technology and high-powered computers. However, these technologies are commonplace today; companies that retain warehousing and delivery services in their own portfolios in which these services do not constitute VACs, and who continue to ignore the economic benefits that outsourcing can yield, dilute their own efforts and incur needless costs.

Such firms tend to maintain rigid, inflexible organizational structures that are not designed to integrate the functionality offered by the market. However, flexible organizations can more easily link with external partners for specific functions with negligible disruption, becoming a more efficient competitor in the process.

Take a look at the securities trading industry. Although investors have traditionally traded shares in public companies through intermediaries, the number and type of such intermediaries has changed dramatically in the last few years. Drastically lowered transaction costs and the abundance of readily available information have together conspired to effect a massive disintermediation in the financial services industry.

Thanks to the Internet, investors can opt out of a brokerage relationship and easily handle their own transactions. Commissions have shrunk from a percentage of the value of the trade to flat fees in the $5 to $30 range. Additionally, individual investors now have access to near real-time information formerly available only to brokers and other investment professionals. The complex monitoring and analysis tools that used to belong solely to the intelligentsia of the investment community are now available to individuals and corporations alike.

In addition to reducing the cost and increasing the amount of information available to the consumer, these new services have put *time* (the most important commodity of all) back into the consumer's hand by making investment transactions much simpler to accomplish.

Retailing provides another example.

As the Internet reaches more and more people, it has proven itself a highly efficient channel for transacting retail business; it has wide market reach and costs little to provide a virtual storefront. Some companies, such as Egghead Software, have abandoned their physical presence entirely; others—the independent bookseller Amazon.com chief among them—never had one. Traditional mail-order catalog companies, such as Lands' End and L.L. Bean, now reap a significant portion of revenues through online sales. Online storefronts give customers a multitude of new options and features: Consumers can find products and information more quickly; they can make more informed decisions without feeling pressured by a hovering sales representative; and they can shop whenever they want—24 hours a day, 365 days a year. Consumers also reap the benefits of significantly reduced overhead expenses and distribution costs.

CASE IN POINT—APPLYING TECHNOLOGY TO REDUCE TRANSACTION COSTS

eRoom is an off-the-shelf, Web-based application specifically designed to help companies manage projects more efficiently through improved communication and collaboration. The software offers extensive groupware capabilities and can be used by a project team which may be scattered all over the globe. eRoom works like a virtual meeting room that is always open: At any time, users can log on to share ideas, resolve issues, and get updates to projects. Users can log on from anywhere, at any time. eRoom removes time, distance, and organizational barriers to quick sharing of information. In short, it creates a more efficient market for intellectual capital within the organization (or group of organizations) that use it.[5] A.T. Kearney consultants have successfully used eRoom to collaborate on projects and have achieved powerful results by capitalizing in its ability to connect consultants with varying areas of expertise on multiple projects simultaneously from all over the world.

The Evolution of Information Technology

As computer processing power increases, as traditional voice communication networks evolve into data networks, and as more businesses become connected to the Internet, an infrastructure is being created for global digital communication. Public communication networks have evolved from being able to carry voice-only traffic to being able to handle both voice and data; by the year 2000, it is estimated that data traffic will outnumber voice traffic by a factor of 10 or more. This increase in data traffic is in direct response to the changing ways in which consumers, businesses, and employees interact with each other.

The rise of the global computer network, the Internet, and its impact on businesses as a low-cost digital infrastructure is driving business-to-business communication and seamless integration between internal departments and external business partners. Businesses no longer view themselves as silos that create value in isolation; they are partners in an integrated value chain. With new technological advances, these value chains are transmuting into entire value networks with indistinguishable individual players.

The increasing use of digitized information to conduct all types of business activity is paving the way toward breaking down the barriers between businesses. As vital information is shared, even more value is created. Businesses no longer need to perform every function necessary to create a particular set of products or services. By sharing information through digitization and computer networks, firms can rely on external partners for noncritical functions and focus more resources on those functions that create the most value and provide the most return on investment.

Transaction Costs

More than 50 years ago, Ronald Coase presented his theories on transaction costs in an article titled "The Nature of the Firm."[6] Coase's ideas were largely ignored until 1991, when they earned him a Nobel prize in economics, and finally brought the issue of transaction costs to the attention of nonacademic businesspeople.

Coase said, in essence, that companies were formed in an effort to minimize the costs of doing business. These costs, he said, are associated with the transactions that businesses engage in—activities that consume time, resources, or money in the process of creating value. Coase identified the specific costs involved in doing business, defining them as "the costs of carrying out a transaction by means of an exchange on the open market."[7] These costs are now referred to as *transaction costs* in both economic and business literature. Transaction costs range from those associated with finding information about available goods and services; negotiating and contracting for them; and acquiring, maintaining, and (eventually) retiring them.

Coase elaborated on the meaning of transaction costs in his 1988 work, *The Firm, the Market and the Law*, stating that, "in order to carry out a market transaction, it is necessary to discover who it is that one wishes to deal with, to inform people that one wishes to deal and on what terms, to conduct negotiations leading up to a bargain, to draw up the contract, to undertake the inspection needed to make sure that the terms of the contract are being observed, and so on."[8]

According to Coase, companies came into existence largely because they could conduct transactions at a lower cost if they owned the resources, and brought those resources together themselves, effectively removing or replacing the price mechanism and the inefficiencies inherent in using such a system for each transaction. Coase's assertion, that individuals organize themselves into firms for the simple reason that transaction costs would be prohibitive otherwise, stands in direct opposition to the one held by traditional organizational theorists. (Traditional organizational theorists say that an organization's main purpose is to reproduce internally the conditions of a competitive market for all the resources the firm consumes without relying on the price mechanism as it creates its products or services.) However, to satisfy Coase's definition, these resources must be reproduced internally at a lower total cost than the open market could profitably provide.

Applying Information Technology to Reduce Transaction Costs

In a 1998 interview published in the online *Context Magazine,* the 87-year-old Coase said that simply obtaining and absorbing information accounts for a large portion of transaction costs, and that transaction costs represent a large part of the cost of production. Coase added that Nobel laureates Douglass North and J. Wallis estimated the magnitude of transaction costs at 45 percent of the total economy.[9] Presumably, companies that handle information better than others are in a position to redeploy the money they save in transaction costs to create more value for their customers and shareholders.

Although the potential cost savings of efficient information processing are enormously significant, amazingly they do not represent the true value businesses can obtain from the strategic use of IT. The real value in such cases comes from the ability to transform an organizational structure from a slow, hierarchical form into one that is fast, flexible, and agile.

Specifically, IT allows transactions to seamlessly transcend the physical (and organizational) walls of any one corporation.

For example, most companies do their own accounting. That is, typically, the job of keeping track of cash flow, fixed-asset depreciation, revenues, expenses, and taxes for a firm is completed by individuals fully employed by the firm. However, few if any firms can truly state that their internal accounting departments are VACs. Independent accounting firms are much more capable of performing the function and, for publicly held companies, indeed are used to make sure that the job of the internal department has been done accurately and according to established standards.

Therefore, what is keeping companies today from completely outsourcing this activity? It is the cost (perceived or real) of the *interface.* The accounting function appears to be woven into the very fabric of the organization, from the finance department to the boardroom, and the size and number of interfaces to the rest of the organization seem too numerous, and too complex, to disentangle.

Consider this however: What if a company specifically focused on automating that interface? If all accounting-related activities were isolated and the relevant information intelligently channeled via IT to a specific (virtual) place? At that point, the accounting function could conceivably be outsourced to any competent external provider.

This is already being done by many small businesses, and it is only a matter of time before the internal bookkeeping departments of larger firms follow suit. The market for accounting services is simply becoming too efficient. The firm that is not willing, or able, to "plug in" this efficient capability will subsequently remain less competitive in its own market—whether that involves selling shoes or repairing washing machines.

It doesn't take much imagination to discern that most business transactions are based on information that can be digitized and communicated over computer networks. As the digital economy evolves and businesses routinely use the common public network infrastructure to link with their business partners, companies will be able to reduce transaction costs to the point at which it becomes feasible, both strategically and financially, to outsource all noncritical business functions. Companies that do this will then be able to focus solely on high value-adding activities.

Although many businesses have already taken the first steps toward reducing transaction costs through the use of IT, most have done so under the standard banners of cost reduction and productivity improvement. Few, as yet, have consciously reorganized themselves specifically to create new value by systematically minimizing transaction costs (and thereby reducing the cost and improving the ability of the organization to interface with other businesses) through IT for the purpose of leveraging external business partners for non-VAC activities. One exception to this is the Automotive Network Exchange.

CASE IN POINT—TECHNOLOGY ENABLING EFFICIENT MARKETS

The Automotive Network Exchange (ANX) is a managed virtual private network that runs over the Internet and links manufacturers and suppliers of automotive components worldwide. The network electronically routes product shipment schedules, CAD files for product designs, purchase orders, payments, and other business information. The automotive industry's network is an example of an extranet that provides automotive trading partners with a single, secure network for electronic commerce and information exchange.[10]

The ANX initiative is about bringing to the automotive industry the full benefits of the digital revolution. The Automotive Network Exchange is intended to deliver the consistent performance, reliability, and security required of a business-quality network supporting all automotive applications.[11]

The Automotive Network Exchange service is expected to become the most prevalent method for automotive trading partners to access each other's business applications. However, using ANX wasn't created to suit the convenience of the "Big Three" automakers and a handful of larger suppliers. Rather, it is an opportunity to solve the data communications problem endemic to the entire industry with one fell swoop, rather than one trading partner and application at a time; to deploy new applications faster; to reach customers and strategic partners more easily; and to reduce communications costs by eliminating redundant connections.[12] The ANX mission is therefore a far-reaching one, indeed: to create a communications environment that maximizes the ability of each trading partner to compete effectively, increasing the shareholder value of *all* participants through innovative business practices.[13]

It is clear from the "Intelligent Markets" section that markets are rapidly forming around value chains. Concurrently, we see IT breaking down the barriers (transaction costs) that exist between internal company operations and the market. Coupled with the ever-increasing efficiency of markets for business services and the added focus on delivering value, corporations now find themselves scrambling in an effort to adjust to the new realities of doing business in the digital economy. The value-based organization is our answer to the question of what your company should look like to remain competitive in this new world, and the focus of the next chapter is on the specific steps needed to transform into a VBO.

9

Transforming into the Value-Based Organization

"If one does not know to which port one is sailing, no wind is favorable."

—Seneca

IN THIS CHAPTER, WE GIVE YOU A FRAMEWORK FOR TRANSFORMING YOUR TRADITIONAL enterprise into a true value-based organization (VBO). The following 12 steps present a series of rigorous exercises, each based upon proven methodologies that have been applied repeatedly in successful businesses throughout the world. The ideas and tools presented here have been in the hands of business executives and consultants for quite some time. The real power in the 12 steps is not the individual methodologies from which the individual steps are built, but from the combination of these proven methodologies into a framework that illuminates an entirely new way of doing business.

The exercises presented in this section are far from easy to complete, and many companies will find that without making a firm commitment (and dedicating sufficient resources), they will be difficult, if not impossible, to complete. They will require management to make some very difficult decisions, and will challenge even the most motivated and ambitious executive management team. If a CEO is not prepared to turn the organization upside down, this book (and therefore the digital economy) may not be for your company.

It's important to note that the 12 steps included here, although presented in numerical order, do not necessarily have to be followed in order, nor is there a definition of "complete" for any one step. It is up to the senior management team to determine how far the company must go to be successful, and every company will be different.

Although we have laid out 12 specific steps, finishing all of them does not assure victory. True value-based or value-centered organizations never stop transforming. They have simply managed to create a corporate structure that is capable of responding to ever-changing market needs.

As a springboard to understanding where we're headed, it's first necessary to understand where we are. Figure 9.1 depicts the current state of most corporations.

The large outer oval represents the company's overall business activities, the inner oval its value-added competencies (VACs). The odd splotch shape represents the activities that the company currently performs, which is some combination of its VACs and the competencies that are better left to more capable business partners, which we'll call non-VACs. (See the sidebar, "New Terminology to Take Note Of," in Chapter 8 for clarification.)

The goal of the 12-step process is to transform your company so it performs only those activities within the inner oval.

FIGURE 9.1
Pre-value-based transformation organization.

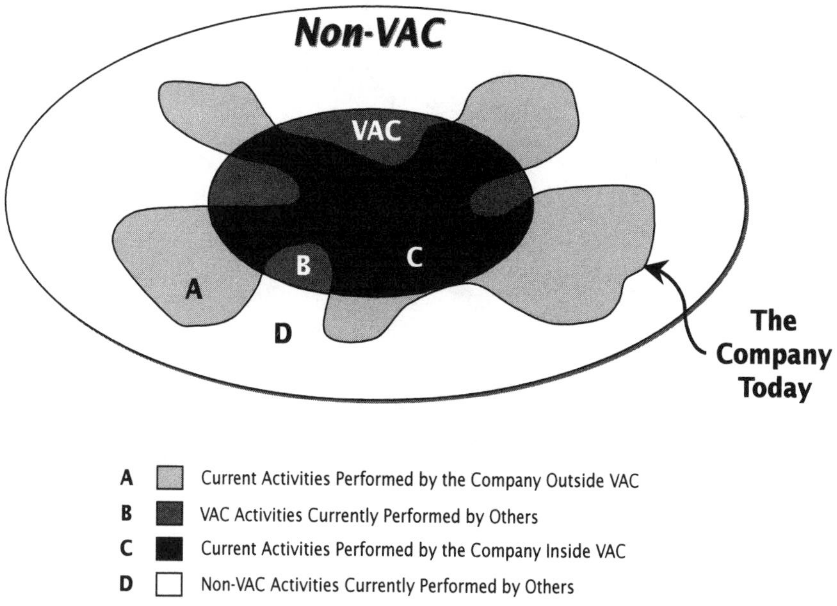

A	Current Activities Performed by the Company Outside VAC
B	VAC Activities Currently Performed by Others
C	Current Activities Performed by the Company Inside VAC
D	Non-VAC Activities Currently Performed by Others

Areas like section A, which reside outside of the VAC oval and within the splotch, represent those non-VAC activities that the company currently performs. These non-VAC activities would ideally be outsourced to external business partners. Areas like section B, conversely, represent VAC activities currently sourced externally that should be brought in-house. The area labeled section C, which is within the VAC oval, consists of the VAC activities currently performed in-house. These activities are core value-added business activities and should continue to be performed by the corporation. Finally, the area labeled section D, which consists of the area outside of the VAC oval and the splotch, represents non-VAC activities currently sourced externally, as they should be.

Figure 9.2 provides a different view of a typical (that is, non-value-based) organization. Understanding this general business model will enable better understanding of the 12 steps to follow.

As you can see, the company's leadership, strategy, and coordination functions at the top of the diagram represent the core of the business. They are woven throughout the entire organization, cannot be separated from any aspect of it, and in fact will be found in both traditional and value-based organizations in much the same way.

The two layers beneath this is where we typically find the true value-adding capabilities and competencies of the corporation. Although strategy,

FIGURE 9.2
Competencies within the standard corporation.

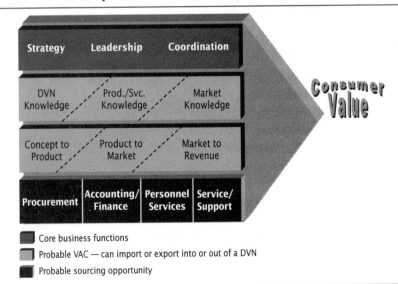

leadership, and coordination are core business functions, they differ from these next two layers because they encompass the entire organization; the functions represented by these two lower layers address specific pieces of the business—those pieces where the business typically differentiates itself from the competition.

Most organizations will find that one or two of these pieces are the true VAC of the business, whereas the others are merely support functions.

Finally, the bottom layer of this diagram represents those functions that all businesses must do, but that do not generally drive revenue generation or profitability. These areas are normally categorized as cost centers and are areas where outsourcing can yield significant benefit in a short amount of time.

It is our belief that the current state of most organizations today is fairly represented conceptually by Figure 9.1 and structurally by Figure 9.2. It's clear that companies are already doing correctly a number of the things they should be doing, while also doing a number of things they should not. The goal is to begin outsourcing the latter activities immediately.

Try to imagine this: as the company becomes more value-based, the splotch (shown in Figure 9.1) will migrate toward the shape of the inner oval.

Contracting with business partners to perform non-VAC functions provides a company with the opportunity to get the most out of the external partner's investments, innovation, and specialized professional capabilities, many of which would be prohibitively expensive or impossible to duplicate internally. Remember, too, that these non-VAC functions are sourced through low-cost, efficient interfaces enabled by information technology (IT), which is what makes this new business model possible, and also is what drives the market toward an efficient state.

Additional benefits of outsourcing include decreased risk, shortened cycle times, reduced investments in peripheral activities, and increased responsiveness both to the market and to high value-adding activities.[1]

All of these benefits are significant, but the real value of outsourcing non-VAC activities results from freeing up financial, managerial, and employee resources. Those resources can then be redeployed within VAC activities to create true value for the customer.

It's not always that simple, however. You may not be able to find a more efficient company to provide non-VAC functionality. Your best option may be to continue performing the activity in the short term while waiting for an efficient market to develop. Alternatively, you could take advantage of the situation by spinning off the internal function as a stand-alone service that then sells the functionality back to your company—and to others. After all, if your firm needs that function, it's reasonable to expect others will, too. The spin-off company could conceivably become the efficient provider for that functionality in the market. This is essentially what American Airlines did with its Sabre reservation system, and this resembles the action General Motors took when it spun off EDS. Companies are doing spin-offs much more frequently now, mainly in response to a renewed focus on the core business. Recent examples include the spin-off of Lucent by AT&T and The Associates First Capital Corp. by Ford Motor Co. In fact, there were 77 corporate spin-offs in 1997 with an estimated market value of $117 billion, according to Securities Data Co., a merger and finance information company in Newark, New Jersey. That compares with 80 spin-offs in 1996 that were worth only $20.8 billion.[2]

Implementing the Value-Based Organization— A Case Study

Much of the discussion in this chapter and in previous chapters has been very theoretical. To help you grasp the concepts more easily, we've included a case study that dramatizes the evolution of a company trying to transform itself into a VBO. It's written from the point of view of a senior executive who has only recently joined the company. You'll be reading successive installments that emphasize some of the more important points of each of the 12 steps using real-world examples.

Step 1: Identify Current Value-Added Competencies and Their Related Skills, Technologies, and Capabilities

As stated previously, a company's VAC activities are those activities that directly support its core or value-added competencies, as shown in areas B and C in Figure 9.1 (see also value-added competencies, pp. 128–131). They are the things the company is particularly good at, that yield a competitive advantage in the marketplace, that have value in the eyes of the customer, and that apply to at least several, if not many, of the company's products.

Value-creating activities that do not meet these criteria are very likely non-VAC activities (areas A and D in Figure 9.1).

In addition, VAC activities are skills and intellectual capital that transcend product families and provide the foundation for future products and services (Figure 9.3). Often these activities derive from intangible assets that other companies cannot replicate, and revolve around intellectual capital assets that the organization has built over a long period of time. Value-added com-

FIGURE 9.3
Value-added activity identification framework.

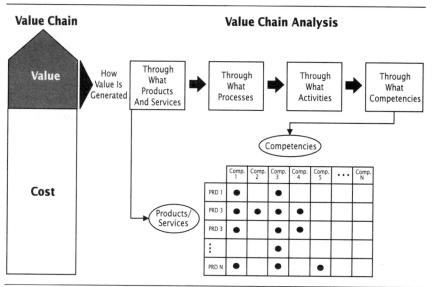

petency activities provide the organization with unique sources of competitive advantage, allowing their corporate owners to effectively compete and even dominate a particular market segment.

It's important to understand that without at least one VAC, a company is destined to fail—and that VACs change as market demands change. For example, a manufacturer of copper wire may have experienced healthy returns and possessed true VACs for generations—but that counts for nothing when the consumer stops attaching value to copper wire when compared with fiber-optic or wireless technology.

As easy as it is might be to define VAC activities, in practice it is often quite difficult to determine whether a specific activity is part of a company's VAC. Much has been written about core competence identification, but until now, no one has developed a surefire way to identify the value-added activities that make up VACs.

In an attempt to remedy this, we offer the following framework.

First, start with the value provided to customers. Which of your products and services provide unique value to your customer? Now, ask yourself: What processes create those products and services? Then, what activities execute those processes? Finally, what competencies do these activities support? You may also ask: What is unique about these activities? What particular strengths does the company exhibit by performing these activities?

In answering these questions, it is possible to create a matrix such as that shown in Figure 9.3. A competence that meets these criteria, and that reaches across more than one product or service, might be a true VAC. To be sure, you have to investigate further.

Each competence that has made it this far (e.g., competencies 1, 3, and 4, in Figure 9.3) must pass a series of quantitative and qualitative tests. If the data is available, perform the combination quantitative/qualitative test outlined in the sidebar, "How to Identify the Value of an Internal Activity," discussed in Chapter 8, and the following qualitative series of questions. If no data is available to perform the "How to Identify the Value of an Internal Activity" test, simply perform the following qualitative test by asking the following questions. (If you answer no to even one of these questions, then the competence in question is not a VAC.)

QUESTION 1

If you removed this competence from the value chain, would the end consumer perceive your product or service as less valuable?

EXPLANATION

This test gives you a quick reading on whether the competence truly adds value. If you answer yes to this question, then you believe that customers can perceive the value that the competence provides.

QUESTION 2

Does the competence add value to the end product that cannot be provided by a competitor at similar cost and quality levels?

EXPLANATION

By answering yes to this question, you believe that the value you add is unique and preferably the best in the marketplace for this particular competence.

QUESTION 3

Is the value that this competence offers so compelling that customers could be induced to switch from a competitor?

EXPLANATION

Few companies are in business to maintain the status quo. Most want to grow. Growth involves acquiring new customers and increasing sales to existing customers. Because costs are almost always involved in switching from one supplier to another, your competence must add enough value to make the switch worthwhile to your customer.

QUESTION 4

Is the market for this competence increasing, and is your share of that market also increasing?

EXPLANATION

If you've made it this far (i.e., answered yes to each of the four questions), then you must believe in your VAC—that it adds significant and discernable value, that it is uniquely yours, and that customers would be willing to incur the costs involved in switching to your product or service because of it. While this would seem to mean that you have identified a VAC, if the market in which that competency exists is static or shrinking, you've got a problem. Imagine, for example, having a unique competence for manufacturing audio-cassette tapes. How much longer do you suppose that's going to keep your company healthy?

A VAC is something that you can use to not only create existing products but also build new products. If this competence will not help you in the growth opportunities of the future (after your existing products die), then you probably want to build a new set of competencies that will.

When you complete this process you will have a list of VAC activities, as well as non-VAC activities.

Now, it's time to address the non-VAC activities. Later (beginning with step 8), we will dig deeper to identify the skills, technologies, and capabilities that make up these VACs. That process is likely to consume weeks, or even months, if your company is of significant size. Top management will have to meet repeatedly to brainstorm, aggregate, and evaluate iteratively to truly understand the multitude of activities in which the firm engages.

At this point, you may find that you have few or no VACs. This is a troubling situation—and a serious one. If this is the case, you need to immediately identify and build a core competence in something that customers find valuable.

Figure 9.4 provides an easy map for determining what actions to take once you have the results from completing step 1.

Steps 2 through 7 address only non-VAC activities, providing a framework for outsourcing them. Step 8 addresses your company's VACs and how to invest and develop them to create new value-added products and services. Steps 9 through 12 address risk, performance measures, organizational change, and other issues that are important during the process of transforming into a VBO.

FIGURE 9.4
Competency/value-add matrix.

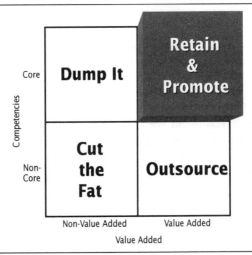

APPLYING STEP 1: AN EXECUTIVE'S PERSPECTIVE

I knew this first step would be a difficult one. After all, everyone wants to believe that what they do adds value. Although everyone adds value in some way, not everyone adds value that a customer can appreciate. Therefore, there were some pretty heated discussions in the first few meetings about who the customer is, what "value-added" means, what value our business really adds to the customer, and why we were really in business. It got a little difficult. People began realizing that the digital economy demands a new way of thinking about the business. I've been involved in this sort of activity at other companies, and I've seen the same reaction time and time again. However, I have confidence that everyone will eventually see the value in making this transition.

At the end of the series of meetings on step 1, the group came to the conclusion that recruiting was one of the VACs within our business. They feel that our methodology for screening, interviewing, and selecting job candidates is what sets our company apart from the competition, and the value our company adds to our customer is a direct reflection of the people we employ.

The payroll processing function, however, was a different story. We went through the steps to identify its economic value, and determined that not only was our business quite unable to compete in executing basic payroll processes, but that each of the test questions received a resounding "no." Therefore, we have put payroll processing in the non-VAC bucket. However, the group seems very unsure of how we can separate out such an integral part of our business operations.

Last, the group concluded that parts of benefits administration were key to our company's value proposition. Happy employees make happy customers, and part of making employees happy is to provide exceptional benefits, which we agreed the company does. That said, there were aspects of benefits administration, such as managing insurance providers, that clearly didn't pass the test. Therefore, the group has broken down benefits administration into individual activities and will put some in the VAC bucket and the rest in the non-VAC bucket.

I have to say, at this point, the group is pretty skeptical of this process and is unsure how we are going to take these disparate results and actually use them, but we're moving on.

Step 2: Identify and Categorize All Non-VAC Business Activities According to Whether They Are Currently Performed In-House or Outsourced

Building on the work done in step 1, you will now determine which tasks are currently outsourced and which are performed within the company. This may seem obvious or simple, but you may believe you currently outsource some activities, only to find that you really only outsource a portion of them.

Because the goal of the next step is to begin deciding whether and how to adjust the in-house/outsource balance for all business activities, a *precise* segmentation is essential.

To complete this step, create Figure 9.5 from the same set of core and non-core activities you identified in step 1.

FIGURE 9.5
VAC/non-VAC versus insource/outsource matrix.

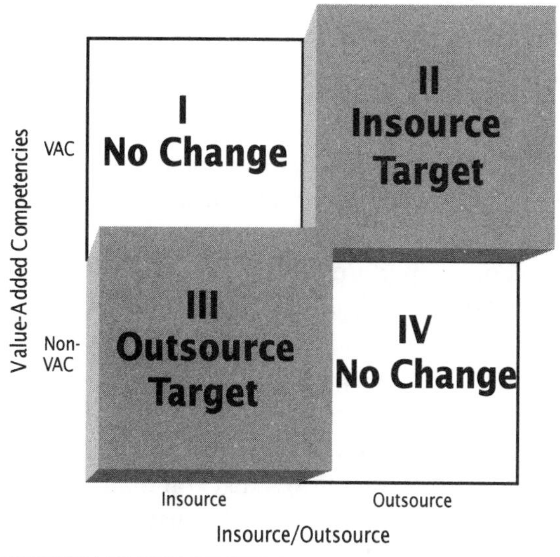

Activities in Quadrant I of Figure 9.5 are VAC activities that the firm currently performs (well). Activities in Quadrant II are VAC activities that the firm obtains from an external provider (these activities need to be brought in-house). Activities in Quadrant III are non-VAC activities that the firm currently performs (they are prime candidates to be outsourced). Activities in Quadrant IV are non-VAC activities that are currently outsourced, which is where they should remain.

In subsequent steps, we will concentrate on activities currently falling into Quadrants II and III. For now, it's your job merely to place the various activities into the correct quadrants.

APPLYING STEP 2: AN EXECUTIVE'S PERSPECTIVE

After step 1, everyone expressed their fears that the 12-step process would take forever, but this step went much more quickly. In fact, it wasn't even apparent initially why this step existed. Wasn't it obvious whether activities were currently insourced or outsourced?

Still, once we began doing the exercise, it became obvious this wasn't such a simple question. For example, in the area of employee benefits, we discovered that although most activities are performed in-house, our company currently outsources management of all pension and retirement plans. Some people knew this, but most of us were pretty surprised. Another marvel—within the payroll function, we actually cut our own checks! Everyone assumed this was outsourced. In fact, it turns out that our company does *everything* related to payroll processing. Already, we're seeing some possibilities. People are even eager to continue.

Step 3: Determine the Most Likely Course of Action for Each Non-VAC Activity

There are essentially three courses of action that can be taken with non-VAC activities. The goal, of course, is to perform internally as few of them as possible. However, due to the efficiency of the market for those activities, strategic decisions and a number of other factors, it may be in the best interest of the company to continue performing some of these activities. Therefore, this step and step 4 will delve into making the determination of whether to outsource an activity, continue performing the activity until some set of conditions change (such as the efficiency of the market or the company's strategic direction), or continue performing the activity on a permanent basis. Note: At this point you may be having difficulty delineating between VACs that your company currently possesses and VACs that you think a company like yours ought to possess. There may also be activities that you have classified as non-VAC (or should have classified as non-VAC) but you believe for some reason that they *should* be core to your business. Be patient. The following two steps will help you clarify these issues, and if there are non-VAC activities that should be classified as core for one reason or another, these activities will be identified by the end of step 4.

Two factors assist in beginning to clarify what you should do for non-VAC activities currently performed in-house. These are *level of interface* and *scope of activity,* and this step helps you understand how they impact your decisions.

Level of interface refers to the extent to which an activity is integrated into current business processes (and, therefore, how difficult it will be to outsource it). For example, the level of interface for procuring office supplies is probably relatively low, whereas the level of interface for procuring accounting services is likely to be high. Therefore, in general, a company is more likely to outsource the procurement of office supplies, while maintaining an internal department for accounting services.

The *scope of activity* refers to how broad the exposure of the activity is to the rest of the business, relative to the product or service being created. For example, the R&D activity within Motorola that is responsible for wireless technology is relatively large in scope (that is, it affects a variety of products), whereas the activity of selling pagers to individual consumers is relatively small in scope. Therefore, Motorola would be more likely to outsource the selling of pagers than the R&D function.

Of course, an activity can have a low level of interface, but a large scope (the final assembly of computers by Dell), and vice versa (the creation of digital signal processors for cellular telephones).

These two metrics assist management in making outsourcing decisions with respect to specific noncore activities. Using this framework, management can map the activities from quadrants II and III in Figure 9.5 onto the matrix in Figure 9.6 to gain a better understanding of the level of effort required to outsource a particular activity. As the level of interface rises, the difficulty in outsourcing rises. As the scope of the activity increases, the difficulty in outsourcing again also increases.

Quadrant I in Figure 9.6 represents activities that consume a considerable amount of resources, but which have a relatively low business impact. These activities are likely to be currently insourced; management should reconsider their value to the business. Quadrant II represents activities that are essentially core to the business, and are most likely currently insourced. These activities should, in most cases, remain insourced for the time being. Quadrant III represents activities that are nonessential, and which are most likely outsourced already. (If not, they will be by the time you complete step 7.)

FIGURE 9.6
Level of interface versus scope of activity matrix.

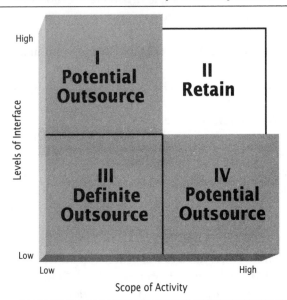

Finally, Quadrant IV represents activities that may or may not be core. For those that the company believes are *not* core, the activity may be partially or completely outsourced due to the low interface costs. Activities that the company believes may be core are likely to be currently insourced; the firm should continue to build and develop these activities for the time being.

At the end of this difficult and often strenuous process, management will have the information necessary to really take a hard look at the enterprise as a whole, and to make the truly critical decisions that must follow.

Still, we'd like to stress that even though the results of this will be infinitely useful, the *process* is where real learning takes place. If management is successful in completing this step, it has accomplished one of the most difficult of the 12 tasks. Other than executing the plan once it is created, there is no single, more difficult task than determining what your future organization should look like.

APPLYING STEP 3: AN EXECUTIVE'S PERSPECTIVE

We were initially uncertain about how to do this. These "level of interface" and "scope of activity" classifications were somewhat vague. Still, once we started discussing specific activities, we began to understand. It helped when I suggested that we start by isolating the top three activities within each of the payroll and benefits functions. For example, the top three functions within payroll were data entry and processing of time and expense information, calculation of taxes, and calculation of deductions such as health and retirement benefits. After that, we began making real progress.

Using Figure 9.6, and plotting the activities on the matrix, the group was able to categorize each activity and determine the likely course of action. We're really beginning to see the emphasis on value as the primary driver. It's clear that even though there are difficult (and painful) decisions ahead, the goal of value creation is properly aligned with the long-term interests of the company and its shareholders.

Still, I sense resistance building in the ranks. From experience, I know it will only get more pronounced as the process continues.

One fact that surfaced in this series of meetings was that if our recommendations are to outsource some of our business functions, how will we handle the very serious personnel issues? No one really wanted to think about this. It was finally recommended that a special task force be created to identify the best way to handle this situation. This task force will begin meeting while we continue with our work. The goal is to find a reasonable personnel strategy before we make any firm decisions to outsource particular activities.

Step 4: Designing the Value-Based Organization

This step builds on information developed in step 3 and delves deeper into determining what activities to outsource, and when to outsource them. In effect, you are now analyzing the *market* to determine how easy, or how difficult, it will be to actually outsource those activities that should be outsourced. (Previously, you were analyzing only *internal* conditions; now, you are examining mostly external ones.)

If markets were completely dependable and efficient, there would be no logical reason for firms to do anything other than their VAC activities in-house. It would make beautiful sense to partner with others for everything else. However, few markets are ideal.

There are essentially three questions you need to answer.

1. How important is this activity to your overall business? (Another way of putting this is: How vulnerable will your business be if your external supplier fails to deliver at promised quality/price/quantity levels?)

2. How *complex* is the market for the activity in question? (As market complexity increases, so does the cost of maintaining an interface to it.)

3. How well, and at what cost levels, can you perform the activity in question as compared with the capabilities of potential suppliers?

It's essential to examine these questions in tandem with each other to arrive at a sophisticated understanding of the best way to proceed.

Business Impact versus Market Complexity

The *business impact* of an activity is simply a way of assessing the importance of a particular activity on the ultimate value of the end product or service. This is a qualitative value determined by examining the percentage of total costs allocated to procuring or performing the activity, the value that the activity provides as perceived by customers, the activity's supporting technology that can also support other activities, and the activity's contribution to the product's differentiation in the marketplace.

Market complexity is determined by three factors: how much competition currently exists among suppliers; the company's own internal requirements and constraints; and the company's bargaining power. Competition among suppliers can be determined by analyzing Michael Porter's five forces: competition among suppliers, supplier bargaining power, availability of substitutes, bargaining power of buyers (both your company and others who buy the product or service), and barriers to entry into the supplier market.[3] A company's internal constraints can include customer requirements, government restrictions, trade and tariff restrictions, and self-imposed restrictions (quality standards, for example). The company's bargaining power can be influenced by its special competencies, innovative technologies, international presence, or relative size in the market.

In this portion of the analysis, you determine the level of business impact and market complexity for each activity, then plot these activities onto Figure 9.7.

Because the analysis for this matrix is very similar to the analysis for the next matrix, the explanation for both matrices will be presented immediately following the next section.

Business Impact versus Relative Position in Market

To understand your relative position in the market for a particular activity, you need a complete picture of what efficient markets and inefficient markets look like. Efficient markets were defined in Chapter 8; however, *inefficient* markets have not yet been addressed.

An inefficient market is an environment in which buyers and sellers have difficulty identifying each other, exchanging information about their wants and needs, or agreeing to a price. Inefficient markets do not readily facilitate the exchange of goods and/or services, nor do they readily facilitate the exchange of funds. Inefficient markets often exchange information, communication, funds transfer, and possibly the goods and services themselves in a manual, physical fashion without the help of IT.

FIGURE 9.7
Business impact versus market complexity matrix.

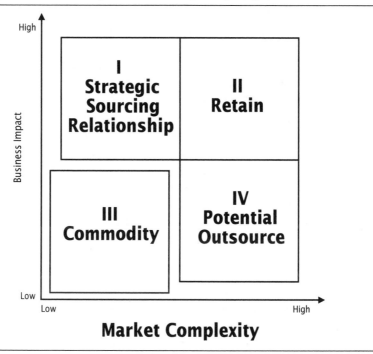

Why is this important? Whether you can outsource a non-VAC largely depends on whether the activity in question is served by an efficient market.

First, you need to determine: Does an efficient market exist with regard to this particular activity? Second, how does your company measure up in its ability to perform this activity when compared with competitors?

If there *is* an efficient market, then you need to evaluate the respective abilities of suppliers to perform the activity in question on the basis of cost, quality, accuracy, response time, dependability, innovation, and flexibility. Doing this requires a benchmarking study that compares the activity within the market against your company's ability to perform the activity in-house.

If the market is inefficient (that is, no viable suppliers exist), you should still create internal benchmarks using the yardsticks (cost, quality, and so on). This way, you can assess just how inefficient the market is, then attempt to predict when it will become sufficiently efficient to warrant outsourcing your activity.

Let's look at a concrete example of how business impact is plotted against the relative ability of your company to perform an activity when compared with competitors. The toll-free customer service function for a beverage manufacturer like PepsiCo obviously has a low impact to the business of making and selling beverages. (PepsiCo customers are unlikely to cite it as a major contributor to how much they value PepsiCo products.) It's safe to say that it's a non-VAC activity. Therefore, strategic sourcing is not a fitting option. Two choices remain. If there's an efficient market for customer service suppliers, and if PepsiCo can't compete with the price and quality of competitive offerings, then it makes sense to outsource this commodity service. If there are no viable outsourcing options, PepsiCo might be best served by spinning off its own customer service arm, creating a new market.

Of course, all these factors are constantly changing, so management will need to continuously reevaluate them.

If we now look at the business impact of the activity in question with respect to the firm's relative position, we can more confidently determine the right action to take.

In this portion of the analysis, you determine the level of business impact and relative position for each activity, then plot these activities onto Figure 9.8. *Note:* Although management has completed a similar exercise with Figure 9.7, it is vitally important that each activity is *also* plotted onto Figure 9.8 to understand the full impact of potential outsourcing decisions.

For example, if management determines that the business impact of the marketing function is high, the market complexity is low, and the relative position is low, it may choose to strategically source the activity to the market. (The strategic relationship in this case is determined by the level of business impact.) However, if the business impact is low and market complexity is high and relative position is high, management may choose to spin off the unit, creating a more efficient market for that function.

Additionally, if the same conditions existed as in the last example, with the exception of a high business impact, it may choose to retain the activity internally until a less complex market develops. At that point it could consider spinning off the activity or forming a strategic alliance with a supplier. In brief, it should be evident that both exercises are necessary if you are to get the complete picture.

The following detailed explanation of the previous two matrices will show activities from Figure 9.7 in bold text and activities from Figure 9.8 in *italics*.

Activities that fall in Quadrant I are those that have a high business impact but low market complexity/*relative position with respect to potential suppliers*. Therefore, the organization should look to outsource them through

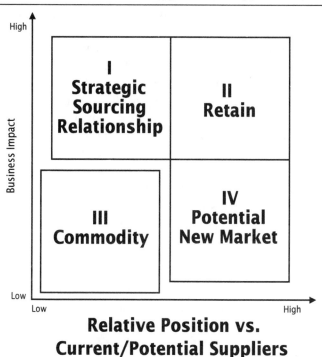

FIGURE 9.8
Business impact versus relative position to suppliers matrix.

strategic relationships to ensure that the company controls the outsourcing arrangement and can procure these activities over the long term. Although these are high-impact activities, the company should not choose to insource or retain them because they are non-VAC and can be sourced in a relatively straightforward market/*from more capable suppliers.* However, management should continually monitor these activities, because at some point the market complexity may rise and the activity may become closer to VAC activities/*suppliers may become less able to efficiently supply the activity.*

Activities that fall in Quadrant II have a high business impact and a high market complexity/*relative position* and are likely to be near-VAC activities. These activities should be retained over the short term. However, management should continually monitor these activities over the long term, because at some point the market complexity/*relative position* may change and/or the business impact may change, possibly creating an opportunity to outsource the activity.

Activities that fall in Quadrant III are those that have a low business impact and a low market complexity/*relative position* and, most likely, are commodity activities that are either already outsourced or that are next in line to be outsourced.

Activities that fall in Quadrant IV are those that have a low business impact and a high market complexity/*relative position*. They are most likely activities that, if the market complexity/*relative position* for these activities decreases through the development of more efficient markets, they would be sourced as commodity items. However, these activities could also become closer to core in nature if their impact on the business rises. Administrative functions such as internal accounting often fall into this category.

Caution! As you complete this portion of the exercise, you will be tempted to put many so-called necessary evils into this last quadrant. Before you do this, explore the marketplace for each activity because sufficiently efficient markets are created for all types of functions and activities on a daily basis. (You might also consider creating a new market for those activities that have low business impact, yet high relative position with respect to the market by spinning this function off into the market.)

Efficient markets are developing constantly for all types of business functions. Fifteen years ago, every business of substantial size owned a mainframe; today, most large businesses outsource entire data centers. Because markets constantly evolve, management must implement programs to constantly review the applicability of decisions made in this step.

The outcome of these two exercises yields a clearer, more concise, and more accurate picture of what should be done with each non-VAC activity over the short term. Management should take the outcome of these two exercises and categorize each activity as to the appropriate course of action. This will either be to outsource the activity to an efficient market; strategically source the activity; spin off the activity into the market; or retain the activity until outsourcing is feasible.

With the list of outsourcing candidates from this step, the company can move onto the next step, which addresses one of the last major hurdles to outsourcing non-VAC activities and functions: transaction costs.

APPLYING STEP 4: AN EXECUTIVE'S PERSPECTIVE

When told to analyze the "business impact" of (respectively) payroll and benefits, the group found that their previous discussion of level of interface and scope of activity really helped them. We came to the conclusion that because these two classifications were the main drivers of business impact, they used the results of step 3 to determine the business impact of each activity. To determine market complexity and relative position, we needed a solid market analysis study. Therefore, the group asked the marketing division to appoint a team and to spend two weeks performing as much research on these two dimensions as they could. When we reconvened, everyone had reviewed the marketing team's results and had begun to formulate their own conclusions. Interestingly, when we began comparing our opinions, we found that pretty much everyone agreed that our company was not very competitive in the area of payroll, and that a quite efficient market for payroll services existed.

The same thing was found to be true for benefits, with the exception of some unique features of our program, such as on-site day care and special arrangements with local health and fitness facilities.

One interesting argument was brought up by one of the middle managers. She was concerned that if payroll were outsourced (and that was looking increasingly likely), we might lose control over valuable payroll information, which could potentially cause a number of problems. Many others voiced the same concerns; therefore, the group concluded that in every area in which we would consider outsourcing, we would need assurance of confidentiality and we would structure the contracts to ensure that we maintained strict control whenever sharing critical information with third parties.

At the end of this step, the group concluded that although efficient markets already existed to turn all of payroll and most of our benefits over to outsourcers, as a company we were far from prepared to separate these activities from the rest of our business. These processes were embedded in our everyday operations, and required a significant amount of human interaction. In other words, there were a lot of manual processes still in place. Even when things were automated, we used proprietary systems. We knew then that it wasn't going to be easy to move these activities outside of our business.

Step 5: Identify the Transaction Costs between the VAC Activities and All Other Business Functions (Non-VAC Activities)

Transaction costs are the glue that holds traditional organizations together, and are a critical component in the transformation of a company from the traditional organizational model to the VBO. As stated in the enablers section of this chapter, not only is the 45 percent of total production cost identified by North and Wallace a significant amount of money, but there is also the fact that these costs prevent firms from focusing their resources exclusively on what they do best.

Although the reduction of transaction costs alone provides the opportunity for significant cost savings, the real hurdle to winning in the digital economy is weakening the glue that holds traditional organizations together and moving the non-VAC activities to more capable partners so the company can focus on its true value proposition—its VAC. The importance of this step cannot be overstated.

Identifying transaction costs is not a trivial task. However, much of the methodology for doing this can be found in activity-based management and activity-based costing (ABC) applications (see Figure 9.9). Activity-based costing requires that a company first identify the activities performed; trace resource costs to these activities using resource drivers; and then use various resource drivers to trace the cost of activities to products.

The resource drivers (for example, the number of persons performing the work or the number of setups required per product) reflect the consumption of resources and activities by the products.[4]

The resource costs identified in ABC analysis, in theory, are very similar to the transaction costs that Coase identified and can be used as relative measures of these costs. Therefore, companies that have implemented ABC as their internal cost-accounting system already have the framework in place,

FIGURE 9.9
Using activity-based costing (ABC) to isolate transaction costs.

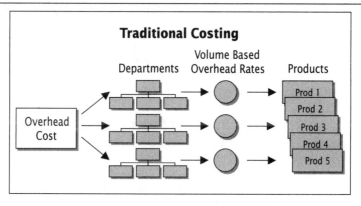

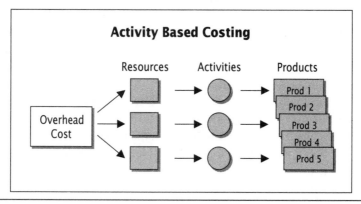

and have to some extent already identified most, if not all, of their transaction costs. All that remains is to categorize these costs as internal to VAC activities, internal to non-VAC activities, or interface costs between non-VAC activities and the rest of the business.

The most important transaction costs are those that arise from transactions between the non-VAC internal functions and the rest of the company's VAC and non-VAC activities. Minimizing these costs will allow the firm to more easily find an external supplier to perform that non-VAC function. If the cost of interfacing to that function is low, it becomes very cost-effective, indeed, to outsource.

Companies will need to implement ABC or use another method of identifying specific activity costs to complete this step. Implementing an ABC system involves gathering information on activities, resources, and drivers of cost; decomposing functions into activities; identifying elements of cost; determining the relationship between activities and elements of cost; and identifying and measuring cost drivers. The result is compiled into a matrix for each product that tracks all activities performed for the product and all the resources those activities consume. This information is probably not readily available and must be identified manually through searching existing documentation and historical cost information, as well as workshops, surveys, and interviews with the people who do the work.

The process for categorizing these costs, once they are identified, is straightforward and should require little time. When complete, you will have a list of interface activities and their associated costs that must be reduced to prepare for outsourcing non-VAC activities. Using the ABC method and model to identify and categorize costs and cost drivers will allow you to paint a complete picture of the true costs inherent in performing non-VAC activities. Once these costs are understood, the company can apply IT and best-practice business processes to reduce these costs. Once these costs are reduced to a minimum, the company is fully prepared to begin outsourcing the non-VAC activities.

APPLYING STEP 5: AN EXECUTIVE'S PERSPECTIVE

Fortunately, the company uses ABC for allocating overhead expenses. Implementing ABC had apparently been difficult—people were still grumbling about it, and it happened more than five years ago—but the information the group now has on the cost of individual processes, and the understanding of the true operation of the business is invaluable.

To begin, the group categorized the resource costs based on their interaction with VAC activities. To do this, the group needed two things. First, it needed to know which activities were VAC activities. Second, it needed to have a list of activities and their associated resource costs and resource drivers,

(Continued)

according to ABC. Then the group ran the list of resource costs and resource drivers against this VAC list to see which costs were incurred through transactions between payroll/benefits and the VAC activities. Once this was complete, the group reviewed the results of the analysis line by line to understand just what sort of costs the company was incurring between these non-VAC activities (payroll and benefits) and the VAC activities.

Many of the group members seemed quite apprehensive at this point because they were afraid of what they would find. They assumed that if their department or function had a high overall cost, then it would immediately be an outsource target. Even the executive management team seemed to be taking a hard look at the cost side and drawing inferences about what to outsource based on cost levels alone. I immediately stepped in and explained that the cost levels were relevant—not as indicators of outsourcing targets, but as indicators of how much work must be done before the functions could be outsourced. In other words, the interface costs represent costs that must be reduced or eliminated to create the opportunity for outsourcing.

What the group found mostly involved information exchange and authorization costs—human intervention costs that probably could be eliminated or significantly reduced if the right technology was used. For example, a major cost driver in benefits comes directly from the large number of personnel needed to assist employees in obtaining information, referrals, and other administrative procedures. Another major cost driver is the fact that hourly employees are still turning in paper time sheets that track the hours they worked. Armed with this information, and the realization that at the very least, significant efficiencies could be obtained by applying IT to reduce these transaction costs, the group seemed united around the platform of cost reduction through technology. Onto step 6!

Step 6: Continually Reduce Transaction Costs between VAC and Non-VAC Activities through the Strategic Application of Information Technology and the Implementation of Best-Practice Business Processes

At this point, you have identified the VAC activities that your company will continue to build upon, as well as the non-VAC activities that it would prefer to obtain from the marketplace. You have also identified the glue that keeps the non-VAC activities inside the four walls—the transaction costs between the non-VAC activities and the rest of the firm.

The goal now is to figure out how to reduce these transaction costs, to dissolve the glue that holds non-VAC activities in-house. In some cases, the transaction costs have already been reduced (that is, through business process reengineering, continuous improvement efforts, or other management tools), but management has rarely focused on the *nonmonetary* costs that prevent outsourcing. This is because transaction costs don't necessarily accrue in hard dollars. Instead, they can add up because a process consumes resources, such as managerial time and employee effort, for which no direct cost-line item exists.

Management has not yet realized that what seemed to be a core piece of the business could be outsourced to a more efficient, higher value-added partner for less than they are currently paying. In some cases, outside firms have gained such a high level of efficiency in certain activities (through specialization, economies of scale, scope, and knowledge) that *not* outsourcing the activity means becoming much less competitive in the marketplace.[5]

This step is about the strategic application of IT and best-practice business processes to reduce the transaction costs of the interfaces between VAC and non-VAC activities identified in step 5.

Information technology and best-practice business processes have been routinely applied to functions and activities to improve productivity and to reduce the cost of personnel or other resources, but *rarely,* if *ever,* have firms *expressly* applied IT and best practices to *specifically* reduce transaction costs.

Although ABC analysis provides a great deal of information that must be digested with respect to cost and resource drivers, the benefit of such an indepth analysis is that you obtain a complete picture on which to base cost reduction/future value creation decisions. The first step in digesting this information is to take the costs identified in step 5 as interface costs and categorize them along the lines of IT/best-practice solutions. Therefore, costs involved in exchanging funds or purchase invoices could be grouped under the electronic commerce solution set. Meanwhile, costs involved in communicating product design details, exchanging CAD information, or analyzing production yields could be grouped under a document management bestpractice solution, perhaps supported by a virtual private network that spans the company's internal network and extends outward to each supplier's internal network.

Once the costs have been segregated, management should assign priorities to the solutions based on available technology, cost of implementation, impact to the business, magnitude of savings anticipated from each solution, and the need or ability to outsource a particular function based on the reduced transaction costs.

Once priorities have been assigned to potential solutions, your next step is to implement the IT and/or best-practice solution.

For example, if you see that your benefits transaction costs are exceedingly high, you could create an internal web site (intranet) that employees could visit if they needed up-to-the-minute benefits information or services previously disseminated via published handbooks, interoffice memos, voice response units, and of course, human beings.

Once this was done, you could decide whether an internal or external benefits coordination group could most efficiently administer that largely automated function. If an external supplier was deemed more efficient, it could access the internal network and manage all of the transactions generated by employees when adding or modifying existing benefits elections, as well as manage the relationships with health care providers and insurance firms, with little need for your company to be involved other than general oversight.

This low-cost, IT-enabled interface would allow the firm to replace the benefits coordination team if another, less costly one appeared, or to provide the same functionality and service with a much smaller team of benefits coordinators, with the added ability to outsource or insource any part of the capability due to the extremely low transaction costs at the interface.

By reducing transaction costs at the interface, you have not only made that function more efficient, but you have prepared the company to outsource that activity from the marketplace when the market is sufficiently efficient.

Many technologies are already in place in most companies to reduce transaction costs at the interface between core and noncore functions. These include enterprise resource planning (ERP) systems, business intelligence systems, electronic commerce and EDI, virtual private networks, and supply chain automation systems. Exploiting these technologies and adopting Internet technologies that link your firm to the market will be critical in effectively and efficiently reducing transaction costs of interfacing with external business partners.

Most important, adopting standard interfaces such as Internet electronic commerce and mainstream ERP platforms whenever possible will ensure that transaction costs will remain low as markets and technologies progress and as other companies look to the market for non-VAC capabilities.

Because the implementation of new technology or best-practice processes does not happen overnight, this step could conceivably take months, or even years.

Still, it is extremely important to prioritize the solutions based not on just the cost savings, but more on the value the organization could create without having a particular set of activities performed inside the four walls. As the transaction costs at the interface between noncore activities and the rest of the business are reduced, the firm is poised to move to step 7, in which the focus will turn to actually outsourcing non-VAC activities.

One note before we move on. You may be wondering that, if everyone implements technology and reduces these transaction costs, then what advantage will you have over your competitors by using IT? The answer is that eventually there will be little or no advantage based on information systems. In 15 years, it is very likely that most businesses will hum right along without giving much thought at all to what computer systems they have or what functionality they provide. They may very likely become commodity items. However, that doesn't mean you can ignore IT. Businesses without this capability will exist only in very small forms and only to fill very specialized needs. All mainstream businesses will employ these systems much like every business today performs accounting, finance, marketing, and the like.

APPLYING STEP 6: AN EXECUTIVE'S PERSPECTIVE

Our team aggregated the individual activities identified by the ABC system for both the payroll and benefits departments. Then, working alongside our IT department and the internal best-practice squad, we were able to come up with some solutions.

For example, the time and expense reporting activity within the payroll function could benefit significantly from an online entry system. The current system has employees manually filling out time sheets, which accounting then enters into the system. If employees could enter their information into an online system that performed automatic checks and balances and looked for anomalies, the employee-intensive process for getting payroll checks cut could be drastically improved. Another example is the vacation and sick day tracking activity within the benefits function. If this process could be incorporated into the online time and expense system, an entire separate activity could be eliminated.

To flush out the details of the IT solutions, I asked a team of IT managers to join our meeting and give us a presentation of some of the potential solutions. I stressed that the presentation be interactive—the purpose was to get businesspeople thinking about the possibilities. We weren't going to hand over IT decisions, after all; we were going to be involved from the beginning. I made it clear to the business managers that this was just a first step in the process of finding IT solutions. There would be interviews, process mapping, and many other activities to perform before any solution could be finalized. I also asked several senior executives who had recently implemented technology solutions for specific business problems to attend the presentation. Hearing their experiences proved invaluable.

Our best-practice team was easier to work with (at least we spoke the same language), but they had less specific solutions in mind. It seems that there are best practices, and then there are ideal practices. Some things we are already very good at, according to best practices, but we know we should be able to do much better.

The last part of this step was the hardest part—implementation. To ensure that the company would do the most important things first, the group mandated that the owners of each area meet together and draw up a company-wide prioritized list of projects. Hopefully, this will keep everyone on track. After several months of analyses and vendor evaluations, the company has begun several of the implementations—both process improvement and IT solutions—and we'll be continuing with these projects as we move on to the next step.

Step 7: Examine the Marketplace for More Efficient Capabilities in Which to Outsource Your Non-VAC Activities

Now that the transaction costs of interfacing to one or more capabilities are being reduced through the application of improved business processes and information technology, the next step is to actually *begin* outsourcing those non-VAC functions to efficient markets.

This involves identifying the functions that will be outsourced, examining the markets that offer appropriate services, and going through an evaluation process to select a supplier.

If there is no appropriate market in which to outsource an activity, you have a difficult decision to make. You may decide to invest in developing such a market, or you may choose to simply keep the activity in-house until a more efficient market develops. Investing in the development of a new market is a difficult and time-intensive process and should be left to those activities that are non-VAC but that have a significant business impact. Deciding to keep an activity in-house until an efficient market develops is an easier decision to make. However, going down this route also means that you must devote sufficient resources to monitoring the market, so you can easily identify more efficient suppliers as they become available.

Because the subject of outsourcing has been covered so extensively in the information industry trade press, this section will address only issues specific to VBOs.

Issues of control and the loss of specific skills are vitally important and must be considered when outsourcing non-VAC activities. The higher an activity's impact on the business, and the closer to the core of the business the activity is, the more important these considerations become. Suppliers' abilities to make decisions without consulting your company should be clearly outlined in the outsourcing contract, lest you lose control over the relationship. The loss of skills being outsourced is a managerial problem related to the issues of risk and performance measurement. These will be addressed in steps 8 and 10.

Efficient markets are already developing for call centers, payroll, mainframe data centers, strategic planning, strategic sourcing and operations consulting, systems development, computer operations, recruiting, clerical work, and manufacturing. For functions that do not yet have efficient markets, such as internal finance, your company may want to help develop one. This could be done by spinning off a world-class internal unit, as AMR did with its Sabre division, or by investing in firms or individual entrepreneurs that have the potential to meet your needs but are not yet fully developed. Although this may be the best way to move an activity outside the company, it is by no means riskless, and management must take the appropriate steps to mitigate the risk. Risk mitigation is discussed more fully in step 9.

Although there are many instances in which efficient markets do not yet exist, markets change rapidly and the company must be prepared to outsource a capability regardless of the current state of the market.

For example, in medical practices, small legal offices, and the like, outsourcing the human resources function by "leasing" office management employees has become commonplace. This rapidly expanding market did not exist just five years ago.

Once you have decided to shed non-VAC activities, a framework for outsourcing is necessary. Potential partners should not only have outstanding capabilities, but they must also be in harmony with your company's goals. Outsourcing arrangements should be flexible enough to accommodate changing business climates and evolving technological environments.

Outsourcing partners should be evaluated for cost, quality, accuracy, response time, dependability, innovation, and flexibility. These dimensions will separate the mediocre market players from the world-class operations.

You will want to perform a series of benchmarking analyses, as follows: First, benchmark potential suppliers against the internal activity to assure that providers in the efficient market are superior to your internal function. Second, benchmark suppliers against each other to determine which should be used. Continued analyses need to be performed, as market capabilities change frequently, as do the needs of your company.

Sourcing non-VAC activities is by definition a nonstrategic decision. Therefore, it is neither necessary nor desirable to attempt to create strategic relationships with partners who supply non-VAC functionality. They are commodity players whose services can be obtained anywhere. Partner with the firm today that has the best price/performance ratio, then switch tomorrow if something better comes along. However, if there is only one or a few suppliers for a particular function, or if the business impact of the activity is particularly high, then outsourcing that function becomes a strategic decision even though it is not part of your VAC, because it cannot be easily replaced. In such a case, you must create a solid relationship while simultaneously encouraging the development of an alternate provider. For example, establishing a just-in-time link with suppliers creates certain vulnerabilities; a company has done an inadequate job of spreading the risk if, when one supplier strikes, the whole supply chain shuts down. It is better to create interfaces that allow easy switching of suppliers. However, the closer you get to the core of the business, the more strategic the relationship becomes—even though the outsourced function is not part of the core business. For example, if Frito-Lay chose to outsource the distribution of their snack products, they would very likely choose a strategic relationship with a partner, and lay out clearly defined responsibilities and performance targets. After all, to Frito-Lay, the distribution of their products is not a commodity service. You must likewise understand the strategic implications of outsourcing based on your needs and the state of the market that supplies that function.

When you're dealing with suppliers in competitive and relatively efficient markets, do not build relationships that would inhibit your ability to switch providers with minimal disruption; otherwise, you may find yourself changing suppliers on a regular basis. After all, you should be focused on minimizing transaction costs, maintaining independence from any one provider, and ensuring that you are always dealing with the highest-value provider. Retaining your prerogative to switch will help you achieve these goals.

As departments, business units, and perhaps even divisions are outsourced to more efficient providers, the role of senior management becomes increasingly difficult. There are political ramifications, as well concerns of corporate image and employee loyalty. However, these are unavoidable side effects of your company's quest for competitive advantage—and, possibly, survival. Once you have surpassed this hurdle, though, you will be on the verge of reaping the real rewards that await the VBO in the digital economy.

APPLYING STEP 7: AN EXECUTIVE'S PERSPECTIVE

At this point we were ready to begin looking for outsourcing partners for almost the entire payroll function (the company would keep some administrative and managerial pieces until it was comfortable with the new way of doing business) and most of the benefits function. The company would keep a few aspects of benefits in-house if it couldn't find an external supplier to fulfill the need, but if another company could manage our more unique benefits, then our company was willing to outsource the whole function.

To ensure the objectivity of the outsourcing process, and to minimize disruptions to the current operations, a new team would need to be created to complete this step. Together with the CEO and CFO, I created a new team and staffed it with members of the senior management team, as well as some of the middle managers of the payroll and benefits functions themselves. The senior executives would own the process; the middle managers were those whom the company would retain internally to manage the interface between the functions and the outsourcer on an ongoing basis. I also retained the strategic sourcing services of a consulting firm to help coordinate the outsourcing process.

We took the change management report created by the task force commissioned during step 3 to identify the best method of handling the personnel aspects of outsourcing. Although we certainly tried to find internal positions for employees that were being displaced, it was clear that the majority of employees in outsourced areas would have to leave the company. Some of these employees found employment with the outsourced service provider. For the remaining affected employees, the company provided retraining, counseling, and placement assistance depending on each employee's needs.

We decided at this point that the company did not have the internal expertise to negotiate effective outsourcing contracts. A consulting firm and outside legal counsel were asked to take responsibility for these tasks as we prepared for the next step.

Step 8: Continually Identify and Develop New Value-Added Competencies in Response to Anticipated Future Market/ Consumer Needs

At this point, we have gone through the process of outsourcing non-VACs and are ready to refocus our efforts on VACs. Companies in the digital age must not only focus their attention on current VACs, but they must also build the competencies necessary to compete effectively in the future. Because no one knows which products and services will be in demand in 2 years, much less in 5 or 10 years, this process is fraught with risk. However, with the proper framework in place, VBOs can minimize these risks.

The process of developing new VACs can be done with a variety of management tools. Whether management chooses to perform classic strategic analysis, scenario or options-based planning, or use some other methodology, the important point is that this process is central to sustaining the VBO. A general framework resembling scenario or options-based planning is presented here, but it is not the only way to successfully develop new VACs. It is up to each management team to decide which method is most appropriate for their specific company.

The goal of the VBO is to mold current VACs into new VACs based on the company's current set of VACs and the expected market demand for similar competencies.

One process that will be described in this section resembles options-based decision-making concepts. Options-based decision making is a process by which multiple outcomes are predicted, and strategies for addressing each outcome are created with the goal of keeping the maximum number of future options available at all times. By performing this type of analysis, the company will develop a variety of possible market evolution scenarios, then create action plans for each scenario.

This options-based process essentially occurs in three phases, as originally outlined by Hamel and Prahalad in their book, *Competing for the Future.*[6] First, you create a vision of the future for the industry, as well as a strategic plan for how the company will compete in new markets of the future. Next, you develop a portfolio of the shortest migration paths from the current industry structure to a particular opportunity within the envisioned new industry structure. This often takes place concurrently with the activities of other firms that recognize the same opportunity. The goal of this phase is to actually *shape the emergence* of the new industry so as to make the best use of your company's abilities. The third phase involves maneuvering within the industry to place your company in a position of power once the market begins to form.[7]

During the first phase, each participating company plays the role of either leader or follower. Some firms believe they should let others create market opportunities while they follow close behind. This strategy attempts to reduce the risks of investing in a market that may never materialize. However, this strategy overlooks the "core competence" development factor and the first-mover advantage. Without the core competence required to develop competing products, a company cannot effectively compete in new markets.

During the second phase, companies formulate the most probable market evolution paths, then attempt to minimize both the time and investment required to develop the industry vision along each path into a tangible market opportunity.[8] This can be done by testing product concepts and prototypes with employees and selected customers early in the development process. Other techniques include small-scale test market experiments, sharing investment risk with alliance partners, and tapping into the knowledge base of alliance partners to gain insights into a new and unfamiliar class of customers or set of technologies.[9]

Finally, in the third phase, companies position themselves within the new market to take full advantage of the competencies they have built during the first two phases. This process occurs when the market evolves to a point at which a particular competence reaches critical mass and becomes clearly valued, and is worth full investment in developing and marketing.

For example, the latter half of 1998 witnessed the evolution and viability of the MP3 music platform. In response, the handful of firms who had developed competencies for this platform began full-scale development and marketing of hardware devices that could play this music format. As of early 1999, there were a dozen or so companies with prototypes and several companies with actual products on the shelf, whereas the consumer demand for this product was still very much in an early embryonic stage.

APPLYING STEP 8: AN EXECUTIVE'S PERSPECTIVE

Although currently in the process of outsourcing both payroll and benefits, we had decided in step 1 to keep the recruiting function in-house. Therefore, to build and improve this process, we needed to understand how recruiting would fit into the company's ongoing value proposition—and commit the appropriate resources to continue building this capability into a true VAC.

The justification for this strategy was a sound one: Employees are central to the company's value proposition; therefore, the ability to continue recruiting talented employees was critical to the company's ability to innovate and create new value in the future.

As a result, we decided to restructure the recruiting function by creating a new position, director of recruiting, that would report directly to the senior management team. Thus, recruiting would no longer be informally coordinated by personnel services and executed with random employee involvement from interested departments. Instead, a team would be dedicated to managing recruiting for the entire enterprise.

In step 6, the original team had created a plan for reducing transaction costs through the strategic application of IT and best-practice business solution. We used this same approach to develop a plan to improve our recruiting competency. Recruiting is a very expensive process, costing tens of thousands of dollars for each employee hired; in addition, hiring mistakes can be extremely costly. To reduce the expenses involved in the recruiting process, as well as to create new value and improve our capability in this area, the team approved the following initiatives:

> The company will develop a recruiting section on its existing web site and will post jobs on other appropriate job-search web sites, to reduce the cost of finding qualified candidates.

> The company can constantly update its web site, so it will be the preferred way to advertise job openings (over newspaper ads, billboards, and so forth). The company will direct all potential candidates to its web site if they seek hiring information.

> The company will redesign its web site so that it accurately reflects the corporate community and culture. Potential recruits can log onto the web site and determine for themselves whether they are a good fit.

> The company will attempt to obtain as much information as possible from web site visitors through forms and surveys. It will also encourage electronic submission of resumes. All candidate data will be stored in a database on which searches can be performed, thus significantly reducing the amount of time the company spends manually looking through resumes and cover letters.

We hope that these specific initiatives will not only reduce the cost of recruiting new employees, but will improve the overall hiring process by screening candidates more effectively. In addition, the team hopes the initiatives will provide more information to candidates so they can prescreen themselves. Because better and more complete information about the company will be available via the web site, we also expressed our hope that we will attract more qualified individuals.

(Continued)

Preliminary feedback from this approach has been very positive. The recruiting team has already created a solid framework for initial candidate selection based on the best practices of several internal departments and third-party best-practice solutions. We finished this step by concluding that recruiting the best and the brightest talent is critical to our future success. Any changes we make in this area will positively affect that process.

Step 9: Employ Risk Management Strategies for Outsourced Capabilities

Although the transformation into a VBO provides tremendous benefits, it also exposes a company to increased risk. These risks arise primarily due to inefficient markets, the loss of control of outsourced capabilities, and the loss of specific skills when capabilities no longer exist internally.

If markets were perfectly efficient, it would make sense to outsource everything except VACs. However, most markets are not very efficient. You may end up paying more than you wanted for an outsourced function or activity; the quality may be substandard; the supplier might not deliver in a timely manner; and so on. Moreover, outsourcing necessarily involves new transaction costs—including searching for partners, contracting with them, and continuing to investigate options. The nature of these specific transaction costs, which do not exist when keeping the activity in-house, can increase the risk associated with maintaining a VBO.

There are also intangible benefits that arise from retaining specific functions internally. For example, technology transfer retains skills and adds to a firm's intellectual capital resources. Outsourcing activities where inefficient markets exist exposes the company to the risk of losing these benefits—and there is always the possibility that a company will need to bring the activity back in-house.

Inefficient markets also create the risk that specific capabilities may become unavailable at some point. Insufficient depth in the market can lead to a small number of overly powerful players who could potentially exercise monopolistic tactics. Another challenge facing CEOs of value-based organizations is that you must occasionally form partnerships with companies that have different priorities. When sourcing strategically, it is absolutely essential to partner with companies who have similar ethics, culture, priorities, and similarly aligned business strategies.

Finding and maintaining a stable relationship with business partners can be difficult when market forces create pools of power within the value chain. For example, some suppliers, after building up their expertise with the buyer's support, will attempt to bypass the buyer directly in the marketplace. Giant Manufacturing of Taiwan was able to bypass its customer, Schwinn Cycles, by first mastering the relevant manufacturing technology, and then entering the retail market. Supplier firms cannot only attempt to integrate vertically around their existing suppliers and customers, but can also limit the availability of their resources, depending on competitive pressures, market imbalances, and strategic changes of direction. For example, automobile manufacturers are often shut down because of strikes at supplier companies. These strikes often result in the automobile manufacturer losing billions of dollars. In such cases, suppliers may be able to charge monopolistic prices in the absence of competition. A supplier may also hide issues related to labor disruptions or raw material shortage until it is too late for its outsourcing customer to go elsewhere.

Your company must do whatever it can to minimize these and other risks. Although standard risk management principles apply equally to traditional and value-based organizations, the *magnitude* of risk increases significantly in the digital age. Whereas most organizations are comfortable managing as many as 10 or 20 outsourcing arrangements at any given time, a VBO could conceivably participate in hundreds or thousands of such arrangements. Consequently, management must spend additional time and effort mitigating the risk of outsourcing with respect to costs, resources, service levels, and communication.

The areas of risk that will be affected most by the VBO are in structuring contracts, delegating responsibility and decision-making authority, and creating appropriate performance measurement systems. Effectively addressing these issues up front will greatly reduce the risk of failure in the digital economy.

APPLYING STEP 9: AN EXECUTIVE'S PERSPECTIVE

We knew, even from our previous limited experience with outsourcing, that there would be additional risks involved. Members of the team were very cognizant of the importance of properly structuring contracts as well as putting backup plans in place in case things did not go as anticipated. To understand the risk inherent in outsourcing payroll and benefits, the team needed to identify what could go wrong, and decided that they would perform some internal analysis, as well as rely on the advice of the consulting firm who was assisting the company with the outsourcing contract/process.

After some debate, we decided that the main risks in outsourcing the payroll function would be the accuracy and timeliness of checks and deposits; the accuracy of tax calculations, reporting, and deductions; and the accuracy of various nonregular payroll events such as disability payments, parental leave, business travel, and other expenses. Although these risks exist whether the function is performed internally or externally, the method of control is much different. To mitigate these risks in an outsourcing arrangement, we appointed a team composed of several senior managers and a core team of payroll specialists who will be responsible for managing the relationship.

(Continued)

Although the risks are different for the benefits function, we decided our approach should be the same. We established a risk management action team that will be responsible for anticipating possible risks, as well as managing the outsourcing relationships on an ongoing basis. We also decided that anticipating the potential risk of outsourced functions involves specifically identifying performance metrics, penalties, and rewards for compliance with stated objectives. For payroll, the team established thresholds for minimum performance levels for check delivery, check accuracy, and tax calculation accuracy. For benefits, the team established minimum performance levels for aggregate and specific insurance benefits, pension and retirement fund management, employee survey scores, cost minimization, and overhead expense minimization. For each maximum target that is exceeded, a penalty will be automatically assessed. For each minimum that is exceeded, a reward will be automatically awarded. These performance metrics, penalties, and rewards are open for negotiation every year and represent a significant level of influence and control from the perspective of the company.

Step 10: Continually Create and Update Performance Measures

Airline pilots, who are the "managers" of the business within the domain of an airplane, have at their disposal in the cockpit a comprehensive set of instruments that provide the information they need to monitor the performance of the aircraft. By contrast, most senior managers of traditional businesses feel they are flying blind. Some of the problems that can be caused by inadequate performance measurement systems include:

- Lack of *focus* on the critical dimensions of the strategy
- Lack of organizational *alignment* around the strategy
- Lack of *insight* into what is actually happening in the business

Lack of Focus on the Critical Dimensions of the Strategy

"I simply cannot get my people to focus on the issues that drive value in our business."
—*Senior executive, manufacturing company*

One common problem is an overabundance of disparate performance measures, leading to confusion, or even cynicism, in the ranks. A classic example is found in companies that have growth strategies but measure only efficiency. Following the restructuring wave of the 1990s, many companies have realized that they cannot create prosperity simply by economizing, and have turned their strategic focus to growth—but without adjusting the balance of their performance measures accordingly.

Lack of Organizational Alignment around the Strategy

"Our people's behavior leads me to believe that they really do not understand our strategic direction."

—Senior executive, automotive company

Clearly articulating the business strategy and getting your top managers to buy in is a difficult and troublesome process. However, the real challenge is getting the entire corporation (organizational units and functions, and ultimately, individual employees) on board and headed in the same direction. If performance measures for different groups are inconsistent or out of synch with strategic goals, inconsistent behavior and disappointing results are likely to follow.

Lack of Insight into What's Really Happening in the Business

"We had reams and reams of financial data. It told us a lot about what had happened in the past, but it didn't show what levers we needed to pull to create future value."

—Divisional manager, large oil company

A strategy is not something that can be carved into stone and left standing as a permanent signpost to competitive success. Companies that want to compete must constantly adjust to industry and environmental changes, and to the actions of competitors. However, companies often find that their ability to change direction is constrained by existing performance measurement systems.

One problem is that in many companies, the majority of the metrics are so-called *lagging indicators:* they document past performance. Most accounting measures fall into this category: return on capital employed, sales growth, asset turn, and the like, which tell you what has already happened. Though useful in assessing historical performance, they offer little insight into how the firm is performing now, or how it is likely to perform in the future if it continues on its current course. Nor do they offer much insight into the drivers of business performance, indicating what actions need to be taken to create additional value for shareholders. Companies need leading indicators as well, tests that measure their progress toward meeting quantifiable goals, if they are to adapt their strategies appropriately and stay a step ahead of competitors as conditions change. The lack of insight resulting from inadequate measures may very well lead a company in the wrong direction.

**CASE IN POINT—THE WRONG PERFORMANCE MEASURES DRIVE
THE WRONG BEHAVIOR**

A printing firm based its reporting systems on conventional operating and financial measures. In its production plants, the company used press speed and press utilization as key performance measures. Over the years, one plant managed to improve press speed and utilization significantly, and this unit was generally considered one of the best performing in the company. What the indicators failed to reveal, however, was that the unit had achieved these apparent performance improvements while concurrently reducing prices to a level at which not even variable costs were covered. Thus, the narrow focus on press speed and utilization actually caused the unit to destroy shareholder value at an ever-increasing rate.

The State-of-the-Art Performance Measurement System: Four Critical Dimensions

Most performance measurement systems come from one of two models: Either they measure value generated, or they measure compliance with a stated strategy. In our view, neither approach alone is sufficient to implement strategic decisions and track results in the digital economy. Value-based measures are good for strategic planning but fall short when attempting to assess execution. Strategy-derived measures are good for execution but typically lack strong analytical validation. We believe a robust performance measurement system that will allow companies to maximize shareholder value in the digital economy must combine the best aspects of both.

Companies trying to succeed in the digital economy by transforming into a VBO structure need also to break the conventional paradigms of performance measurement, recognizing such systems should encompass more than just numbers. To fall back on our airplane metaphor, you must not only design comprehensive cockpit displays, but must also:

1. Apply a rigorous analytical approach to understand the nature and logic of your business model.

2. Use the performance measurement system as the cornerstone of your strategic management and reporting process.

3. Design individual performance and compensation programs for executives and managers consistent with these business measures.

4. Support the performance measurement system with IT, enabling automatic data capture, drill-down presentation, and root-cause analysis.

One method for implementing a comprehensive performance measurement system is the Integrated Strategic Measurement toolkit. This toolkit attempts to mold the performance measures around a business's strategy, operations and information architecture, and includes one of the most critical but often overlooked dimensions of performance measurement: organizational change.

INTEGRATED STRATEGIC MEASUREMENT

At first blush, selecting a handful of performance measures for a business may seem like a straightforward exercise. However, designing and implementing a performance measurement system that successfully focuses on the key elements of the strategy, aligns the organization behind those elements, and provides valuable insight into the performance of the business proves to be a rather complex task. It requires a deep understanding of:

- The strategy of the organization
- The organization's operations and business processes
- The current and potential information architecture
- The dynamics of creating change

Strategy of the Organization

We have found that the team designing the performance measurement system needs to be able to articulate the business vision clearly. The team must also segregate the system into strategic objectives, critical success factors, and ultimately, through a path of *root causes* as opposed to symptoms, into the potential measures.

The Organization's Operations and Business Processes

Developing a sophisticated performance measurement system is rarely worth the effort unless it is embedded into the heart of the organization—in the very business processes. Mapping the processes, identifying the process drivers and outcomes, and understanding the interactions and interdependencies between these processes requires a thorough understanding of the firm's operations.

Current and Potential Information Architecture

It is no use designing a brilliantly insightful set of performance measures if the data they require are unavailable at reasonable cost. In practical terms, the process of identifying and ultimately selecting the most appropriate measures is constrained by current and future information architectures: What kind of information is available, and where it can be captured. The architects of the performance measurement system must be able to find the right data in the typically wide array of systems and sources that most companies have.

Dynamics of Creating Change

Designing a state-of-the-art performance measurement system is not just about periodically printing out new reports with new numbers in them. The

(Continued)

new system may significantly change the way the business is managed, the way resources are allocated, the way task priorities are set, and the way individuals are rewarded. In our experience, understanding the dynamics of and obstacles to change in the organization is often the single most decisive factor for success or failure.

Implementing a forward-looking, strategy-encompassing performance measurement system that provides the right information to the right people at the right time is an arduous task and is never really complete. However, there is no alternative. If you want to play in the digital economy, you need these particular toys.

APPLYING STEP 10: AN EXECUTIVE'S PERSPECTIVE

Looking back, I realize that trying to develop a performance management system from scratch was an impossible task. The business environment was changing much too rapidly to build a system from the ground up—and we had so little to start with. Therefore, we once again solicited the help of specialists.

The consulting firm began by analyzing our basic corporate strategy. Our company is committed to top-line growth through new products and services focused around the time-value proposition. We are also intently focused on building additional content around existing containers, as well as building new containers and new content. We intend to capture new markets and customers based on leveraging our core competencies in innovative ways; internally, we continue to develop a set of core competencies that will sustain growth and profitability in the future.

Once the strategic intent of the organization was identified, a team of executives was selected to design a strategic management and reporting system with the help of specialists in the business intelligence systems arena. This system will be the foundation for executive information, in addition to providing companywide decision support. This tool will be responsible for providing real-time information on current business performance, the capability for analyzing good or bad performance, identifying key performance drivers, and the capability for performing "what if?" analyses and scenario planning activities.

The executive management team then aligned individual incentives with business performance metrics by creating new performance evaluation criteria. Future compensation systems will be based on performance metrics such as percentage of revenues and profits from new products and new features in existing products. Other criteria will be: new markets entered, customer base growth, profitability per customer growth, new product introduction frequency, and brand equity growth. Although this is an abbreviated list of the full performance evaluation criteria, the message is consistent for all of them. The new system will be based on pure business performance, and each employee will be compensated based on his or her individual contribution to that performance.

It should be painfully obvious that none of these performance management measures can be performed without IT. Information technology must permeate each and every solution, and will be both an enabler as well as a driver in the further evolution of performance management and monitoring.

Step 11: Continuously Use Information Technology to Enable Business Strategy

Throughout the 1980s and early 1990s, it was widely accepted that a company must align its business strategies, technology strategies, business processes, and organization. Aligning IT strategies to existing business strategies was once sufficient to achieve competitive advantage—or at a minimum, afforded a position of parity within one's industry.

Alignment was important because of the traditional gap that existed between business and technology communities, which resulted in IT investments being made in areas inconsistent with the strategic direction set by executive management.

The good news is that these principles are still fundamentally correct. Companies that have followed this direction have achieved tremendous marketplace success. Numerous examples exist; companies such as Wal-Mart, USAA, and FedEx formulated winning strategies and then created the technology to support the desired business capability.

However, for tomorrow's winners in the digital economy, it is no longer sufficient to support existing business strategies; they will have to use IT to enable new business strategies and capabilities that, in many cases, weren't even imagined—much less planned for—by management. The digital economy thus poses new challenges to IT alignment due to a rapidly changing business and technology landscape.

Changing industry structures and rules of competition are causing companies to rethink traditional paradigms and develop new scenarios for their future business direction. To adjust to these changes, industry leaders must focus IT alignment as detailed in the following text.

Define and Measure the Value Contribution of IT Initiatives

In the digital economy, the means by which we measure IT's contribution must change. Until recently, when large-scale enterprise transformation replaced narrower initiatives, most companies treated IT as an independent investment separate from the business capabilities it enabled, and measured it with internal criteria, such as return on investment (ROI). The problem in calculating ROI for IT investments is that IT is inseparably linked to all areas of a business. It is difficult to separate the return on an IT investment from the return on other investments.

For example, is a faster product delivery cycle a result of the new delivery tracking system implemented two months ago, or the change in delivery procedures mandated last week? It is commonly accepted that measurements that look at the cost of an investment relative to revenue generated, like ROI, are meaningless in measuring IT investment because many of the benefits of IT are not quantifiable in the traditional sense.

Companies therefore need to measure IT's value contribution with more market-oriented, external criteria, such as the impact on the company's ability to innovate, grow, and improve shareholder value. Companies should look at other aspects of IT investments, such as its impact on employees and learning, innovation, and of course, customer value, to determine IT's total impact. In the digital age, companies are forming new relationships and communities with consumers, suppliers, and other associates to extend the boundaries of their enterprise. Because IT provides a company with the capabilities to achieve these objectives, it should be valued as more than achieving short-term cost-reduction objectives.

Develop Winning Strategies for Exploiting Enabling Technologies

Companies must become skilled at exploiting enabling technologies. In the near term, these enabling technologies are solutions to enterprise challenges such as globalization and business process integration. Even today, such technologies provide opportunities to link together customers, suppliers, and business partners—to extend the boundaries of the enterprise into a virtual community. Extending one's reach with virtual products and services, understanding the competitive landscape, and simultaneously understanding your customers' needs and understanding how those needs are changing will provide the degree of customer intimacy and marketplace intelligence required by winners in the digital marketplace.

Exploit Virtual Relationships with Technological Experts to Maximize Profitability and Minimize Risks

Due to the speed of technological development, most companies have formed relationships with multiple service providers, software vendors, and other specialized technology entities to gain access to the requisite skills and resources. These relationships will become increasingly necessary if VBOs expect to stay on top of new, enabling technologies. Whether these relationships are viewed as strategic partnerships or as contractual agreements will depend on the kind and importance of the enabling technologies in question.

Over the years, companies have stepped up efforts to align technology initiatives with strategic business directions. The challenges of the digital economy, however, add to the complexity of performing such alignments. Instead of forming a singular view of the future, companies in the digital economy must develop scenario-based business plans, involving multiple business scenarios supported by multiple technology strategy scenarios. Companies must shift from thinking in terms of implementation plans to incremental *development* plans based on ever-evolving business scenarios. This makes IT alignment a continuous activity, not something a company does every five years.

Scenario-based business plans are created as follows: The business plan is first broken out into key decision factors. These decision factors represent the directions in which the business could potentially head. Next, it's necessary to create a comprehensive list of possible events; for each event on this list, a separate scenario should be formulated. Then, for each scenario, a set of decision implications should be created. These decision implications should be factored back into the key decision factors, and the process should repeat itself until management is satisfied that all probable scenarios have been identified and planned for.

This type of scenario-based business planning ensures that most of the probable business scenarios have been taken into account and a plan created for each one. In the event that an unexpected event occurs, most of the decision factors will likely be known—they will just need to be combined to formulate a new scenario based on current events.

APPLYING STEP 11: AN EXECUTIVE'S PERSPECTIVE

After discussing the issues raised by this step, we concluded that far more issues involving IT and its integration with business strategy existed than had been raised. After all, the company was experiencing firsthand the fundamental ways that new technologies such as ERP systems and electronic commerce were changing the way it did business. Already, a number of business units were clamoring to test leading-edge emerging technologies with the hope of finding new ways to bring products to market. The team knew that technology would be the key to the digital economy, but what criteria should be used to determine which initiatives will grow the business and which could put the company into bankruptcy? After agreeing that this was a critical step, indeed, our team created a set of general guidelines to direct future IT investments.

The first step in obtaining funding for an investment in IT would be to write a business case that would address the business need, the proposed IT solution, and the expected value created by the investment. This could be written by anyone and would be submitted to an IT steering committee. The IT steering committee would be composed of senior business and IT executives who would meet once a week to review proposals and evaluate ongoing IT initiatives.

This steering committee would be chartered with the directive that the following criteria be used in evaluating the business cases for IT investment. First, would the IT investment contribute to the evolution of a VAC? Second, would the IT investment reduce the cost of interfacing to a non-VAC? Third, would the IT investment contribute to the growth of a product or a family of products, or did it enable the business to develop new products or new content for existing products? Fourth, would the IT investment incorporate a time-

(Continued)

value proposition? Fifth, was the IT investment aligned with the existing business strategy? Each business case for IT investment would be objectively evaluated against this criteria from both a quantitative and qualitative perspective.

We concluded by deciding that the IT steering committee would also be responsible for bringing in industry and IT specialists when necessary to address significant investment requests and to keep nontechnical executives abreast of developing technologies and their potential impact on the business.

Step 12: Undertake Change Management Processes and Techniques to Ensure Successful Migration from the Current Organization to the Value-Based Organization

Transformation to a VBO poses a difficult question to management: How best to conduct change of this magnitude, especially when it has such far-reaching human consequences?

As a direct consequence of the digital economy, people everywhere must unlearn past habits of thinking and adopt new ways of cooperating with one another. This won't be easy. Implementing change can be fraught with peril.

We have identified four steps in the management of change brought about by the digital economy:

1. Complete the past.
2. Stand in the future.
3. Design and implement the change.
4. Align measures and rewards with the new rules.

Complete the Past

The organization has evolved to its current state for good reason. This is the company's culture, and it should be understood and acknowledged before attempting to move on. You must get at the hidden assumptions that have created these traditional ways of doing business. The first step is to review the company's history, and make people conscious of their culture. In other words, answer the question, "How did we get where we are?"

For example, people may hold odd assumptions: that quality assurance people have sole responsibility for product quality, or that only PhDs have truly useful ideas about product innovations. Assumptions such as these are entrenched in many businesses today. They need to be identified and then challenged.

Stand in the Future

The ideology of the digital age is to cherish impermanence. The old notion that stability is good is itself dysfunctional. To achieve lasting change, take advantage of informed communication among functional teams, and capitalize on the diversity of information people naturally use to assess company performance. Think of an organization that will come into being as you create a design for it. As part of the business process redesign, state explicitly which rules no longer apply, and what patterns of behavior are to replace them. Identify and discuss the rules by which your company operates. Ask which of these moves you toward your goal. Decide which are dysfunctional and hinder you from reaching your goal. Then consider which rules and behaviors are simply obsolete—the ones people know don't work, and are already working around or ignoring.

A classic example is the hard-to-eradicate belief that suppliers can't be trusted. The resulting rule of behavior is to reinspect all materials received or work performed by outside vendors. Another is that only your company knows how to specify components. This leads you to miss opportunities to embed the supplier's manufacturing and materials know-how into new product designs.

In a stressful situation, an authority figure can easily revert to being directive, critical, or worse. Identify and understand negative feedback signals; they tend to drive people back to their old ways of doing things. Responses such as "It's the other guy's fault"; "Don't stick your neck out"; "Kick it upstairs for a decision"; "They don't pay me to think"; and "Outsiders can't be trusted" are all too common, particularly among middle managers. Without a clear directive to the contrary, lower-level employees will wait to be told what to do. It's not enough to tell employees that they are now empowered to make decisions. They must be assured that they will not be punished for making mistakes as long as they can explain what led them to the decisions they made. Thus reassured, an employee who interacts with customers may decide to offer a replacement item rather than requiring the customer to file a complaint and await judgment by some invisible corporate official.

Design and Implement the Change

The following are levers that upper management can use to implement change:

- *Markets and customers.* Use new market opportunities as the impetus to change. Egghead Software, unable to compete in the retail software market through its physical outlets, closed its brick-and-mortar stores and opened a virtual storefront online.

- *Products and services.* Create new products and services made possible by new business partnerships. The OnStar system by General Motors, as discussed in Chapters 2 and 3, was made possible through a three-way collaboration among General Motors, Hughes, and Electronic Data Systems.[10]

- *Business processes.* Modify the existing process or replace the process entirely with a new process that aligns the activity with the intended change.

- *People and reward systems.* Alter incentive systems to align the goals of individuals with the goals of the business after the change. Train, reclassify, or remove people when they represent individual barriers to change.

- *Structure and facilities.* Move to a new physical facility that is better suited to teamwork and that facilitates employee interaction. Oticon A/S, the Danish maker of hearing devices, moved from its office building to a renovated warehouse that had no internal walls and in which all of the furniture was movable. This environment encouraged collaboration and teamwork among employees both within functional units and across functional boundaries.[11]

- *Technologies.* Use technology to support and drive the new way of doing business. Using the Internet as the first stop for customer support questions, Cisco has been able to reduce customer service headcount by more than 1,000 engineers. These 1,000 engineers have been redeployed to develop new Cisco products for the future.[12]

Any or all of these levers could be used in the process of transforming a company into a VBO. For example, if a business identifies its VAC as the ability to create trendy, low-cost alternatives to existing products, much as Swatch did with the Swatchmobile, then entering new markets and garnering new customers could be one way to begin implementing the transformation. Another way would be implementing technology in the form of an ERP system to nudge the organization into a new way of doing business. Most corporations will find it necessary to employ more than one of the above levers, so in the following text, we've included examples of ways to use (and to combine) the individual levers.

Align Measures and Rewards with These New Rules

An essential aspect of change is to modify the rules by which people are rewarded, psychologically as well as financially, and to align the consequences of their behavior with these new rules. Human resources policies must be consistent with new organizational structures. Explicit criteria in appraisal and compensation schemes reinforce desired behavior.

Often those on the front lines are best able to relate the organization's shortcomings to their impact on individual customers. A case can be made for giving the frontline employees greater responsibility for change. To make this work, though, may require intensive reeducation and reassurance. At this point you may ask, "How do we convince our people to back the change initiative?" We suggest rephrasing the question as, "How will people convince themselves that this change is worth undertaking? How can management help them to do so?" Conviction comes from within. You can't force someone to be motivated; you can only provide a motivating environment. The key is to remove barriers to motivation, rather than to attempt to motivate. The typical organizational change spiral moves swiftly from planning to forgetting. The challenge is to create a circle of learning, changing, and communicating, in which people within the organization can commit to the change program.

The first step in building a motivating, convincing environment is to manage and overcome fear. Often those at the top have grown up in the organization. Culturally, it suits them and they are afraid to see it change.

In trying to counteract these effects, it is important to differentiate between paralyzing fear and fear that makes you act. There is fear that acts as a trigger for change, and there is fear that simply causes inertia. To distinguish between the two—and, whenever possible, to convert paralysis into action—senior managers need to understand fully what people within the organization are feeling. That includes their peers, those who work for them, and those for whom they work; there is no monopoly of resistance and fear at any level of the organization. Fear is difficult to identify; it is rarely manifested as such, but it is expressed through other minor issues and complaints. Still, even petty grievances are a good place to begin bringing problems to the surface and removing barriers to commitment and motivation. To motivate effectively, we must employ tools aimed at individuals instead of organizations:

- Communication (not broadcasting) in a way that encourages dialog
- Individual counseling that addresses personal responses to change
- Team briefings that build group consensus and airs group concerns

- Anonymous surveys that allow the airing of more contentious reactions
- Focus groups that work toward promoting a common understanding of the change
- Published request, review, and response channels so that everyone involved in the change has a structured, formal system through which to ask questions

If these actions provide employees a chance to let off steam, but achieve nothing concrete, they are valueless or worse. They yield only a mass of tiny detailed complaints that management will find difficult to interpret. Interacting with employees isn't enough; neither is conducting surveys if you do nothing with the feedback. You must understand what employees are doing and feeling; you must engage in a two-way communication with them.

APPLYING STEP 12: AN EXECUTIVE'S PERSPECTIVE

Even before we began meeting to discuss this notion of transforming into a VBO, our CEO had spearheaded a communications campaign that he hoped would foster awareness of the upcoming dramatic effects of the digital economy. This message was put on posters, integrated in the weekly bulletins, and included in corporate communication to the rank and file. Every employee was exposed to the idea that our market was experiencing rapid change brought on primarily by IT—and that our company would need to respond to this new reality.

Throughout this campaign, the CEO was careful to reiterate the company's values, goals, and ambitions to demonstrate that the company would not lose its identity, but was simply going to operate under new rules.

After we began meeting and going through this 12-step process, the CEO altered his message slightly. He now was sending a clear signal designed to bring home the message that our company would not survive without change. Those of us on the senior management team were encouraged to begin speaking about the inevitability of changing the business model, and it soon was quite clear that changes—big changes—were under way. Employees were asked to provide feedback through town hall meetings, e-mail suggestion boxes, and an open-door policy by the senior management team. Issues that seemed important to all employees were addressed in corporate bulletins and other companywide communications. In this way, our CEO successfully created a vision for the future that focused everyone's attention on our common goal.

To further motivate employees to accept the upcoming changes, we rolled out a new *innovation incentive* system to all functional units. Employees were rewarded for coming up with new ideas that were actually used in implementing the change, and for going above and beyond the call of duty in ensuring that the change process went smoothly. These incentives were incorporated into employee evaluation forms and would directly impact the employee ratings for bonuses and special awards that were handed out twice a year.

10

Obstacles to Reaching the Value-Based Organization

"Only those who dare to fail greatly can ever achieve greatly."
—*Robert Francis Kennedy*

THE BENEFITS OF THE VALUE-BASED ORGANIZATION (VBO) MODEL ARE CLEAR, BUT THE ROAD to digital age readiness has a few barriers to overcome:

- The bigger-is-better mentality
- Organizational inertia
- An emphasis on assets over information
- Difficult-to-change employees and corporate culture

These roadblocks are keeping companies today from achieving the ideal organizational structure. Successfully addressing these roadblocks will allow companies to move toward a VBO much more easily and with greater speed.

Bigger Is Better

The bigger-is-better mentality and the impetus to merge or acquire are rooted in old ways of doing business. Digital technology can enable companies to gain the same benefits through strategic partnerships and alliances with third parties. Past limitations, such as access to capital and extensive distribution channels, no longer keep small businesses from attacking new opportunities aggressively and with force. As the digital economy evolves, industry behemoths will rarely be the first who are prepared to attack new opportunities.

If technology really has reduced transaction costs enough that companies can incorporate the services of external businesses for non-VAC functions, why isn't it happening faster? To be sure, many companies now outsource data center operations, help desk and customer service operations, accounting, and legal services among others. Merger and acquisition activity, however, has continued to rise, and most firms have done everything but get smaller. Regarding the recent megamergers (BP-Amoco, Bell Atlantic–GTE, Citicorp-Travelers, Mobil-Exxon, and Boeing–McDonnell Douglas), we believe these aggregated organizations will have even less entrepreneurial capability to respond to changing markets than the formerly separate companies would have had. These deals were struck with a misunderstanding of the new forces in the digital economy. Mergers and acquisitions will undoubtedly continue as companies strive for the apparent benefits consolidation seems to offer. However, the resulting megacorporations will eventually fail if they do nothing to strengthen their core capabilities. We present seven typical reasons behind mergers, and why they are wrong.

The Seven Reasons Why Megamergers Do Not Work

1. The presence of immature and inefficient markets leads firms to join forces to exploit these markets. However, they fail to recognize that maturing and more efficient markets are being developed every day without mergers. Merger and acquisition activity is rampant in the online market for information services with mergers between portal sites and more traditional businesses, with these traditional businesses paying billions of dollars simply for the market presence these portal sites have in the immature online marketplace.

   While these portal sites may turn out to be instrumental in reaching the online consumer, companies could save a lot of money by forming relationships with these sites instead of purchasing them and squandering them like Compaq has done thus far with Alta Vista.

2. Regulatory changes often encourage corporations to merge or acquire as a hedge against uncertainty and in an attempt to control the market and defend their positions. However, it is more important—and more financially rewarding—to take advantage of relationships with external partners and focus on the core business to create new products and

services, than to defend the existing business, which may involve markets that are dying or that the company should not be in for strategic, operational, value-added competency, or other reasons.

3. Companies demonstrate an apparent need to pressure suppliers and other third parties by consolidating and using economies of scale. However, partnering and investing in a relationship with those businesses will be much more likely to provide higher overall returns than creating an adversarial relationship.

4. Companies seeking more physical assets often merge or acquire. The consequent utilization of fixed assets justifies retaining what in many cases would otherwise be useless and simply written off. For example, railroad companies merge or acquire to consolidate and better utilize existing railroad tracks. However, unless access to these tracks could not be had through partnerships, the resources required to manage the additional fixed assets will likely exceed the value of simply accessing additional assets through partnerships. Through strategic relationships, companies can obtain access to any fixed assets they do not own. This is similar to the now standard lease-or-buy decision, with leasing being the better option for physical assets which may have short useful lives in the digital economy.

5. Firms can merge and acquire without exchanging cash, as in stock-for-stock deals that make the process painless for management. This allows companies to transact deals that their cash flow would not otherwise allow, while at the same time having little effect on earnings. Some companies, such as Internet stocks, are making multibillion-dollar acquisitions before ever reporting a profit. For example, as of September 1998, Yahoo! Inc. had never reported a profit, had year-to-date sales of just $125 million; yet in January 1999 announced a $5-billion acquisition of the Internet home page builder GeoCities. This was possible due to Yahoo! Inc.'s market valuation of over $30 billion, giving it the ability to acquire another company for approximately 25 times its annual revenue. Although there are many factors involved in purchases of this type, the risk involved in making acquisitions and assuming the entire load of organizational baggage and dead weight that companies maintain is far greater than the gains possible through strategic partnering for specific competencies. Companies can achieve the same objectives through partnering that are achieved through mergers and acquisitions, but avoid the cost of managing and controlling a larger, slower, more bureaucratic organization.

6. Firms merge in an attempt to globalize operations. However, the expanding global network infrastructure provides the ability to compete globally without being joined at the hip.

7. Consolidating operations appears to spread overhead costs over a greater number of revenue dollars. However, by divesting noncore activities, a company can drastically reduce overhead costs without the need to merge or acquire. Mergers and acquisitions are attractive only when the goal is to strengthen the core while simultaneously shedding noncore activities. Adding noncore functionality in-house is counterproductive.

Organizational Inertia

Organizational inertia is the intangible force in the conscious and subconscious mind that says that things are fine the way they are, so don't make any big changes. This mentality is a giant-killer in the digital economy. All companies must reinvent themselves from time to time, some more often than others.

The list is long of firms that lost their focus and died, as evidenced by the constant churn of the Fortune 500. Although the digital economy revolves around information technology (IT), technology in and of itself cannot solve the problem of organizational inertia. In fact, a large number of modern information systems add to it. The availability of more information and more advanced ways of delivering that information about the same business does not necessarily make for better or more enlightened decision makers. The answer is in looking outside the business—at the markets, the consumers, and your competitors. Figure out how to adapt to and even lead the markets and the consumers faster and more effectively than your competitors.

In addition, CEOs need to look beyond the markets they are currently in, toward markets they *should* be in or would like to be in. Similarly, they shouldn't spend time looking at all consumers, or even all consumers of their products or services. CEOs should look at their most demanding consumers and figure out how to satisfy *their* needs.

The new digital economy moves much faster than the industrial economy; firms only a few years old can quickly obtain multibillion-dollar market capitalization values—witness Netscape and eBay, among so many others. Therefore, firms must address organizational stagnation, find their real value in the market, and begin building innovative products and services that will satisfy the next generation of consumers.

The quality that separates the organization of today from the organization of tomorrow is agility. Agile organizations are very aware of their place in the market. They are constantly alert to any developments that may affect their current products or services, or that may present opportunities for new products or services. Agile organizations also understand that the market will always be more powerful than they are in the long run, and that rather than controlling the market, the market controls them.

Consider Microsoft. Microsoft was slow to realize the revolutionary importance of the Internet—and actually thought that a viable Internet-based market would not develop without its blessing. Those who argued successfully for the delay could hardly have been more wrong. It took a set of radically different business practices, such as software giveaways, to change the course of mighty Microsoft. Every agile company understands that no matter the degree of influence on the existing market, things can always change.

In the digital economy, every business model is at an almost immediate risk of obsolescence. Inefficiency becomes much less important when your product or service, and hence your company, becomes irrelevant due to innovation. Change is a necessity, and those companies that cannot change will die. As Microsoft's CEO Bill Gates often quotes, "We are always two years away from failure."

Valuing Assets over Information

Few executives have shifted their focus from managing fixed assets to managing intellectual capital resources, despite the fact that the most important activity in the digital economy is the creation and management of information. Traditional methods of measuring productivity (such as return on investment, return on assets, return on equity, return on capital employed, and even Economic Value Added^{sm} and net present value) all have one thing in common: They attempt to measure performance based on employing physical assets.

Although these measurement tools do a good job, they miss several points relevant to the digital economy. First, attempting to measure performance based on capital employed never considers the real possibility that the market could change, leaving the invested capital stranded and without a use. Second, it focuses managerial time on effectively using that capital once it has been invested in, creating a backward-looking measurement, which is hardly in the best interest of value creation. (This is called the pitfall of sunken costs, and it has lead to some disastrous business decisions.) Last, these measures do not take into account the increasing value of intellectual capital assets within the company, which in the digital economy will become one of the most valuable assets.

We believe the demands of the digital economy will force corporations to reduce the attention they currently pay to fixed-asset management and adopt intellectual capital asset management practices to remain competitive.

Change-Resistant Employees

The saying, "Old habits die hard," is especially true for employees. The inability of people to embrace change and the absence of change as an integral component of corporate culture creates a real and significant barrier to achieving a VBO.

Competitive advantage today is more than just a matter of determining the *right* strategy; it's also about executing faster and *more smoothly* than your competitors. Competitive advantage of technology does not arise simply from owning technology; it grows out of strategic implementation, from the human resources and organizational systems that are already in place.

An organization's culture is difficult to study and impossible to quantify because it fundamentally represents a broad aggregation of individuals' beliefs, values, and personal assumptions. These philosophies eventually become deeply ingrained in an organization. Both invisible and intangible, a corporate culture is difficult to manage or to change. As such, corporate culture constitutes one of the most powerful obstacles to organizational transformation.

People fear and resist change. Biologically, as well as psychologically, the human organism is hardwired to seek homeostasis—a stable state with minimal change, if any. Employees initially see new organizational structures or any threat to the status quo as dangers, not opportunities. Following is a list of several key manifestations of resistance to change.

Denial. People deny that change is necessary. If employees refuse to try and understand why the current structure is unsatisfactory, any change will be considered unnecessary. Unnecessary changes can lead to resentment, anger, and refusal to cooperate.

Confusion. People are often unclear about how the proposed change will solve the problem. Although the need for change may be evident and accepted, the proposed solution—a new organizational structure—may not be understood. Management must communicate clearly the project's vision and goals, and how the proposed change will address visible organizational problems.

Fear and anxiety. People get anxious about what will happen to *them.* One of the most common roadblocks to change is uncertainty. Employees fear the new organization because they are afraid of how it might detrimentally affect them. They are concerned that they do not have the right skills or may not receive the necessary training to adapt and remain in the new structure. Employees at all levels worry about losing their jobs, about having to change positions, or embark on a new career path. Furthermore, they worry about losing contact with peers and superiors with whom they are accustomed to work.

Lack of trust. People don't always have faith that things will work out the way you say they will. Denial, confusion, and fear all manifest themselves in mistrust. Employees concerned about maintaining career expectations and job security will actively seek to preserve the status quo. For example, they may conceal critical information or sabotage projects so as to hinder the change process. Outsourcing and merger-driven reorganizations additionally evoke external mistrust—doubt that third-party providers or new partners can perform their roles correctly, accurately, and confidentially.

Inertia. People are slow to change. To combat fear and anxiety, they cling to familiar values and behaviors. Inertia is the most powerful force in human nature. If changes seem too dramatic, many employees will just drag their heels and refuse to cooperate.

CASE IN POINT—CHANGE GONE AWRY

National Semiconductor (NSC) learned that change must be moderated when it attempted to reengineer its entire IT organization practically overnight. The company established 38 challenging objectives, redefined roles, eliminated some positions and created others, and forced all 250 members of the IT department to reapply for their jobs. When only 70 people received their first choice of a new position, the entire process degenerated to chaos within five months. NSC tried to do too much, too fast.[1]

It's no surprise that companies in long-standing, traditional markets often have the hardest time adapting to rapid changes in environments. Cultural myopia is especially prevalent in monopoly industries, such as electric utilities, that are now undergoing deregulation.

An entrenched *customer* culture can also make organizational change extremely difficult. For example, practically all companies that have built sophisticated Internet-based ordering systems staff and operate a parallel process for manual input of orders that still come in by phone or postal mail. This system is necessary because certain customers still demand a "personal touch." Many customers, particularly those who are less technologically savvy, still require human interaction. In addition, of those who are connected to the Internet, many customers continue not to trust the security of online ordering and thus prefer not to transmit credit card information electronically.

Although these sorts of scenarios are becoming less common, market culture nonetheless continues to be an impediment to implementing fully digital systems.

Another relatively new phenomenon is challenging organizations' ability to change. Many large companies are losing their best people (those who would otherwise spearhead corporate reengineering efforts) to start-ups and new ventures. Because the Internet revolutionized the global supply chain, individuals now have ready access to instantaneous, worldwide distribution networks. Creating and running a new business is becoming less difficult each day and requires much less investment than a traditional enterprise. With capital markets paying enormous multiples for shares of Internet IPOs, the allure of instant riches is rapidly drawing away talented people from the less risky and lower-rewarding corporate world. The result is that the very people who least fear change, and hold the key to successful reengineering, are also the ones most likely to abandon the company in its time of need.

Although executive leadership is critical for successful change management, senior managers can also present the greatest roadblocks. Often with long-running tenures, senior managers can attempt to use political influence to derail projects that may detrimentally affect them or their division. An uncommitted senior team can foil unpopular changes in vision or direction, such as the management breakdown that led to the fall of People Express.

CASE IN POINT—LEADING THROUGH CHANGE[2]

Donald Burr, founder and CEO of People Express Airlines (PE), built an empire by developing a team-based, consensus-management culture, and by staying away from popular routes to avoid head-to-head competition with the big airlines. As the airline grew rapidly, it exceeded its limits. Unable to staff up quickly enough, it placed excessive workloads on staff. In a companywide memo, Burr acknowledged that PE was "operating beyond our practical capacity." Nonetheless, the airline continued to grow and to increase shareholder value.

Although part of Burr's strategy included a commitment to not buy other airlines, PE decided to fuel its growth by purchasing several regional carriers, including Frontier Airlines. Frontier's high operating costs and unionized labor force made it the polar opposite to the People Express organization. The vastly different cultures put a tremendous strain on PE and its distinctive environment. Many senior managers questioned the strategy and were troubled by the cultural divide. In less than one year, the discord, along with other factors, brought down People Express.

Managers can also hinder change efforts by simply remaining distant. If projects are conceived and run solely from the top, employees may not understand the realities driving change. Without employee buy-in, change is impossible.

The ability of companies to create a culture of change within their organizations and their ability to effectively address each employee's concerns during this transition will greatly improve the ability of the company to complete the transformation into a VBO.

Lessons for Modern Management

Some firms will manage to survive for quite some time without changing their organizational structure. Still, inevitably, the digital economy will force all businesses to move toward VBOs. As the digital economy pervades even the most resource-intensive industries, non-value-based firms will become increasingly less competitive and will eventually be forced to make radical changes or die. The following are several of the lessons we have learned from helping companies make this sort of transition.

On Managing the Business Portfolio

Look at your company as a portfolio of business opportunities, each one evolving at a different rate. Value is created by manipulating the portfolio, applying the know-how derived from one opportunity to the next, from one cycle to another. In this way, for example, brand equity in a mature business can also pave the way for launching new products, concepts, or extensions. Conversely, technology developed to exploit a new opportunity may be injected into a more mature opportunity cycle to restart it as a new business.

On Using Sophisticated Management Tools

Dealing with complexity requires using sophisticated management tools, such as Integrated Strategic Measures, as discussed in the previous chapter. Without the proper tools, management is deprived of the ability to quickly and accurately make correct decisions.

On Outsourcing and Relationships

The most significant advantage to outsourcing is that you can gain access to the latest technologies and benefit from economies of scale without having to invest in infrastructures or competencies. To obtain these advantages, fast-moving companies should spend energy and resources on building alliances and partnerships, not on making noncore components.

To ensure that these competitive advantages are sustainable over time, your company must regularly evaluate corporate relationships, looking for opportunities to improve and strengthen contracts. The company must also regularly evaluate its value proposition. It must be prepared and willing to reshuffle the organizational structure, bringing outsourced functions back in-house if necessary, while possibly outsourcing former core competencies that may have become commodity items.

On Innovation

Do not get bogged down in managing the present. Keep focused on the demands of the future. Although it may seem that current products are the most important item on the agenda, it is the products you will sell in two or three years that should concern senior management today. The most important factor in moving from today to tomorrow is the company's ability to innovate. However, whereas it is important to be innovative and embrace new ideas, it is also critical to be able to shed old ways. Success breeds complacency in every company; do not let prosperity cause you to avoid change.

On Focusing on Value First and Costs Second

Value-based companies cannot be developed simply by cutting back on costs, capabilities, or investments. Rather than curtail capital investments, VBOs are willing to redirect them if new assets or improved infrastructure is required. Lean and mean cost-cutting concepts are abandoned because the returns on cost reduction alone do little more than place a company in a holding pattern. Although value-based companies emphasize value and opportunity first, they are nonetheless careful to analyze the cost structure of each business they run. They retain only the best performers. They pay attention to reducing fixed costs and divesting assets. The by-product of outsourcing noncore activities is the natural divestment of many fixed costs that drain the investment coffers. Companies that move swiftly also derive value from resources in new ways, recognizing that one can view ownership of physical assets as a liability since they represent significant investments which in some cases never provide an adequate return. Value-based companies often divest nonstrategic assets to focus investment-building efforts on their brands, know-how, and strategic alliances.

On Optimizing Tangible and Intangible Assets

Reliance on physical assets and the associated high-fixed-cost structures often drag down the ability to move into new opportunities. Assets—tangible or intangible, owned or externally accessed—are managed for revenue today and to build value tomorrow. Value-based companies have a knack for tapping whatever resources they need—technology, production capacity, proprietary know-how, licenses and physical assets—when they need them. Actual ownership of resources is not critical to business success; access to them is.

That is why a nimble company often places as much value on intangible assets (its ability to forge relationships with allies or to manage a brand, for example) as it does on ownership of tangible assets like a factory.

On Embracing Change Management

The ability to jump on opportunities quickly can be achieved only when an organization is structured to innovate. Roles and relationships among key executives should be fluid and always changing. "Dynamic," however, is not to be confused with "unmanaged." Responsibilities, decision making, and information flow still need to be orchestrated by creative leaders.

On Inertia

Beware of organizational inertia, and specifically, cultural inertia. Inertia is the greatest threat facing your company. Management must clearly communicate its vision and goals while simultaneously listening to the pulse of the organization. Neglecting to communicate clearly and to listen with an open mind will result in employees who resist change. If necessary, create an emergency situation. People respond to emergencies; even if your company is the market leader and highly profitable, create a crisis or you risk falling behind your competitors.

On Nurturing Human Capital

Companies must instill, encourage, and utilize entrepreneurial energy and resourcefulness in their people. Recruiting, developing, and retaining a high-performing workforce—from leaders on down—is essential. A company's workforce must take ownership of the results of their actions; only then can they become value creators, whose individual contributions add substantive value to the business. Managing accelerating, overlapping business opportunity cycles calls for finding and developing managers who are adept at accommodating incompatible practices. The best procedures for managing a start-up may be the worst for guiding a mature business line. Executives must develop management styles to govern businesses effectively at all opportunity stages: in earlier stages when quick decision making and action taking are paramount, and in more mature stages when formal reporting and budget processes are needed.

On Empowering Managers to Seek Opportunity, Take Risks, and Operate Flexibly

Executives who grapple with the implications of dramatic change must learn to recognize and address emerging business opportunities. Businesses poised to jump when they see opportunities are managed in an unfettered, risk-tolerant style. Entrepreneurial spirit is nourished and supported by encouraging freedom in decision-making, trusting managers to make the right decisions and permitting them to act quickly and decisively. Decision making is based on feasibility of new opportunities, not cost; committing to decisive action is crucial. Excessive testing and pilot programs, rather than helping to manage the risk of launching new ideas, may actually delay results, giving managers an opportunity to create excuses for nonexecution. In the new digital economy, executives practice a form of just-in-time decision making, often operating on a planned-but-only-when-needed basis. For example, progress reviews may occur on a virtual, ongoing basis as key decision makers monitor results online, and structured reviews occur only as exceptions.

On Managing Knowledge

Nimble companies manage knowledge as a corporate asset, and will emphasize innovative ways to capture, develop, and use it. Finding the means to share intellectual capital and know-how throughout an organization is crucial for creating new opportunities. Willingness to change rapidly means respecting the value of intellectual capital and routinely evaluating its contribution to total business value, just as companies continually measure the worth of more concrete assets. The search for an edge from intellectual capital goes far beyond passive brainstorming.

Intelligent Organizations Conclusion

Today's corporate leaders are having to make tough decisions about what value a company really delivers (for example, what business activities the company should do to increase the value it delivers to its customers and shareholders, and what activities it should *not* do but rather leave in the capable hands of partners, contractors, or the open market).

The digital economy has allowed another economic leap, one in which more efficient markets are driving businesses to reduce transaction costs through the intelligent use of IT and the leveraging of market efficiencies to improve their market competitiveness. This has created a demand for an organizational structure that is nimble and can quickly adapt to the dynamic changes and demands required of a consumer-driven value network. Such "Value Based Organizations" are possible because of the sophisticated connections that technology provides, enabling them to form alliances with other businesses to leverage each other's strengths instead of integrating vertically. For example, Microsoft-Intel and Intel-Compaq alliances are partnerships that eclipsed the PC originator, IBM, who stuck too long with its own proprietary chips and system software.

The foundation of intelligent organizations lies in establishing the nimbleness and flexibility necessary to adapt to the digital economy. Successfully transforming into a VBO ensures the success of the organization in the future. Whereas the discussion on intelligent products provides a framework for creating the new products and services that will drive the organization's profits in the digital economy, the discussion on intelligent organizations attempts to provide a framework for understanding the forces that are driving the evolution of the organizational structure which will drive the organization's ability to adapt to rapidly changing market dynamics. The goal has been to help you apply the new rules of the digital economy to decisions about how to organize your enterprise and provide specific, detailed guidance on how to create an organization adept at reacting to the market by delivering high-value-added new products and services as quickly as possible. Your goal should be to take these concepts and the 12-step process and guide your organization to a more capable, productive state. The value-based organization is a great model to use, but your organization will most likely look somewhat different at each step in the transition. The bottom line is that the digital economy demands that your organization change to survive. Therefore, the question is not whether to change; it is, "How fast can I change and survive?" Good luck. It will not be easy.

Mastering the Digital Marketplace

11

Mastering the Digital Marketplace

"The best way to predict the future is to invent it."

—Alan Kay

December 5, 2003

It is a beautiful winter morning in Silicon Valley. Outside, the California sun is shining, a fresh breeze is blowing over the newly decontaminated waters of the San Francisco Bay, and Intel's stock is (again) up a full five points. Heather Caldwell, the CEO of @WarpSpeed walks briskly down the hall of the @Warp-Speed executive suite. Her smile does not betray the nervous excitement she feels, and as she greets her staff, they see nothing but her usual confident and energetic self. After all, Caldwell has many reasons to be pleased. Since taking over the reigns of the floundering computer graphics company in late 2002, she has transformed it once again into the undisputed market leader, consistently producing excellent returns and robust profit margins. In one short year, @WarpSpeed has been transformed from a dying dinosaur to a media and stock-market darling.

All good—but today represents a significant milestone for Caldwell. She has good reason to be nervous. True, she's been successful at turning @Warp-Speed around, but she wants to do more—much more. Specifically, she is about to take @WarpSpeed where no computer graphics manufacturer has gone before. Would she succeed? She thought so. All the building blocks were now in place.

Just a year previously, before Caldwell was promoted to CEO, the company had been hemorrhaging cash in an ill-considered foray into the video games market. Simultaneously—and more disastrously—it was experiencing significant market share loss in its traditional industry niche, high-power computer graphics equipment. Its stock price was at an all-time low. The company's lack of strategic focus at a critical time in the market was causing consumer confidence to suffer. Formerly the acknowledged technical leader in a highly technical industry, @WarpSpeed had fallen behind competitors in its ability to deliver the latest and greatest products to market.

There were other key factors that together caused @WarpSpeed's rapid fall from grace:

- It had ignored the fact that its customers were increasingly unhappy with its traditional proprietary (i.e., closed) operating platform. After all, this meant that @WarpSpeed products could not be easily integrated with products by vendors who were conforming to open systems specifications and accepted market standards. Rather than paying attention to this shift in customer needs, @WarpSpeed decided to ignore it, believing it had sufficient power in the market—and that its customers were sufficiently loyal—for it to go its own way.

- @WarpSpeed had lost its strategic focus. By diversifying into too many product lines and markets, it found itself the proverbial jack-of-all-trades—and master of none. Its exceedingly demanding customers quickly noticed and took their business elsewhere.

- The massive infrastructure investments and overhead costs associated with its venture into video games diverted cash (as well as management attention) away from its core business areas. @WarpSpeed wasn't operating up to previous standards in many functional departments that had previously been hailed as industry best practices.

- Although the overall quality of its products remained high, @WarpSpeed was taking far too long to develop new products—twice as long as competitors needed to get a new design out the door.

- Employees and managers alike expressed strong not-invented-here contempt for any products or ideas that had not originated within @WarpSpeed. This made it difficult for the company to form effective alliances with business partners, even when there was a significant (and obvious) competitive advantage to such an alliance succeeding.

Some pretty major challenges here. Yet Caldwell managed, within the space of just 12 short months, to effectively address and solve each of these seemingly insurmountable roadblocks. How exactly did she accomplish this? Let's take a quick inventory of her strategic actions:

- First, she *listened* to her customers—and reacted accordingly by creating products that delivered value based on the consumer's definition of value—not some engineer's notion of what was "cool."
- She looked for innovative ways to address those demands within a timeframe that still allowed for sizeable (if temporary) profits—before the fickle customer decided it needed something *else.*
- She created a new organizational model for @WarpSpeed—one that focused on doing fewer things well, doing them quickly, and partnering with other companies whenever necessary to create truly compelling products. @WarpSpeed was now exceedingly nimble, flexible, and specifically structured to be hypersensitive to ever-changing market demands.

Pushing the Envelope Further

Caldwell knew that her investors were happy with all she'd accomplished. Now, she knew, it was time to push the company even further. She walks toward a set of double doors; the entryway to @WarpSpeed's main conference room where her eight-person management team was already gathered. She could hear them excitedly talking and laughing; they knew big changes were afoot. When Caldwell entered the room and began detailing her newest plan, a hush falls over the room. Could what Caldwell is suggesting be possible?

Caldwell's latest strategy had been originally inspired by a discussion she'd had with an old friend and colleague, Barbara Kelly, CEO of retail giant TJMiller (and its related cyberstore, TJMiller.com). Kelly had a vision for dramatically restructuring her business, which was currently centered on hundreds of brick-and-mortar retail stores around the country that sold brand-name designer clothing at steeply discounted prices. Although TJMiller transacted a fair amount of business via its web site, consumers were understandably hesitant to buy clothes unless they could see them, touch them, and try them on. Kelly had a revolutionary idea. She thought she might be able to encourage more of her customers to shop "virtually" by incorporating some of the more exciting new multimedia technologies now available.

Specifically, in mid-2003, virtual-reality technology finally entered the mainstream. Consumers were able to buy new digital entertainment products that allowed them to virtually climb Mount Everest, play tennis against Chris Evert, or fly the space shuttle to Jupiter. Manufacturers were able to use virtual-reality systems to help their designers more accurately envision what their cars, aircraft, houses, and boats would look (and feel) like. Kelly thought she could use these same technologies to revolutionize the retail experience. She called her concept VirtualShopper, and she needed the help of @WarpSpeed to make her vision a reality.

Caldwell laid the idea out before her management team. The essence of the VirtualShopper idea was this: When entering a retail store, instead of wandering through the usual merchandise-filled rows and floors, consumers would first go to a "virtual" shopping space—a room equipped with a state-of-the-art virtual-reality projection system that also contained a comfortable chair, attractive lighting, and soft soothing music. The consumer would swipe his or her TJMiller smartcard through a terminal reader that would immediately bring up their specific profile: style preferences, color preferences, detailed size information, and of course a history of previous purchases. The customer would then be placed in a three-dimensional virtual world specifically suited to his or her tastes. It could be a Greek island beach, for example, or a breathtakingly beautiful mountain top in Japan. Everything from background sound, to lighting, to temperature would be adjustable—whatever the customer needed to enjoy a comfortable shopping experience. Then, the shopping begins. Using simple voice commands ("show me a blue dress") and body gestures (pointing to things, nodding or shaking the head), the customer indicates what he or she would like to see. Past purchases can be used as a starting point. ("I liked that polka-dotted shirt I bought for my husband last Christmas. Do you have one in my size?") However, any request can be accommodated. ("Show me that black bathing suit that was featured on the latest cover of *WiredVogue*.")

Because these are not physical products, but virtual ones, there's no limit to the type, style, or size of apparel that can be viewed. After selecting the desired products, the customer can view an image of himself or herself wearing them. This three-dimensional persona mimics the customer's every move and gesture, and is viewable from all angles. The customer can try on any number of outfits: replacing a blue baseball cap with a low-slung cowboy hat, or making dirty white sneakers morph into a pair of sequined ostrich boots. Rumpled khakis and a torn sweater turn into a crisp denim shirt and a pair of perfectly fitting denim jeans, with a little extra room in the seat, just the way this customer likes them. The customer can then see himself or herself walk down the streets of a mythical town of the Old West, or through the busy streets of Manhattan.

By this point in Caldwell's presentation, her team is nearly jumping out of their seats. "Just hold on," she says, "there's more." The customer can make any desired purchases instantaneously and be guaranteed that all clothes ordered will be delivered the following day, precisely as specified. Best of all, clothes ordered via VirtualShopper will fit perfectly based on the consumer's current measurements, using off-the-shelf inventory if possible, but custom-manufactured if necessary.

Caldwell finishes and looks at her team. "Our job," she tells them, "is to build a prototype for the VirtualShopper platform. Can we do it?" There's silence for 30 seconds in the @WarpSpeed boardroom. Then her vice president of manufacturing speaks up. "When do we get started?" he asks.

Only then does Caldwell break the news that she's already committed to delivering the prototype within three months. If that can be successfully accomplished, TJMiller will commit to ordering 10 VirtualShopper systems for each of 500 of her most successful stores by the end of 2004 in an aggressive pilot program. Eventually, Kelly hopes to equip every one of her stores (and there are currently more than 4,000 TJMiller outlets worldwide) with the systems.

"If all goes well—and there's every indication that it will—the Virtual-Shopper platform could then be licensed to just about every other kind of retail business," Caldwell concludes.

The meeting is over, and the room has been emptied before Caldwell sets her pen down. She smiles. She knows what's happening.

Most businesses, even high-tech enterprises, would say that this sort of deadline was extremely unrealistic. However, the @WarpSpeed team was by now, thanks to Caldwell's leadership, comfortable to moving at the speed of light. Within an hour, the head of design had organized a videoconference in which potential business partners from around the globe joined in. Participants included HumaForm, a London-based ergonomics and human design firm with expertise designing systems for simulating human movement and interaction; Virtuality.com, a Chicago-based manufacturer of computer games and maker of holographic three-dimensional projection systems; and Warnes-Time, the media giant that owned necessary music, video, and other digital content. (Interestingly, Virtuality.com was a direct competitor of @WarpSpeed in several existing markets, but Caldwell insisted that its technology was critical to making VirtualShopper a viable product within the required timeframe.)

Although lawyers were present at the videoconference, the preliminary deal was cemented in relatively short order. Each of the partners was extremely familiar with the others' capabilities, and all were confident they had a common goal. By the end of the business day, a new extended enterprise was beginning to take form. A collaborative workgroup system purchased from Sunny Design Systems (another competitor of @WarpSpeed) was immediately installed at all sites to allow employees of all partner companies to work around the clock from their respective locations.

Eleven weeks later, a working prototype of VirtualShopper was assembled in @WarpSpeed's R&D labs. After witnessing the initial demo, Barbara Kelly and her team immediately ordered 5,000 production units to be delivered over the next 18 months. She swore all members of the VirtualShopper team to secrecy, until she got the first working models into her stores. After that, she knew, it would be impossible to stop her competitors from playing catch-up.

A Quick Review

Sound too far-fetched? We don't think so. Pioneering companies have been launched using similar models for decades. As James Brian Quinn wrote in the March-April 1990 issue of *Harvard Business Review:*[1]

> Apple bought microprocessors from Synertek, other chips from Hitachi, Texas Instruments, and Motorola, video monitors from Hitachi, power supply from Astec, and printers from Tokyo Electric and Qume. Similarly Apple kept its internal service activities and investments to a minimum by outsourcing application software development to Microsoft, promotion to Regis McKenna, product styling to Frogdesign, and distribution to ITT and ComputerLand.

In Chapter 1 of this book, we introduced you to the idea of the digital marketplace, and subsequently laid out a framework that attempted to help senior managers such as yourself make sense of it with the eventual goal of mastering this new marketplace (Figure 11.1). We've come a long way since then, and in the process provided you with a gamut of ideas, terms, and potential actions to take.

With this in mind, let's reflect on some of the lessons that can be learned from the fictional experiences of @WarpSpeed. We think there are three that merit special attention.

First, the company made the wise decision of actually *listening* to what its customers were asking for. Barbara Kelly was the partner/customer that could make VirtualShopper a reality. Developing VirtualShopper as a stand-alone

FIGURE 11.1
The dilemma faced by senior executives in the digital economy.

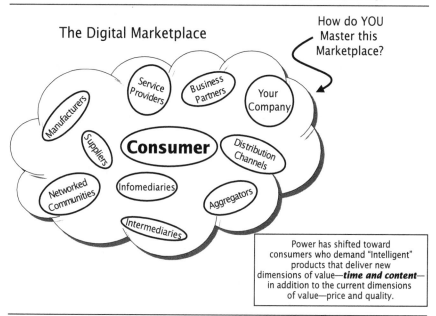

The Digital Marketplace

How do YOU Master this Marketplace?

Manufacturers

Service Providers

Business Partners

Your Company

Suppliers

Consumer

Distribution Channels

Networked Communities

Infomediaries

Aggregators

Intermediaries

Power has shifted toward consumers who demand "Intelligent" products that deliver new dimensions of value—*time and content*—in addition to the current dimensions of value—price and quality.

product in search of a customer would have been fraught with risk and would have required market knowledge that @WarpSpeed didn't possess. [It was well outside of their value-added competency (VAC) of engineering and developing world-class graphics systems.] No doubt, it makes sense to deliver your products or service at the lowest cost, but it is significantly more important to figure out what the customer "values" about what you sell. Whether it be time, content, price, quality, brand, reliability, or any combination thereof, it is critical to understand this, and crucial to incorporate these value drivers into your product. Barbara Kelly clearly saw the value of @WarpSpeed in developing graphics systems, just as @WarpSpeed clearly understood the value of HumaForm, Virtuality.com, and Warnes-Timer for their respective competencies.

It is imperative for executives to start with the end consumer and work toward devising an organization and a market that is aligned with the dynamics of the changing economy. In this instance, TJMiller provided the hook to the consumer, and based on market research and their intimate knowledge of their consumer segment, they knew the potential of VirtualShopper. Companies need to realize that traditional models of consumer needs and behavior no longer suffice. Quality and price remain important, brand names still attract loyalty and status, but time and content will become the fundamental drivers of purchase decisions. @WarpSpeed recognized this and, in concert with Barbara Kelly's vision, developed a product offering that not only saves significant browse time for the consumer, but offers the ability for sophisticated decision making through the use of digitized content. VirtualShopper took a conventional offering, namely the retail outlet, and transformed the buying experience into a multifaceted, versatile, and significantly *faster* event.

The customer-centric theme of this book was reinforced in Part Two, "Intelligent Products," which highlighted the value-add of products/services and provided a framework for creating value-added, intelligent products that the consumer wants. We discussed both new and conventional arbiters of consumer value in the context of the digital economy, and we identified steps that can be taken to ensure digital preparedness.

Second, @WarpSpeed understood the changing dynamics of the market they were playing in and appropriately identified how it could add value within the larger context of the marketplace. It realized that the best way to do this was to align itself with appropriate partners, even though some of these partners were also direct competitors in other market niches. Part Three, "Intelligent Markets," outlined why these sorts of partnerships and alliances will be essential in the digital economy.

Chapters 6 and 7 analyzed the various roles of these digital value networks (DVNs) and gave guidance in how companies can establish their position in them. It described these roles and their interactions in a model we call a digital value network—a model for mastering the digital marketplace.

Thus, even though the "traditional" product of @WarpSpeed was a high-performance graphics workstation, they created another digital value chain by bringing together multiple digital players across a digital platform provided by Sunny Design Systems to produce the VirtualShopper in "Internet time."

The third and final lesson is that @WarpSpeed created an organization that was flexible and nimble enough to react to a highly dynamic market, and to the ever-changing consumer demands. Learning from the mistakes of her predecessor, Caldwell had put the right organizational structure in place that leveraged the very real value @WarpSpeed could offer. Although @WarpSpeed possessed impressive technical design and manufacturing capabilities, Caldwell knew she would need to seek partners if she wanted to be able to create an extended organization capable of delivering the new kinds of integrated digital products increasingly demanded by its customers. Part Four, "Intelligent Organizations," provided a step-by-step framework to achieve an intelligent value-based organization (VBO) much like @WarpSpeed.

Your Wake-Up Call

What will *you* do next? What is the first step for *your* business? Only you can decide.

If you've followed our arguments this far, the one thing you'll realize is that we're not promising a one-size-fits-all solution to making sure your company can make the transition to the digital economy. Unlike the total quality management (TQM) or business process reengineering (BPR) management initiatives of the last decade, instead of offering "the answer," we have attempted to assemble a portfolio of strategies that will allow a broad array of companies to assemble their own answers to the complex questions raised by emerging digital technologies.

Two things you obviously *can't* do: dig your heels in, hoping to hold onto your current market position; or simply react when absolutely necessary to the strategic moves of your competitors.

For some companies, they should first focus on the *product or service* they currently offer: How can they transform it to meet the more stringent (and diverse) requirements of digital consumers?

Other companies will need to begin by exploring (and hopefully exploiting) the new electronic *markets* made possible by advances in digital technologies; and many others should first take a hard look at their organizational structures, making sure they are structured around the customer, and that they are flexible and nimble enough to respond to changes in the marketplace.

In short, tailoring a strategy for mastering the digital economy that will work for your company requires insight and knowledge that only you have. To help you out, we've included a step-by-step diagnostic blueprint in Appendix A that should help you apply the book's concepts to your particular situation. Now, read on. You're about to get the last few pieces of the digital economy puzzle. It may seem that there is little left to discuss, but in fact we've left a large part of the economy out up to this point—namely, public institutions. These institutions and areas of public concern, such as the public education system, health care, and the good old IRS are inspected to understand how they will be different, or how they should be different, in the digital economy. This is the topic of Part Five, and last but not least, the ever-important topic of security, privacy, and the government's role in the digital economy will be addressed in the last section, Part Six.

PART
SIX

Intelligent
Society

CHAPTER

Creating Digital Value

"The excellence of every government is its adaptation to the state of those to be governed by it."
—*Thomas Jefferson to Pierre Samuel Dupont de Nemours, 1816*

IN PREVIOUS CHAPTERS, WE'VE DISCUSSED HOW THE DIGITAL ECONOMY WILL REQUIRE CEOS to transform their existing products, markets, and organizations into *intelligent* ones that deliver true value to the consumer.

In this chapter, we will build on these concepts by dramatizing how the digital economy is already forcing massive changes on three existing industries: education, health care, and federal tax collection (the IRS). We focus on education because without an educated society, consumers and employees alike will be ill equipped to deal with what the digital future has in store. We put a spotlight on health care because it provides a fascinating case of public and private enterprises cooperatively leveraging new technologies so that *all* parties can benefit. Also, we zero in on the transformation of the tax collection function of our government—yes, the good old IRS—because just as businesses must transform themselves in the digital marketplace, so must the government, as it, too, strives to be a more efficient and effective provider of consumer services. Although the government is not exposed to the same market pressures for efficiency and effectiveness, individual government programs are constantly scrutinized and reviewed for budgetary purposes.

Interplay between Public Business and Private Enterprise

Private and public businesses share a common ancestry. Both formed because people came together as a group to address a financial, physical, or emotional need they would not have been able to satisfy individually. Such groups would then *aggregate* the various resources belonging to their individual members to address the need in question. Although resources are commonly thought of as capital assets (things) or monetary wealth (cash), it's important to keep in mind that a resource can be anything that can be used to satisfy a need. For example, physical strength is a resource (a group of men and women coming together can move a fallen tree, whereas one man would not have sufficient resources); so is intelligence (hence the adage, "Two heads are better than one.").

Typically, a private business is a group that has been organized specifically to manipulate resources in the pursuit of providing shareholder returns. A public business, on the other hand, has generally been created with the goal of providing a service to members of a particular community, society, or politically organized state.

In either case, both the infrastructure and management requirements are remarkably similar. In fact, there has been a significant push to privatize many public service institutions to emulate private industry's more efficient way of managing similar resources.

As we've discussed, business practices in the digital economy center around a new kind of resource that is shaping the future of public and private organizations alike: *access to information.*

Interestingly enough, the Internet, which has been the key factor in making this powerful new resource available to profit-minded businesses around the world, was originally conceived of for private use. (The U.S. government needed some way of maintaining communications in case of national emergencies.) However, the similar needs of both private and public organizations meant that the Internet could be easily transferred into a commercial resource while keeping its original design intact.

The Internet now represents a global resource for consumers and businesses alike; whether their need is fulfilled by a public or private organization is becoming less obvious and less important. The government now has access to an efficient medium for communicating *information* to its constituents, and can benefit greatly, just as private enterprises do, by doing so.

We're already seeing vast amounts of information being put on the Internet, from tax guidelines, forms, and interactive forums to huge repositories of information on legislation, governmental filings like 10-Ks and 10-Qs, and detailed information on entitlements like Medicare, Social Security, and the like.

Not surprising, these massive infrastructure and business process changes in the public sector are having an enormous effect on private enterprise. For example, many government agencies are now maintaining public web sites on which pending legislation and proposed regulations printed in the *Federal Register* are freely available for public view. Private enterprises no longer have to weed through the unending maze of public institutions to find legislation and other information important to their business or their industry. The White House home page is now the gateway to thousands of government pages ranging from press releases to presidential speeches. This information can be useful to for-profit businesses and consumers alike.

Consequently, all information disclosed to a public body by a corporation is now truly public. Even though the Freedom of Information Act was enacted back in 1966, there existed no sufficient infrastructure to distribute public records. So-called *public* information could easily be hidden in obscure (and dauntingly massive) paper reports.

Now, through the widespread digitization of data and the emergence of powerful search engines, this information has become easily accessible to one and all. Unless the information is explicitly protected by legislation or regulation, records submitted by corporations can now be scrutinized—by members of the public, as well as competitors. Private enterprise needs to be extremely cognizant of this.

Similarly, as more public institutions encourage (or even require) electronic filing of corporate data, we will see an increasing *standardization* of both data format and content. For example, anyone can quickly find executive compensation information for public company executives by simply visiting the www.sec.gov web site and performing a "quick forms lookup" on the company of their choice (executive compensation information is located in the DEF 14A proxy filings—this is explained on the web site).[1] Thus, data standards will emerge for individual industries (and across industries) simply because the government is requiring that certain things be publicly reported. Companies are already spending millions of dollars to reengineer their data collection, analysis, and reporting processes to meet government requirements. (Because it is inevitable, the sooner they do it, the better off they will be.)

On the upside, access to government-funded research has never been easier. Interested commercial organizations can gain access to specialized research the minute it becomes available, rather than having to wait months or even years for it to be collected, edited, and published. Thus former barriers to leveraging government research (usually with military, public health, or safety aims) with private research, which usually has more commercial goals, are rapidly collapsing.

To summarize, digitization will have massive effects on both public and private enterprises, and the informational codependencies that already exist between the two sectors will only become more significant.

It is, therefore, urgent for CEOs to understand the extent and complexity of these interdependent relationships, and to keep an eye on the changing digital infrastructures and policies of public organizations, as well as their competitors in the private sector.

Education Value Networks

As we've discussed, information will be the single most critical resource of the digital economy—not capital assets (factories, printing presses, or trucks), not monetary assets (cash), not even labor (the physical efforts of employees). That being the case, *education* is now more crucial than ever to ensure the continued health of our economy and, indeed, society in general.

Yes, education has always been a significant contributor to economic well-being. According to a report by the President's Council on Sustainable Development, a council that advises the President on sustainable development of the U.S. economy, "The Council had hard and frequent debates about the term economic growth . . . In the end, we found agreement around the idea that to achieve our vision of sustainability some things must grow—jobs, productivity, wages, profits, capital and savings, information, knowledge, education—and others. . . . The issue is not whether the economy needs to grow but how and in what way. . . . A society that invests in its children and communities, equitably providing education and opportunity, is far more likely to prosper than one that does not make such investments. . . ." The article goes on to state that, "Knowledge has become the economy's most important and dynamic resource."[2] Likewise, it's essential in the digital age.

Why would this be? Simply this—Only an educated and technically literate population will possess the fundamental tools necessary to absorb the vast quantities of information that will be increasingly available. Only when we have an educated population can these massive reservoirs of information be fully exploited, exchanged, and added to, thus creating a worldwide pool of true *knowledge*.

Both public- and private-sector leaders have been proclaiming the need to educate, educate, educate. Martin Carnoy, professor of economics at Stanford, writes, "[Some are convinced] that the main function of the nation-state in the new world economy is to *educate* [emphasis added] its citizens for participation in the world labor market."[3] We see schools increasing their investments in communications technology despite overall funding inequities. The *Condition of Education Report 1998,* prepared by the National Center for Education Statistics, reports that between 1985 and 1995, government appropriations for higher-education institutions fell almost $1,400 per year per full-time student. However, between 1994 and 1997 Internet access in public schools jumped from 35 percent to 78 percent. President Clinton and the U.S. Secretary of Education Richard Riley in 1997 announced that there were currently seven urgent priorities for education, and that one of them is that "every classroom will be connected to the Internet by the year 2000 and all students will be technologically literate."[4] Some $75 million has been allocated under the National Activities Authority, in partnership with private industry, to award grants that will provide extended technological training for teachers.

When schools invest in technology to offer better educations (their prime directive, after all) there is another significant benefit: They can leverage the digital infrastructure to streamline nonacademic functions as well. A "wired" school can improve its procurement processes, can perform more effective fund-raising, fund community projects more effortlessly, and much more.

In other words, the increased technological sophistication of educational institutions, faculty, staff, and students alike creates a digital value network (DVN) in which all stakeholders (anyone involved in the educational process) can actively create additional value for everyone else.

This works precisely the way it does in the private sector. The Internet forms the backbone of this value network; to use the term introduced in Chapter 6, it's the relevant digital function platform (DFP). A single campus would be analogous to a digital value chain; when multiple campuses collaborate and collectively create value for each other (such as in interuniversity alliances), then the individual digital value chains evolve into a true value network. In this case, we call it an *education value network.*

PRESS RELEASE—UNIVERSITIES SPACE RESEARCH ASSOCIATION AWARDED $484.2 MILLION FLYING OBSERVATORY CONTRACT BY NASA

Washington, D.C., December 16, 1996. The Universities Space Research Association (USRA), heading up a team that includes United Airlines and Raytheon E-Systems, announced today that the National Aeronautics and Space Administration (NASA) has awarded them a 10-year, $484.2 million contract to design, assemble, test, and operate the Stratospheric Observatory For Infrared Astronomy (SOFIA), a modified Boeing 747 equipped with an 8-foot (2.5 meter) diameter telescope. SOFIA, expected to begin flying in 2001, will be the world's largest flying astronomical observatory.

As part of NASA's privatization program to lower costs and improve efficiency, the SOFIA program has been contracted out to this consortium of companies, scientific institutions, and universities, who will work in cooperation with NASA's Ames Research Center. The prime contractor, USRA, is a 26-year-old consortium of more than 80 universities set up to manage scientific research programs. USRA will have overall project responsibility and will manage the scientific operations of the observatory. United Airlines, the world's largest air carrier, will supply the Boeing 747SP to NASA, then manage SOFIA's flight operations out of the Moffett Federal Airfield near San Francisco, California. Raytheon will modify the aircraft extensively for its new mission. The specialized computer systems needed to operate the telescope will be designed and integrated by Sterling Software. Instruments to be attached to the telescope will be built at the University of California, NASA Ames Research Center, and other universities. An extensive education and public outreach program will be run by a partnership of two private nonprofit organizations, the Astronomical Society of the Pacific, and the SETI Institute.[5]

The Need for More Technical Education

Just as private companies tailor their offerings to meet customer demand in the digital economy, government agencies do the same thing in the public sector. The U.S. Department of Education, for example, hears its customers (U.S. citizens) demanding more practical education for their children—education that will lead to gainful employment. As a result, U.S. schools are improving the degree of *technical* training, even at the elementary school level. Likewise, the European Commission, a government agency of the European Union, has also set forth a digital education action plan designed to speed up the process of creating a technically literate population. The action plan includes ambitious connectivity goals for all schools, extensive technology training for teachers, and widespread use of multimedia tools in the classroom.[6]

Many experts recommend introducing students to technology as early as possible in their educational careers—if possible, at the primary school level.

New Jersey is redesigning its core curricula for students in kindergarten through 12th grades. The new curriculum addresses traditional areas such as math, science, and languages; it also includes a new discipline called "workplace readiness." The goal is to graduate students who are immediately able to become contributing members of the workforce.

Prudential Life Insurance Co. works closely with the New Jersey Department of Education and the Business Coalition for Education Excellence to address the issue of education and workplace readiness. Acting as an infomediary, Prudential sponsors an annual summit between the business community and New Jersey educators. A recent summit agenda featured best practices in workplace readiness education across the country, and resulted in recommendations for reforming existing curriculum standards.

Although traditionally a customer of the educational system (it hires graduates to work in its offices around the state), Prudential thus created a novel way to impact the educational process and increase the value of the product they would ultimately receive: workers with a more appropriate skill base for their market.

Some educators fear that too-strong an emphasis on technical education will diminish the resources available for traditional liberal arts instruction. However, visionary alliances made up of private-sector leaders and respected educational authorities are beginning to combine strategies to construct curricula that balance technical and liberal arts agendas. After all, success in the digital economy demands not only technical expertise, but also the ability to innovate, create, and digest an ever-changing spectrum of new ideas. True, a narrow emphasis on technical training (such as a Java programming class) may generate some short-term benefits for an individual and a business. However, true value in the year 2000 and beyond will only be delivered if individuals can draw on a wide variety of experiences and backgrounds to create powerful new products. Narrow minds have narrow thoughts and create narrow products with limited applicability.

If we look at the New Jersey educational alliance, we see the potential for immense and varied benefits from fostering responsible, self-motivated citizens who have the ability to meet their own needs because they have both a desirable skill set (specific technology skills) combined with a broader knowledge base.

CASE IN POINT: THE CLASSROOM OF THE FUTURE

A testament to the benefits of applying information technology (IT) to the classroom is provided by the EDS Financial Trading and Technology Center, located in the College and Graduate School of Business at the University of Texas at Austin. The Center takes advantage of computers and telecommunications to create the learning environment of the future.

The Center has a state-of-the-art trading room that receives live data feeds from four leading providers of financial information—Bloomberg, Bridge, Dow-Jones Telerate, and Reuters. Students use these live data feeds to direct the first and only student-managed investment fund, the $3 million MBA Investment Fund, LLC. In the adjoining classroom, each student is provided with a computer on his or her desk; the work generated by any student can also be projected onto a large video screen for the whole classroom to see. Professors can manipulate information on a touch screen and project this information down to the student terminals or onto the main video screen to facilitate truly interactive learning. A video teleconferencing capability, coupled with satellite access, allows the facility to be used as a truly global educational resource: faculty members can open up lectures to remote sites around the world; they can respond to questions posed by individual students, can review student assignments, share slides, overheads, and handouts, just as in a real classroom.

This teleconferencing feature also provides the students with direct access to investment professionals anywhere in the world, giving them the benefit of "visiting professors," who are truly the hands-on experts in their field.

Using the terminology we introduced in Chapter 3, the concept of the classroom has been extended into cyberspace; the traditional physical *container* characteristic of the classroom has acquired *content* through broadband teleconferencing capabilities across the globe.

The Virtual Classroom

Exactly how can our current educational system be transformed into one that will meet the stringent requirements of the digital economy? As seen from the preceding examples, positive steps are already being taken. The key to continued success will be in our ability to craft a common vision of the future; identify barriers to be overcome, competencies to be developed, and resources to be marshaled; and then launch incremental educational projects that build these competencies and create assured migration paths to the future.

Certainly, educators and curriculum planners must understand how the needs of their customer—the student—are evolving. The student, however, is not the only customer. Society is a customer as well, and its long-term needs must be considered as well as those of the individual. Therefore, the common vision and the resultant migration paths are instrumental in this effort.

One such incremental step is the development of the virtual classroom, as a variety of educational institutions attempt to find new ways to meet the demands of students in an increasingly time-strapped society.

For example, the continuing education requirements for many professions cause working men and women to continue taking college-level classes long after they graduate with bachelors or even masters degrees in their fields. New "virtual" classrooms are a logical result of this new kind of market demand. By attending classes remotely (through videoconferencing, videotaped lectures, electronic forums, or other technologically enabled means), working students are provided with easier access to education than was previously possible. Many schools are developing electronic ways for students to fulfill academic and administrative requirements without ever physically setting foot on campus.

By participating in a virtual-classroom environment, students not only have access to a richer educational experience (through multimedia, targeted information streams and access to an infinite amount of reference material through the Internet), they also are exposed to state-of-the-art tools and technologies while obtaining that education. By helping students become familiar with such things as global satellite technologies, worldwide videoconferencing, computer-generated simulations, and Internet search tools in their academic disciplines, educational institutions are also offering students a stepping stone to the potentially lucrative *commercial* opportunities of the digital economy.

The virtual-classroom idea is extremely compatible with two of the basic premises of the digital economy: that fixed assets should be minimized and non-VAC activities be outsourced. Virtual classrooms fulfill both directives. If classes are conducted via video streaming or two-way videoconferencing (or even delivered via inexpensive CD-ROM disks), the need for the fixed asset of brick-and-mortar classrooms is eliminated, as are the myriad support services associated with those fixed assets (desks, chairs, blackboards, janitorial services, security, and so on). Classes conducted this way also eliminate the need for one institution to provide all of the necessary functions to deliver content to the student. Through technology, each of the content providers (or VACs) can be linked and appear as one organization to the student. In this scenario, non-VAC activities have been replaced or eliminated, making the process much more efficient and much more valuable as a learning tool.

Entire libraries can be made available via the Web with improved accessibility to even the most ancient texts through portable document (PDF) technology. Computer modeling allows students to perform the sort of "hard" scientific research that was too costly to attempt just a decade ago.

In Part One ("Intelligent Products"), we explored why market offerings will become increasingly customized to the needs of individual consumers. This will also happen within the education industry. Students will be able to more precisely demand the kind of education they want, and the ways in which it is delivered to them. Forget the one-size-fits-all lecture so common today. As education becomes more highly interactive and personal, the individual needs of individual students will be satisfied with the help of IT. Most educators agree that one of the least effective methods of teaching is lecturing to a roomful of students; one of the most effect methods of teaching is simply *doing,* combined with rapid and highly personalized feedback. We're already seeing computer-based training (CBT) systems being used in mathematics, language, history, geography, and science classrooms. Eventually, most classrooms will be technically enabled; teachers will still be vital, of course, to provide expert help, direction, and facilitation of the learning experience, but the majority of students will learn (and be tested) in ways that meet their special, individual needs. This can only benefit the students themselves.

For example, a friend's child recently signed up for a seventh-grade typing class. The class was taught using a traditional lecture format, in which the student was *told* how to type with the aid of visuals and was then given a keyboard and computer with which to practice. Within six weeks, her grade had dropped to an all-time low (a traumatic experience for a straight-A student). Obviously, the lecture format was not effective for this student or subject. The student's father bought her "Mavis Beacon Teaches Typing"—a basic computer typing program—as a possible studying aid. This PC product used artificial intelligence (AI) concepts to identify student weaknesses, customized lessons directed at those weaknesses, and compiled a database that tracked progress (or lack of it). Within four weeks, her typing speed had more than doubled (to 50 words per minute), and her grade eventually improved to an A. This is a classic instance of customized and focused CBT outclassing the conventional mass-learning approach.

Online customization of course content has been made possible by entrepreneurs such as Professor Morris Shepard. Through his online business, Book Tech, professors can replace traditional textbooks by going to Shepard's web site, browsing through a database of thousands of articles and papers, and selecting a specific group of these for inclusion in a course pack. These course packs are prepared by Book Tech and delivered to the local university bookstore for purchase by the students. Book Tech takes care of the royalty and copyright arrangements with the authors or other relevant parties. Students can also order articles and papers online. The search database contains more than 25,000 articles that are categorized by copyright status, royalty cost, and names of universities where they have been adopted.

Shepard foresees tremendous growth opportunities for the online course textbook business. By outsourcing the printing and binding process to Xerox, he plans to go global, offering this service to academicians all over the world. This is true customer service in the area of delivering relevant and topical texts.

Global Digital Literacy

Information is power, and the society that can take maximum advantage of technical infrastructure to obtain the most valuable information will be the ultimate winner. Three things drive effectiveness in using information: the ability to easily access it, the ability to assimilate and analyze it, and the ability to *act* on it. Thus, the most powerful societies in the digital economy will be those with large populations of skilled *information users*.

At the 1998 State of the World Forum, Oracle Senior Vice President Marc Benioff discussed the phenomenon of *digital apartheid,* his belief that social power is (and will continue to be) largely a function of access to information. "The truth is that this is about those who can and those who cannot [use computers] in the new age," he said. "It is a question of empowerment. The harsh reality this century is, if you don't have access to PCs and the Internet, you cannot participate in commerce, education, entertainment, and communication."[7]

Issues of digital literacy have naturally surfaced in countries such as the United States, which are already technological leaders. However, this is rapidly becoming a *global* issue.

Historically, technical expertise has been grown in just a handful of nations and exported only to where it could be profitably employed. This can no longer be the case. From now on, digital literacy must be a global priority, especially for the populations of technologically underdeveloped nations. Already, we're seeing joint initiatives between educational institutions and corporate sponsors create opportunities for students where local governments are not equipped to drive change. This has nothing to do with altruism (although it does benefit individuals). This is necessary for the continued economic health of everyone who participates in the digital economy.

CASE IN POINT: UNITING TO PROMOTE DIGITAL LITERACY

The 2B1 Foundation exemplifies unified educational and corporate innovation. Chaired by Nicholas Negroponte, founding director of the Media Lab at MIT and a member of the board of directors of Motorola, this nonprofit organization has a global mission: "To initiate and to support actions aimed at preventing a growing abyss between the digital haves and the digital have-nots."[8]

The foundation's Junior Summit project is especially noteworthy, as it seeks to address technology issues affecting the 1 billion children between 10 and 16 years of age worldwide.[9] The Summit actually incorporates the voice of youngsters from around the globe into the process of change by providing computers and Internet links to over 3,000 young people from 136 countries, creating a multimedia, multilingual online community.

A group of 100 of these young people were selected to attend a six-day meeting at MIT in November 1998, where they discussed topics such as cross-cultural communication, new technologies for children, and countries without borders. Participants were asked to document the state of children in their community, to focus on how computers affect them, and to share their vision of a global community. At the end of the summit, their work was to be presented to leaders in industry, government, and education.

The Health Care Industry

The constantly rising cost of health care, combined with the development of new medical treatment technology and the constantly changing demographics of society, has created an immensely large void that can only be filled by exploiting the opportunities the digital economy provides. No one should be denied access to adequate health care, yet in thousands of ways this happens every day. On a global basis, access to even minimal levels of health care for the majority of the world's population is far from reality. New medical treatments are developed every day, but the extremely large investment required to create these treatments requires a hefty price tag, which the consumer is repeatedly faced with paying. Those that cannot pay are often denied this treatment, and society accepts this as an inevitable reality of life.

Fortunately, the digital economy provides real, tangible answers to these problems. Digitization of the health care value chain could yield immediate and significant benefits. However, the major barrier involves getting all the stakeholders to proactively undertake technology and modernization initiatives. It is important to understand the innumerable social, cultural, administrative, technical, political, and financial stumbling blocks that act as disincentives to adopting an end-to-end health care DVN.

Still, it's important to understand that despite these barriers, tremendous benefits will accrue to all participants in a true DVN in the health care industry. Many companies already recognize the opportunities. Witness how several large non–health care companies (Reuters, Hewlett-Packard, Sprint, AT&T, IBM, and G.E., among others) have already tried to create the appropriate technological infrastructures. These infrastructure improvements include value-added networks (VANs), health information networks, and master patient data repositories.

These initiatives have sometimes encountered opposition from various stakeholders in the value chain. For example, physicians are not very receptive to suggestions from either nonmedical organizations or insurance companies, and are reluctant to change the way they do business. However, these barriers have not stopped the drive toward digitization. Billions of dollars are being invested annually in infrastructure improvements, enhancing connectivity, offering Internet access, and enabling online transactions. The goal is to eventually provide value to all members of the health care industry through the use of IT.

Take the growing trend toward interactive settlements. By eliminating the manual transaction and recording of patient services and payment, massive costs can be eliminated from the current system. Such a consumer-enabled model could usher in an era of medical savings accounts as more consumers self-manage their health care investments.

Access to current information is essential to providing quality care. It also results in reduced health care costs throughout the system. Sharing of such information in remote, third-world communities has historically been problematic due to a lack of resources (engendered by prevalent poverty levels and general corporate apathy), as well as time delays in the normal information dissemination components, such as publishing and mailing.

However, as technology becomes more affordable, communities and nations that have lagged behind in information services can suddenly close the gap in a few huge leaps. This means that more and more health care providers can now participate in research and avail themselves of best practices on a real-time basis. Medical information is now readily available across the globe to both providers and consumers. Benefits accrue for the consumer of health care services, the provider of health care, and for the community that underwrites the system.

What may be less apparent, however, is how these things will also benefit the international business community.

We've discussed in earlier chapters that for IT to maximize its potential, a critical mass of connectivity must be established. In developing nations, however, government resources are limited and often must be devoted to critical daily needs rather than long-term infrastructure development. Local business communities, although eager to grow, may not have either the financial resources or the political influence to develop necessary infrastructure and connectivity on their own. Although multinational corporations are investing in technology in developing countries where they see a potential return on investment, poorer countries or those in political upheaval may not be candidates for such investment.

In these cases, liaisons between government, private enterprise, and public businesses on both local and international levels can build multilayered intelligent markets that will serve immediate needs for health care services; foster midterm goals of growing local business capabilities; and advance long-term plans for bringing entire nations online so they can participate in international commercial activities.

A recent study by the Institute of Medicine openly discussed the link between global health and U.S. economic interests, stating that "by investing in the health of other populations, the United States is investing in their economic development too, and therefore in its future trading partners."[10]

CASE IN POINT: SATELLIFE (HEALTHNET)[11]

Visionary Beginnings
If you want a digital-age example of "doing well by doing good," just take a look at the efforts of not-for-profit SatelLife. The initiative was founded by the International Physicians for the Prevention of Nuclear War after being awarded the Nobel Peace Prize in 1985. In 1986, the group called for the creation of an

international communication system for exchanging information between health care workers in developed and emerging nations. Currently, the system operates in over 30 countries in Africa, Asia, and Latin America, and has an estimated user base of 4,000. One of the features of this communication network is HealthNet, which uses low-earth-orbit (LEO) satellites, simple ground stations, and radio- and telephone-based computer networks. Currently sponsored by NEC and GTE, the system targets areas with little or no telecommunications infrastructure. Users access the network via nodes, which act as electronic distribution centers (computers that relay messages and other data to and from each point in the network, much as a local post office collects and distributes mail).

Integration

HealthNet functions as an *infomediary,* maximizing international integration between corporations and charities. In Uganda, the Ministry of Health and the Makerere University in Kampala jointly leveraged HealthNet to create a Master of Public Health program that is funded by the Rockefeller Foundation, UNFPA, and the Government of Uganda. The program is part of a movement to educate public health care professionals while they are on site in the communities they will serve, rather than on a university campus. HealthNet is the link that provides the students with technical information about medical issues and also allows contact with doctors and educators around the globe through e-mail and online discussions. For such people, access to information is essential, according to George W. Pariyo, field coordinator for the MPH program, who states "We are using HealthNet to get access to technical information . . . and for e-mail, overcoming a major problem for the program, which was communications."[12]

Value Added

The benefits don't stop there. The Bugando Hospital, Mwanza, Tanzania, an 800-bed Catholic hospital serving 7 million people, previously used telephones and faxes to solicit much-needed donations of materials and funds. It could cost as much as $180 to send a six-page fax from Mali to Zambia. Now, by using the Internet connections originally established to access HealthNet, hospital workers can more easily—and much more cheaply—raise funds, recruit personnel, and acquire materials.

Health Care Value Networks

Each of the players in health care DVNs will eventually reap substantial benefits through digitization, even if short-term barriers exist for some of them. Following, we've considered the pros and cons of digitization for each of the DVN participants.

Provider organizations/physicians. The provider community has been experiencing massive consolidation in the United States for several years now. These organizations either purchase or merge with large physician and/or hospital networks and then create governing bodies to help establish and manage the administrative aspects of the health care process. Not surprising, these kinds of organizations are aggressively pursuing digitization.

By digitally sharing information ranging from patient histories, to referrals, insurance eligibility, medical charts, lab results, diagnostics, prescriptions, patient identification, drug protocols, and claims processing, such organizations are already reaping tremendous benefits, both in terms of reduced costs, more efficient operations, and superior patient care.

The major barriers for these kinds of organizations for adoption are cultural, geographical, and regulatory. For example, although it would make sense to directly connect to group purchasing organizations, pharmacies, and insurance companies, the current system of kickbacks, payment delays, rebates, and loyalty incentives reduces the likelihood of early adoption.

Another key barrier is the disparity/lack of technological platforms. For example, admitting labs and operating rooms are often managed using incompatible systems.

If we look at some of the past pre-Internet electronic solutions in health care, the most successful ones are those that have been anchored by a large providing organization with a near-monopoly position. New technology developments were underwritten by this organization; it recovered its costs through its ownership of the information infrastructure—it could leverage the infrastructure by developing other applications to run on top of it.

Most of the efforts that have failed tended to be joint efforts in which individual participants were unable to get adequate return on their investment in infrastructure.

The algorithm for success is complex here: Any Internet-based DVN solution needs the buy-in and participation of all players; roles and responsibilities must be clearly defined; and future ownership rights for building on that infrastructure must be carefully spelled out.

Group purchasing organizations. These are large groups representing hospitals and/or employers. These organizations buy drugs, equipment, medical supplies, and other items in bulk from pharmaceutical companies, hospital supply companies, and so forth, and obtain some kind of a rebate in doing so. These organizations are starting to extend their role in the value chain and expand into new areas. For example, large associations such as the AHA and VHA are beginning to develop extranet capabilities, offering ISP capabilities to their members, along with additional digital products and services that will retain them.

Pharmaceutical companies. Continued consolidation continues to occur in this industry. Pharmaceutical companies have always been interested in capturing end-consumer usage data to better protect their market share. There is a trend nowadays among pharmaceuticals to expand into the area of proactive *disease management* (using their expertise to manage a specific population of individuals on behalf of an employer). Obviously, technology plays a critical role, due to the need for sophisticated data mining and knowledge management.

Insurance companies/payers. An immediate benefit of digitization in the insurance industry is in online claims management. Almost half of all claims today are processed online; however, these are typically done through VANs and claims clearinghouses. There are obvious benefits to moving to the less expensive Internet; however, there would be significant switching costs to be overcome in the form of payer system modifications and web enablement of hospitals, physicians, pharmacies, payers, and third-party administrators.

Many payers already offer online benefit information to their members to facilitate membership enrollment and claims processing. However, it is important to remember that if an insurance company (or other organization that is responsible for making payments for services rendered) is the anchor behind the development of the DVN, then it is important to build an all-payer capability into the infrastructure. For example, a typical physician's office deals with around 100 payers, once you add up all participating insurance companies as well as the patients responsible for some (or all) of the fee. If there is a separate system or application to learn for each of these payers, then the solution is infeasible. It is, therefore, important for any Internet-based DVN solution to be all-payer based—and have the infrastructural capability to interface with different physicians' practice management systems (some of which are not Internet enabled).

Already, emerging technologies such as smart cards are expediting the infrastructure development process. They also present opportunities for disintermediation. For example, complex formularies, histories, allergies, pharmacy records, and claims eligibility could be encoded on the cards, obviating the need for retail pharmacies and wholesalers, and allowing direct-order processing to and from pharmaceutical companies.

Some international health care communities are already creating DVNs comprising manufacturers and patients. These networks are designed to link the two groups more directly to lessen the need for government interaction. The European Commission is promoting the direct link as a way to support "one of Europe's best-performing high-technology sectors and to encourage innovation, which many see as crucial for profitability and return on investment."[13]

Another way that health care can benefit from digitization is in greater cooperation between private and public medical research institutions.

> . . . the existence of a vibrant public sector, its interest in working with private-sector research and its importance to drug research, allows private firms to create *within the firm* many of the mechanisms . . . (that) allow these firms to access public-sector research effectively and to sustain a level of flexibility and responsiveness that gives them a significant edge over their rivals.[14]

CASE STUDY—CORNELL MEDICAL COLLEGE

Visionary Beginnings
Cornell University Medical College has a novel method for keeping physicians in contact with specialists who perform *grand rounds* (formal presentations designed to update fellow physicians on important news in medical research or patient care).

Traditionally, grand rounds have been conducted in a hospital amphitheater, requiring participating physicians to leave their offices and patients and come to the hospital. Now, they can view the lectures and photographic material using ordinary PCs, telecommunications equipment, and streaming video technology.

Integration
Geography becomes irrelevant; physicians anywhere in the world can join Cornell Medical College's grand rounds at a time and place of their choice. More physicians can participate, sharing their expertise while posing questions as part of an expert community dedicated to exploring new options in health care delivery.

Value Added
According to Antonio Gotto, M.D., dean of the medical school, "The demands on a physician's time are such that there are almost always conflicting priorities." The beauty of the digitally enabled grand round process is that "now it is no longer necessary to choose between continuing medical education and patient care. Doctors in our network can tend to their patients and attend grand rounds at their convenience."

The Internal Revenue Service

It's a bitter fact of modern life. Most governments collect taxes from their citizens. They then use the resulting funds to maintain public structures and works, to fund educational endeavors, provide financial and medical support for certain segments of the population, to encourage advancements in the arts and sciences, to protect the state using military means, and so on.

The current procedure of calculating and collecting federal taxes in the United States is, as we are all well aware, a mind-boggling, cumbersome, and complex information transfer process. Yet advances in IT promise to ease even this process—one that many organizations and individuals currently consider the bane of their existence.

The IRS has already begun an ambitious attempt to automate the formerly manual tax-collection process through the widespread use of IT.

Individual taxpayers will benefit in a number of ways: They will receive faster service, be provided with better access to public information, and have increased confidence that their returns are being processed correctly. The IRS benefits by increased compliance with its regulations, and by dramatically reduced processing expenses. Private enterprises benefit as well because not only will the difficulty in complying be significantly reduced, but new services are being invented by and outsourced to commercial businesses, thus creating more economic wealth for them to share in.

When the first income tax return was filed in 1913, it was a simple 2-page form based on 15 pages of tax laws. Less than 1 percent of the U.S. population was even required to file. In 1998, the number of individual income tax returns alone is projected to encompass more than 120 million filings. The warehouses full of paper schedules, forms, and explanations for filing maintained by the IRS must be distributed to all tax-paying citizens—and are based on some 9,000 pages of tax code. Any intelligent observer would conclude that the current tax reporting process has essentially become unmanageable in a paper medium.

Recognizing this, the IRS has started to make changes, including allowing certain individuals to file their returns electronically.

In 1997, the Internal Revenue Service processed more than 200 million tax returns of varying length and complexity. Of those, 4.7 million of the less complicated individual returns were transmitted via touch-tone phones throughout the Telefile service; another 19 million were transmitted electronically via modem. This transition to digital filing is just the first glimpse we're seeing of a new customer-oriented attitude within the IRS, one which, according to IRS Commissioner Rossotti, will be committed "to making filing easier, and providing first-quality service to every taxpayer needing help."[15]

Key to first-quality service will, of course, be making tax filing much less time consuming.

Economist James L. Payne, in a 1992 study, estimated that Americans spent 5.4 billion man-hours calculating their income taxes. Those that sought professional help for the process paid over $25 billion to third-party preparers. The most common form for filing personal income taxes, the 1040, comes with a 55-page booklet of instructions that estimates the time for record keeping, reading the instructions, preparing, copying, and mailing the return to be 11 hours and 34 minutes. To complete this basic tax return, the average person would likely have one or two income statements W-2(s) and perhaps several 1099 forms that report bank interest. However, if a taxpayer's situation were even slightly more complex—if he or she owned a home, for instance, and wanted to deduct mortgage interest—they would probably spend at least twice the amount of time, or a minimum of 23 hours, to complete the return.

How the IRS has gone about transforming its "product"—tax collection—into a more valuable one proves an important point of this book: Transforming your market offering into an "intelligent" one doesn't always mean that the latest or most expensive technology will be required. In fact, the IRS had to be very careful to use only the *minimal* technology that was currently being used among its customer base (taxpayers). The IRS had to find a feasible way that *any* citizen could file a tax return, whether they were technologically enabled.

Thus, when designing a virtual way to file the 1040EZ, the agency was careful to use existing mainstream technologies. After all, citizens filing the 1040EZ have simplified income reporting requirements usually because they have lower incomes or because they are at the periphery of earning potential due to age (either younger or older than most income-earning taxpayers). This customer base was not likely to have access to sophisticated or expensive technological equipment, but still the IRS was able to find a technology most of these customers owned and used—the telephone.

With the TeleFile service, a taxpayer simply goes to any touch-tone phone and dials in all the information needed to file the tax return. At the core of this service were three basic building blocks:

1. Informational database that has preselected certain citizens to receive a TeleFile security code.
2. Basic public communication infrastructure (telephones).
3. Citizens had sufficient trust that the process will work.

The appeal of TeleFile to its target customers is apparent. First, the IRS does all the math (no more hours at the kitchen table on April 14 armed with pencil and calculator). Second, taxpayers can file from anywhere—from a friend's house or the student union between classes. No need to go to the post office to get a paper form, fill it out, and then return it to the post office to get that all-important April 15 cancellation on the envelope.

There are other advantages, also—especially for more severely underprivileged citizens. For example, persons who have difficulty seeing or holding a pen would greatly benefit from this service (no need to read or fill out forms). Language barriers are reduced because citizens can indicate their preference for English or Spanish phone instructions. Educational disparity is leveled because there is no need to perform mathematical calculations, read complicated instructions, or even write down basic alphanumeric data.

But in a true DVN, value accrues to all participants. We've seen how the customer benefits. How did digitization help the IRS? As we'll see, it has helped in a very substantial way.

Tax returns are typically filed between the end of January and April 15, with the vast majority arriving in the last few weeks of tax season. If tax information is keyed into a database over the phone by the taxpayer, there is less need for a large, seasonal administrative staff hired by the IRS—and paid for, ultimately, by the taxpayer.

The CEO of H&R Block testified before the National Commission on Restructuring the Internal Revenue Service that keypunching the data from paper returns into the IRS computer system costs taxpayers $700 to $800 million dollars per year. Filing returns electronically would eliminate much of this cost.

Automating the filing of the 1040EZ was relatively straightforward. Now, the IRS has its eye on offering similarly superior services to more demanding customers: taxpayers with infinitely more complicated returns. To accomplish this, the IRS has begun aggressively partnering with third-party providers.

Working directly with software developers, the IRS is creating interfaces designed to help citizens navigate the filing requirements, either with the help of a paid preparer or on their own. As the digital economy progresses, there could well be increasing layers of processing between the taxpayer and the IRS that will fall into the domain of for-profit businesses partners. The IRS is eagerly inviting interested parties to participate in this new industry opportunity.

A number of software packages exist that help individuals prepare and file tax returns on a PC; professional tax preparers can transmit tax returns as well, but the process is more complicated than simply transmitting a file to the IRS. Most electronic tax return files must first go to transmitters for conversion to the proper IRS file format. At this point, this is a specialized fee-based service, but the IRS is encouraging tax professionals to become authorized e-file providers by helping with marketing materials and logos that can be downloaded directly from the IRS web site, as well as other incentives.

The IRS has been extremely aggressive in other ways to encourage online filing. It has put up Volunteer Income Tax Assistance/Tax Counseling for the Elderly (VITA/TCE) web sites that can transmit electronic returns; it even helps elderly taxpayers get free access to tax preparation software. Employers who offer e-filing services can get reduced rates on necessary software, and tax deductions as well.

More recently, the IRS has enabled electronic employer withholding returns (941 series) via the Simplified Tax and Wage Reporting System (STAWRS).

Perhaps the most striking example of this new customer-friendly, digitally enabled IRS is the Tax Refund Express program, which is a private (that is, for-profit) partner (the IRS actually advertises the services of this company on its official government web site). Tax Refund Express promotes e-filing via alliances with participating financial institutions. The bank gets the software and marketing materials for free, and can decide if they want to charge for the service or not.[16]

Finally, FileSafe is a truly innovative new program that allows individuals to file returns via the Internet. You don't need to download any software or even go outside your home. Don't have a computer? Use one at the public library! It's up to banks to decide whether they exact a fee from taxpayers for transmitting a tax return via FileSafe. If a refund is due to the taxpayer, any filing fees can be automatically deducted from that—if the refund is electronically deposited into a member bank, naturally.

Think of the ways that this process fulfills all the requirements of a DVN by providing true value to each of the participants: The IRS gets its money; taxpayer gets faster and more efficient service; third-party partners reap either direct or indirect revenues.

Probably the most forward-thinking thing that the IRS is doing is proactively figuring out how to track (with the ultimate goal, of course, of taxing) digital transactions. Some analysts believe that we will soon see new legislation enacted that will require all taxpayers to obtain a digital ID to use when making and receiving electronic payments.

By using these ID numbers, the IRS would be able to keep detailed records of all online purchases. The IDs would conceivably be issued by IRS-certified agencies, and all holders of these numbers would have to prove their identities before being allowed to engage in electronic commerce activities. The IRS would enforce this plan by issuing its own digital certificates to issuers of digital IDs so that they can electronically prove they have received IRS certification.

Clearly, the IRS is actively involved in leveraging the digital economy to make tax filing a less painful process. Both public and private businesses, as evidenced by Tax Refund Express, TeleFile, Intuit and other tax software developers, and FileSafe, are actively involved in creating DVNs to simplify and enhance the tax filing process. The benefits for taxpayers are obvious, the most important being time—a major theme of this book—and others including money, in the form of reduced IRS expenditures translating to reduced taxes (or improved government—however you want to look at it). The IRS benefits by improving its service and reducing the size of its organization. (Of all electronically filed tax returns, 99.5 percent are filed accurately, compared with 82 percent of all mailed tax returns. This 18 percent error rate is due to manual data entry errors by either tax preparers or IRS employees themselves.[17]) Clearly, digitization has created tremendous value throughout this supply chain, and the further exploitation of the opportunities present in the digital economy will only enhance this value.

CHAPTER

13

The Power of Information

"Information is the oxygen of the modern age. It seeps through the walls topped by barbed wire, it wafts across electrified borders."

—*Ronald Reagan*

IT SHOULD BE CLEAR BY NOW THAT THE DIGITAL ECONOMY IS ABOUT ONE THING: INFORMAtion. In Part Two ("Intelligent Products"), we introduced the notion that products of the future will involve combining physical *containers* with digital *content*—and how the content of such products will increasingly be more valuable than the containers themselves. In Part Three ("Intelligent Markets"), we discussed how the most successful companies in the digital age will be those possessing *soft* rather than *hard* assets. In Part Four ("Intelligent Organizations"), we elaborated on this idea by explaining how increasing emphasis on intellectual capital over physical infrastructure will require new kinds of organizational structures.

The common thread in all of these discussions was, of course, the fact that there is already a perceptible shift in what consumers *value,* and that this shift is most heavily dependent on information and will only become more pronounced as the digital age matures.

This shift in value has profound implications for consumers, businesses, and governments alike. This chapter discusses many of the larger social concerns that will inevitably arise.

As will be obvious, these are complex and difficult issues; many additional books will need to be, and already have been, written to complete the discussion. Rather than attempt to provide definitive answers (if that were even possible), we decided to simply frame the overall scenario, posing the associated—and exceedingly far-reaching—social questions within a clear business context. Our hope is that this will provide business leaders with enough insight into the relevant issues to spark discussions of how they should act to advance the common good, as well as their own corporate interests.

Law and Public Policy in the Digital Economy

As discussed in Chapter 1, the digital economy is developing at a much faster rate than past economic eras did. Unfortunately, political leadership has a tendency to operate at a moderate, predictable pace—first getting a sense for the will of the people, then building consensus, then finally enacting relevant law and policies. The challenge in the digital economy is that business practices are evolving too fast for this process to be effective; government agencies and society in general are being challenged to respond more rapidly to the new economic, social, and political realities.

Law and social policy are reactive. When a new type of crime is enabled by technology, and the crime is committed frequently enough to appear on the radar screens of legislators, laws are drafted that will enable prosecution of the offense. When a new communications medium such as e-mail is introduced, society must experiment with various uses of the medium before deciding what proper and improper uses are. (Witness the ongoing debates about spamming and flaming in cyberspace—behaviors that were specifically enabled by e-mail technology.)

CASE IN POINT—CONTROLLING CONTENT ON THE INTERNET

In an attempt to curb the growth of the online pornography industry, the U.S. Congress passed the Communications Decency Act (CDA) that tried to make illegal the electronic dissemination of obscene or indecent materials via the Internet. Although signed into law by President Clinton in February 1996, the legislation was overturned by the U.S. Supreme Court on the grounds that it was unconstitutional. Still, there remain multiple ongoing initiatives within Congress to develop similar legislation that will pass constitutional muster.

The problem is finding the right balance of social and legal policy to protect children from the obvious dangers of online pornography (and related activities)—and the need to ensure that the basic rights of all citizens are not stepped on. Numerous corporations and action groups such as the Electronic Frontier Foundation (*www.eff.org*) are staunchly opposed to the government's various proposed methods for protecting minors from pornography and have vowed to fight future legislation that broadly restricts dissemination of information via the Internet. One obvious major flaw in any bill that Congress enacts is the lack of any real ability to enforce it globally. Partly in reaction to the public and corporate backlash over the CDA, the Clinton administration is considering altering its stance to encourage less, not more, Internet regulation, and to solve this very real social problem in other ways.

The enormous body of law that has developed in and between countries throughout the world over the last 50 years largely focused on supporting and propagating an industrial-age economic model. This is a real problem, considering the creation and exchange of *information* forms the basis of the new digital economy.

Take the telephone industry, a classic industrial-age business. The U.S. government regulated the telephone industry decades ago, restricting access to one company (AT&T) and mandating the development of a single network. AT&T was allowed to make a "reasonable" profit and was protected from all competition. In this case, the government thought it best to control the market through legislation rather than allow competitive forces to battle it out.

Increasingly, however, the government has recognized the need for competition within the telecom realm, and has moved away from legislated solutions. Witness the breakup of AT&T starting in 1984, and the opening up of local telephone markets to competition as legislated in the Telecommunications Act of 1996.

CASE IN POINT—THE STOCK MARKET

No market better dramatizes that government and business can interact in a mutually constructive way than the stock market. The stock market is highly efficient, providing a mechanism for trading by both institutions and individuals in thousands of investment instruments, and yet it does this with significant oversight and regulation from government institutions.

The key to success has been the government's recognition that an efficient market that can openly respond to all external influences is most desirable, even when that leaves the possibility of significant losses for organizations or individuals. What if the Securities and Exchange Commission tried to influence which companies "won" in the stock markets (the way the Federal Communications Commission had previously determined that AT&T would be the "winner" in the telecommunications market)? We'd have a dramatically different sort of stock market today.

While there are obvious differences that exist between the stock market and other industries, there are also many alternatives in the ways that government institutions can act to facilitate free and open markets to meet the best interests of both consumers and corporations.

But the U.S. government's approach to regulation has been schizophrenic and often unpredictable. When the cable television industry was first evolving, it followed a highly regulated model similar to the telecommunications industry. In 1994, DirecTV from Hughes Satellite began to compete directly with the cable companies. Other would-be players soon followed. Rather than allowing the various interested parties to compete openly for the consumer's dollar, the government attempted to protect the cable market by placing restrictions on the satellite industry; for example, satellite providers were not allowed to retransmit local television broadcasts—an obvious competitive disadvantage. Once again, the government was legislating the desired outcome (a healthy and protected cable industry) rather than providing rules for a level playing field.

Now, other technologies, such as the Internet, are providing alternate ways for these sorts of media to come into the home. (Video and audio broadcasters are already bypassing all sorts of government regulations by webcasting their content over the Internet.) As these and other technologies continue to evolve, government regulation will continue to lag behind business's ability to innovate.

Given the government's inability to regulate new technical advances, and given the technological uncertainty (and the unpredictably innovative ways that entrepreneurs will inevitably exploit it), in existence today, governments worldwide must understand that the laws and policies they develop should facilitate free and open markets rather than attempt to predetermine outcomes. If laws and policies are created in this manner, government, businesses, and consumers all stand to benefit.

Protecting the Most Valuable Resource of All—Information

Current laws were simply not designed to deal with—and protect—the single most important resource of the digital age: information.

The copyright, trademark, and intellectual property legal practice is swimming in chaos due to the changing needs of individuals and businesses to access, exchange, and protect information. International law is being overturned as nations attempt to balance domestic regulations with global economic forces.

The ramifications in terms of collecting appropriate tax revenues (how do you tax an information exchange in the digital marketplace?), as well as the difficulty in enforcing compliance across national borders, are too numerous to list here. For example, in current radio and television broadcasting law, the country of origin imposes the legal standard. On the Internet, however, even that fairly simple fact (where did the broadcast come from?) can be difficult to pin down.

To further complicate matters, some countries have only recently begun adopting any sort of copyright regulation at all. China has had domestic copyright laws in place only since 1990.

STRENGTHENING INTELLECTUAL PROPERTY LAW

In late October 1998, the U.S. Congress passed and the Clinton Administration approved the Digital Millennium Act and the Term Extension Bill. The Digital Millennium Act is designed to address the World Intellectual Property Organization (WIPO) Copyright Treaty, which was negotiated in Geneva in 1996. Its provisions include making it illegal to break encryption to access copyrighted materials, and protection for online services that unknowingly store materials that infringe on someone's copyright. David McClure, executive director of the Association of Online Professionals, said of the law, "It's probably the single most important piece of legislation in the history of the Internet."[1]

The Term Extension Bill would extend the length of U.S. copyright protection from life of the author plus 50 years to life of the author plus 70 years for work created on or after January 1, 1978. However, the sections covering protection of databases were tabled.

Here's an example: A writer electronically searches databases from numerous sources and gathers relevant information from a broad array of sources to create a new and "original" work. Does that writer "own" the material?

This issue takes us to the heart of copyright protection laws, which were originally established to *promote* information distribution by providing a way for creators of intellectual property—authors, playwrights, artists, composers—to share their creations while also collecting profits from their work. (A playwright allows her or his play to be performed by theater companies around the world because she or he is paid an appropriate fee for each performance.)

A copyright is not a single right, but a group of exclusive rights, owned by the creator of the work, unless that individual chooses to sell them to another entity. Among this bundle of rights: owners with the right to reproduce the work; to prepare derivative works; and to publicly distribute, display, and perform the work. The law also protects the work from modification by anyone other than its creator.

However, in a database, vast amounts of data are stored in a particular pattern and configuration. When a query is made against that database, the result is an original document, in the sense that the data is now stored using a different pattern and configuration. Under U.S. law, any original work is automatically given copyright protection the moment it is released to the public; however, a database does not enjoy the same protection.

There have been various legislative efforts in the United States that attempt to extend copyright protection to databases, but the problem is quite complex, because there is nothing truly original in a database, except for the fact that it uniquely aggregates material whose copyrights are held by multiple individuals. To make this tangible, imagine empowering a program, a software agent, to scour the Internet for various texts on options-based pricing methods used in financial markets, and then to automatically write a paper that integrates the various sources, perhaps making changes to verbiage and style to arrive at an "original" document on the topic. Is this work original or is it simply plagiarism?

These are the types of issues that legislatures and businesses will have to address to ensure that intellectual property can be disseminated widely and yet protected.

Information Segregation

If information is the most valuable resource in the digital economy, then it stands to reason that those who own the information will be the new wealthy.

This has created a new social class distinction: information *haves* and *have-nots*. This distinction is not dissimilar to the traditional class distinction between those who possessed monetary wealth and those who did not.

Information haves either already are, or will become, the wealthy elite of the digital economy, whereas information have-nots will struggle. This is true for both the United States and other developed nations, but will be more exaggerated in developing economies. In economically advanced countries, even the poor have access to computers and other information technologies (ITs). In a country where the vast majority of citizens already possess telephones, reliable power, and televisions, a computer is not far behind. The ever-decreasing price of entry-level machines (approximately $500 in early 1999) brings computing into the grasp of all but the most destitute. Computers have penetrated the classrooms of schools in even the most economically disadvantaged communities.

As more people recognize that information and its proper use will be the keys to economic success and wealth in the digital economy (and there are few who doubt this even now), access to IT will become a priority, and computers will be considered necessities, much as running water and electricity are now.

In the developing world though, this is not the case. After all, before you can give someone a computer and expect them to use it effectively, you must first provide them with basic clothing, food, shelter, and education. You must provide them with access to basic infrastructure, such as telephone service, electricity, and so on. In countries where these basic necessities are being met, the people have a chance to keep up in the digital economy. For citizens of those countries still struggling with these basics, the digital economy will only widen the already broad economic gap between the wealthy and the poor.

Information for Citizens

In an age that provides a revolutionary degree of access to information, citizens can be both beneficiaries and victims. The ability to plug into the Internet and obtain information on products and services from companies, independent third parties, and other consumers has resulted in a significant increase in consumer power. Although the digital consumer is newly empowered, the increasing use of once-private or inaccessible information also poses significant threats.

The New Consumer Information

Consumers have always been sensitive about their privacy. In the digital age, this raises two critical questions: Who possesses information about you, and how is this information being used?

The principle of free distribution of information gets complicated when the information being distributed is personal in nature. This raises a question that will be of increasing importance as the digital era progresses: How do we differentiate between private information and information that is properly in the public domain?

As we go about our daily lives, we leave a digital trail that can tell others intimate things about our personal habits, our health, and our personal preferences about anything from food to sex. These clues are digitized in transactions we make at stores, work, and with government institutions. Who owns this transactional data is often not clear.

Due to mounting public pressure, companies are increasingly giving consumers the ability to restrict the use of their electronic transaction histories. Often, however, the default is to allow companies to use this data as they see fit, and exercising your right to privacy requires doing such things as reading the fine print and checking an innocuous box at the end of a lengthy form. A single piece of information may appear insignificant by itself, but when put together with information from other sources, it may be a serious threat to privacy, indeed.

For example, say you use your frequent purchaser card at your local grocery store to purchase an abundance of unhealthy junk food. You also go to the neighborhood bookstore and, using your credit card, buy a book on relaxation techniques to deal with stress in the workplace. At the same time, you cancel your membership at your gym, which eliminates the automatic monthly fee that is billed against your credit card. Unfortunately, in the weeks that follow, you also miss an unusual number of work days. When it's time to renew your health insurance, you find that all this data was aggregated and available to the insurer. Deciding that your lifestyle has taken an unhealthy turn that makes you a risky customer, your policy is downgraded. In reality, all that happened was that you took a long-needed vacation. It also just so happens that a new gym opened around the corner from where you live, unlike the gym you used to go to which was 10 miles away.

Although this might seem far-fetched, the days are fast approaching when this sort of data collection and analysis will be both simple—and routine.

THE MOST PERSONAL OF INFORMATION—YOUR HEALTH

Nowhere is the topic of privacy more hotly debated than in the medical community. If there's a single industry in which a complete and accurate transaction history on a consumer is of greatest value, it's in health care. Mostly, this will benefit the consumer, the patient, because the more accurate the information, the better the medical care that can be provided. Yet, this very transaction history, in the wrong hands, can be used against the consumer.

Now that DNA analysis techniques exist that can identify defective genes, we see how a source of good medical information can also be used against the patient. Several law enforcement agencies have pushed for the collection of DNA samples for arrested citizens as part of standard processing, ostensibly for DNA fingerprinting of criminal suspects. However, with ever-increasing DNA databases in the hands of law enforcement, and with other personal genetic materials readily accessible via other means, personal privacy could easily be violated in ways not previously imagined.

The U.S. government's answer to this dilemma provides both a potential blessing and a curse. In an attempt to protect privacy, the government is attempting to pass legislation that will restrict improper use of personal medical information (good), but it would also create a unique medical identification number for each citizen and a standard medical digital dataset for each citizen. The existence of such a database would provide a one-stop shop for both legitimate health care providers, as well as criminals. The U.S. government intends to finalize legislation on these issues by late 1999, but the debate is raging now, and the technological developments that influence the debate continue at a blistering pace.

Even when the consumer data is used to make commercial, rather than medical or social, decisions, there are privacy concerns.

Many companies are starting to use sophisticated data-mining techniques and other technology to pull together detailed customer profiles based on internal information sources that were previously disconnected. Banks can now make decisions about whether you are a profitable customer in an instant by looking at your frequency of expensive teller visits, number of telephone inquiries, frequency of overdrafts, and average balance. Based on a combination of these factors, you might be deemed a low-value customer and consequently charged higher fees. With these new insights, companies won't be universally applying the axiom "the customer is king," but will be more discriminating in their approach to attracting and retaining customers. In short, consumers can no longer count on poor communications between a company's different lines of business.

Call centers today often have detailed records of all outbound and inbound communications with customers, as well as all transaction histories. Claiming ignorance of company policy, blaming a company employee for failing to make something clear, or claiming that the check was sent to a different department won't work when evidence to the contrary exists in the files.

WHAT HAPPENS TO THE PROVERBIAL "SECOND CHANCE?"

If at first you don't succeed, try try again. Sound familiar? It should. Humans are big believers in second chances. In the predigital economy, individuals generally had the ability to leave their pasts behind, reinventing themselves if they so chose. Countries such as the United States and Australia were originally populated by people looking for a place to start over. What you were was largely what you presented yourself as. Who would know?

Even today, when looking for a job, you create a resume that is your personal interpretation of your past employment history. You emphasize the high points and de-emphasize, or even skip, the low points. When you meet a potential partner (business or romantic), you do much the same thing.

In the digital economy, we will all have a digital paper trail, and a large part of it will be accessible by anyone else at any time for any reason. The Fair Credit Reporting Act restricts credit reporting agencies to no more than 10 years of data, but this applies only to these agencies. There is no general rule about the aging or deletion of consumer data. What happens when we no longer get a second chance, when youthful indiscretions or mistakes are never forgotten?

A Digital Bill of Rights

The idea of consumer data being truly private is quickly becoming an illusion. Consumers can no more restrict the collection of their personal data than they can stop breathing air and hope to live.

Some people believe they can still take control. We recently heard of a case in which a woman asked her husband not to subscribe to a certain magazine for fear that he would be profiled in such a way that telemarketers would "find out about him." She didn't understand—they already knew. That's why the magazine subscription offer (30 percent off!) was sent to her husband in the first place.

Telemarketers already work from lists that contain everything from your income, to your family size and status, to your career choices, to your neighborhood demographics, and much more. Rather than attempting to pretend that such information will *ever* again be private, we should be making sure that consumers have rights over how their data is used, and by whom—and legal recourse if this is abused by unscrupulous companies or individuals.

One aggravating factor is the sheer number of places that personal information can reside—and the ways it can be used, exchanged, and even corrupted. When a piece of information about you exists in a database, it is often copied to the point that it's impossible to track down. (When someone dies, it can take years before their name is deleted from direct mail and telemarketing lists.) If your credit history became incorrectly blemished, how many companies might have obtained an incorrect credit report, used it, filed it, and sent it on to others? These issues necessitate a new set of rules for the digital economy—a digital bill of rights.

The right to see your information. Many institutions hold vast stores of information about individual consumers, but without being able to see the data, there is little opportunity to spark customer concern. The right to know exactly what personal information a company maintains on you is fundamental.

The right to correct your information. Although we may not be able to restrict companies from collecting and using personal data, all consumers should have the right to ensure that their personal data is correct. They must have the right to make corrections when appropriate.

CASE IN POINT—ACCESS TO CREDIT REPORTS

Credit reports have been maintained on individuals for many years. Before the Fair Credit Reporting Act (FCRA) was passed, individual consumers had no rights to the information that credit reporting agencies maintained on them. Prior to the passage of this bill, there were numerous instances of consumers with improperly blemished credit histories that were rebuffed by credit agencies when they attempted to correct the information. The FCRA was substantially amended in 1996 as the Consumer Reporting Reform Act to further strengthen consumer's rights and ensure that consumers can see their credit histories, as well as have ways to make corrections to them to ensure accuracy. Similar legislation that applies to other collectors of consumer data will go a long way toward protecting individuals.

The right to know where your information resides. As the types and quantity of consumer information increase, it becomes increasingly difficult for individuals to comprehend who knows what. Database records are copied, bought, and sold to the point that the origin of much consumer data is lost. Consumers should have the right to know who has information about them.

The right to know how your information is being used. If a consumer knows who has information about them, often they have no idea what those companies are doing with it. Fortunately, recent legislation is giving consumers more control over how their information is used; still, these assurances aren't universally available. (See the P3P topic, which follows.)

The right to own and protect your own time. As discussed extensively in this book, time is an incredibly valuable resource in the digital economy. For consumers, personal time is perhaps the most precious commodity. Organizations and individuals who use information to steal time from consumers are the pariahs of the digital economy.

CASE IN POINT—TELEMARKETING

For many years, telemarketers have been the bane of consumers. The frequent interruptions of the telephone at the most inopportune times, typically in the middle of dinner, has risen to the point that many consumers and consumer advocacy groups are fighting back with legislation. The Telephone Consumer Protection Act of 1991 gives consumers some limited protection against intrusion by telemarketers (consumers now have the right to be put on a telemarketer's do-not-call list). However, the consumer must explicitly state this during the call, or write or call the offending firms. Unfortunately, telemarketers often hang up or fail to identify themselves so that taking such consumer action is difficult, if not impossible. Organizations such as Private Citizen (*www.PrivateCitizen.com*) have put together directories of off-limits consumers and sent them to many of the most active telemarketers to great effect. They've also empowered consumers with the information they need to pursue legal action when their rights are violated. Telemarketers and others that involuntarily take consumers' time will be under increasing scrutiny in the digital economy.

The right to protect, secure, and in some cases hide your identity. Trusted and verifiable consumer identification has always been a fundamental requirement in legal proceedings and business transactions. The right to anonymity in certain situations is also fundamental. Being able to maintain both of these rights/requirements in cyberspace is essential.

CASE IN POINT—INTEL

In January 1999, Intel was threatened with a boycott of its latest chip (the Pentium III) when it released plans to include an identification feature in the processor. The identification feature would have allowed the activities of individuals to be verified and tracked on the World Wide Web. Although the feature, planned for Intel's next-generation chips, could be electronically disabled by the consumer, the default configuration was to have the feature active. Most users of the Web take for granted that they are anonymous and assume they can view and download materials without revealing their identities. Intel's plan would have made this assumption invalid. In response to the threatened boycott, Intel has announced that this feature will be turned off in its default configuration, ensuring that consumers must make a conscious decision to be identified while on the Web.

Consumers and businesses can come to amicable agreements about the proper use of personal information. Technology tools are already being developed to help this process. A company called Firefly Network Inc. (recently acquired by Microsoft) has developed a way for consumers to create a personal "Firefly Portfolio," in which the consumer explicitly gives permission for any included information to be used by approved businesses. (The Firefly Portfolio data is chiefly used to create a profile of a consumer that automates many of the otherwise cumbersome steps involved in online purchases and other electronic transactions.)

This aforementioned digital bill of rights is not fundamentally different than the basic rights granted to citizens in the U.S. Constitution and its amendments. However, the extrapolation of these rights to the new digital world will require new legislation and new business policies to be enacted.

This has already begun to happen. The World Wide Web Consortium's (W3C's) Platform for Privacy Preferences Project (P3P) will provide web users with the privacy practices of individual sites. Consumers can then make more informed decisions as to whether they want to visit or interact with a particular site. Applications that conform to the P3P specifications will allow users to actually program their browsers accordingly. For example, if a web site assures a visitor that their information will only be used within the corporation for marketing future products and services and will never be shared externally, the visitor might elect to offer specific demographic information that would allow the company to tailor their future offerings to the individual's specific interests. Enabling the software agent of the consumer to make these decisions in an intelligent manner will ensure that consumers' interests are protected without burdening them with whether to provide personal information. Then there's the growth of a new type of infomediary, one focused on giving consumers total control over their personal information. Lumeria is one such company. They're developing a service in which consumers would control their complete portfolio of information and would decide which companies had access to which information, and the consumers might even make a few dollars in the process.

Industry initiatives such as the P3P, products such as the Firefly Portfolio, and the development of appropriate legislation will go a long way toward ensuring that the digital consumer has the tools, technology, and legal protection necessary to operate safely in the digital marketplace.

New Ways of Capturing Business Information

Thanks to advances in technology, we are finding that the same kind of information that was freely exchanged in the industrial age becomes much more powerful when captured, digitized, indexed, and stored in electronic form.

Take the sort of informal business communication that has existed since the industrial age, before e-mail was invented. People have always talked to each other. They've always bumped into each other in hallways, made impromptu phone calls, and sent memos. However, very little of this information was formally recorded. There was no record of conversations taking place in the elevator or around the watercooler. Telephone conversations largely went unmonitored.

Today, however, the e-mail archives of companies are providing a new source of value—and of possible liability. They record the interactions of design teams with manufacturing teams, managers and employees, customers and suppliers. E-mails pulled out of musty digital archives have begun to form the basis for both legal prosecution and defense strategies where necessary to reconstruct how certain events took place or decisions were made.

CASE IN POINT—CONSULTANTS UNDER FIRE

In March 1995, UOP, a petroleum-processing joint venture of Allied-Signal and Union Carbide, filed suit against Andersen Consulting, alleging breach of contract and fraud. Andersen was engaged by UOP in 1992 to develop a new customer service system in an attempt to improve customer responsiveness. After several months on the job, UOP removed Andersen Consulting from the project.

The interesting element of this case is the evidence that was used in court. UOP system administrators were able to retrieve several e-mails from their servers documenting interactions between Andersen Consulting employees who were using UOP's e-mail system. These e-mail conversations reportedly showed conflict between UOP and the Andersen team and allegedly demonstrated that the Andersen team did not perform as required in their contract with UOP.

Recent videotaped testimony to the court overseeing the Microsoft antitrust case shows an uncomfortable Bill Gates viewing incriminating e-mails he crafted in years gone by. In the same case, Microsoft used other e-mail records to support its innocence. The point is, e-mail didn't even exist for most businesses five or ten years ago, but it's already dramatically changing legal prosecution and defense strategies. The broader implications of how digitally recorded interactions between various parties in business and social interactions are just starting to be contemplated.

The greatest new source of information for most companies already resides in their own computer systems. The transactional data captured in all of their dealings with customers, suppliers, partners, distributors, subcontractors, and banks has traditionally been stored online only as long as they are required for processing and historical access. Since the early 1990s, however, companies realize they can employ data warehouses, data-mining tools, decision support systems, executive information systems, and other forms of business intelligence products to glean new value from old data that previously would be considered obsolete after just a few years. New tools that perform statistical analysis on volumes of old transactional data can find new market opportunities, ways to reduce cycle times, improve customer service, and eliminate costs. In fact, companies that fail to leverage the historical data in their transaction systems for more than basic business operations will fail to see or predict future curves in the road that more information-savvy competitors will easily avoid.

CASE IN POINT—THE MISSING FILBERTS

One January, management at a particular baked goods manufacturer found sales had inexplicably dropped 3 percent from the same sales period of the prior year. The decrease could not readily be explained. In their region of the United States, bakery sales are typically flat and infinitely predictable: they tend to rise or fall only as inflation and population levels fluctuate. There are only two seasonal trends: sales rise before Christmas and fall thereafter. They fall again on Ash Wednesday and rise again at Easter.

The CEO demanded to know what had happened. Marketing looked to see if a new competitor had invisibly penetrated its market. Sales looked for a large account that had unexpectedly cut the volume of its orders. Finance looked to see whether people had slowed down payments. No one saw anything that explained the sales drop.

Happily, the company had just installed a business intelligence system that was designed to analyze information at a much more detailed level. The database administrator decided to see whether this new system could help unravel the mystery. First, he looked at overall customer activity. No big changes there.

Then he looked across bakery operations to see whether there was a strike or some breakdown in the overall manufacturing process. Again, nothing. Finally, he looked at individual product categories. He began to see some differences. Sales of cakes and pies were up slightly, but sales of breakfast goods were down more than 5 percent. Heartened, he looked at more detailed data. Finally, he was able to see that sales of uniced coffee cakes were off a whopping 40 percent (sales of all other breakfast products were either flat, or slightly up). He also saw that returns of stale, uniced coffee cake merchandise had gone to zero. Eureka! The entire exercise had taken him less than an hour; he now understood that the problem wasn't that customers had suddenly decided to buy less coffee cake, but that the company wasn't making enough coffee cake to satisfy market demand.

Armed with this information, he phoned a friend, a baker. The database administrator explained his findings and asked how the baker expected the company to make profit if the bakers did not build enough product. The baker replied that uniced coffee cakes fell into two separate product categories, or SKUs. One was a filbert coffee cake that required Turkish filberts. Recently, though, the cloud from Chernobyl had drifted over Turkey. The American and Turkish authorities had banned the export of all Turkish agricultural products to the United States. The bakers had tried to make the coffee cake with Oregon filberts. Oregon filberts had a different oil content, and the recipe did not work. The baker assured his technical friend that as soon as the Turkish and American authorities were convinced filberts were safe, the bakery would start importing them again.

Meanwhile, marketing had already started putting together a campaign designed to try to stimulate additional demand among customers. After the database administrator reported his findings, this campaign was recognized to be useless (customer demand already existed) and aborted. The money saved more than paid for the development of the business intelligence system.

The Information Conflict

As discussed previously, although consumer information is of great value to businesses, the corporate desire to know the consumer is often directly at odds with the consumer's desire to protect his or her personal information. Consumers like to have companies know just enough about them to service their needs without pestering them, but they want strict boundaries to be placed on the use of that information. This tension is apparent by increased consumer frustration with surveys and telemarketing calls intended to gather information from them, and their suspicion when such information is gathered without their conscious approval.

CASE IN POINT—CREDIT CARD DATA

In January 1999, MasterCard International announced plans to begin leveraging its massive transaction histories of consumer purchasing information in a new way: through a product it is calling Merchant Advisor. The plan is to use aggregated and anonymous information on consumer credit card purchases to give profiles of consumer buying patterns. The credit card purchasing information will be cross-referenced with other demographic data on credit card users to develop a new, richer set of consumer buying data. Retailers can use the data to understand their competitive positioning and design marketing programs to attract desirable consumer segments. The intent is to turn the valuable data that currently resides in MasterCard's databases into a new source of revenue for the company.

Of paramount concern to MasterCard when designing the product was consumer privacy. To that end, MasterCard had a team of lawyers review the product plan in detail to develop an eight-point privacy policy. A major plank of the policy is that no consumer-specific information (for example, name, address, phone) will ever be released. It appears that MasterCard has struck the right balance in the conflict between leveraging consumer information while maintaining consumer privacy.

Protecting and Sharing Information

A major area of concern for many business and IT managers is how to best protect this new and extremely valuable resource. After all, the tenets of the value-based organization (VBO) outlined in Part Four specifically say that company walls should be more easily permeated. When you make a decision to outsource a competency, for example, implicit in that decision is the requirement to share with an external firm some pretty sensitive information. Otherwise, the outsourcing agreement is likely to fail.

A major challenge, then, is to simultaneously protect and leverage information. These needs are often at complete odds. Information is most valuable when it is shared among a group, added to, and combined with other data. Implicit in this process, though, is granting access to the information to an ever-widening audience. Granting this access can mean losing whatever advantage was formerly gained by being the sole owner of the data.

Yet, this very notion of keeping information secret is self-defeating. Information is only of value when used, and the shelf life for certain high-value information is often short. As much as they focus on how to secure and protect potentially value information, organizations should be focused on extracting the value of this information by disseminating it to all parties that can best leverage it to the betterment of the entire company.

Much has already been written about ways of protecting your information from being stolen or improperly used. Encryption, firewalls, and other data security tools and techniques are becoming increasingly sophisticated, and network and computer system security is a major business concern.

Headlines about hackers, corporate espionage, and electronic eavesdropping are frequent. Although theft of data by those outside of the corporation is often of paramount concern, evidence shows that the theft and illicit use of corporate data is most often perpetrated by employees rather than outsiders.

We believe that apart from physically securing your data, there are three relatively simple steps to make sure your information is adequately protected. First, only store that data that you intend to use; second, assume that all of your mineable data is accessible to the marketplace; and third, treat your employees fairly and with enough respect to avoid providing them with motivation to want to harm the company.

The Role of Government

Rather than pontificate on the right or wrong forms of government interference, it makes more sense to focus on ways the government role is changing as a direct result of the new digital economy. Although many traditional responsibilities of government will remain intact, other factors will force governments at all levels and in all geographies to modify how they best serve their citizens.

Collecting and Disseminating Information

As far back as the days of the colonial town crier, governments have had responsibility for notifying citizens when important information came to light. The growing influence of the mass media has shifted much of this responsibility away from the government. Nevertheless, government databases, educational institutions, and public libraries still exist largely to fulfill this primary goal.

Still, just as the mass media has already assumed some of the responsibility for information distribution, so will the Internet further erode the government's role in this area. We believe that, in the future, the government will both voluntarily and involuntarily shift from being an aggregator/disseminator of information into a *regulator and facilitator* of the information markets.

For example, the Environmental Protection Agency's Toxic Release Inventory database is used by environmental groups to monitor the activities of polluting businesses and industries. Obviously, much of this data would not be available unless the government mandated its collection. Likewise, the way that states and counties control development activities (through issuing construction permits and other real-estate documents that are, in turn, stored in databases), empowers individuals, as well as consumer organizations, with the information they need to manage critical aspects of community growth.

It's important to understand that consumers won't get less, or lower-quality, information as a result. Instead, they will get more information, presented in ways they can use, and at the times that they need it. The result is an *empowered citizen.*

Government actions themselves will be placed under myriad microscopes in the digital economy. Whereas the mass media and courts have historically been responsible for keeping government honest, as the consumer becomes more empowered, individual citizens will be able to take action. The Freedom of Information Act, passed in 1967 and amended in 1975, has forced once recalcitrant branches of the U.S. government to open up their records to the public. This information has been used by both business and consumer groups to change government practices and further improve access to public information.

Protecting Social Welfare

The government's role of providing a social safety net for its citizens will be required in the digital economy, just as it has been required in previous economic eras. The expanded use of technology and overall transformation of the economy will not result in eliminating the disappearance of poor or disadvantaged individuals who require governmental assistance. What *has* changed, however, is the government's ability to perform these functions more effectively using the tools and techniques of the digital economy.

Historically, the government has often treated people as members of various groups: poor or rich; residents of this community or that community; belonging to this race or ethnic category, or that one. Aggregating people into groups simplified the process of creating laws, identifying who the laws applied to, and actually applying the laws.

In the digital economy, the government increasingly has the ability and responsibility to treat people as individuals rather than as members of a group. Witness the recent backlash against affirmative action programs. The goals of such programs are noble—to reverse historical inequities. However, by applying laws broadly to entire races and categories of people rather than to individuals based on their individual needs and histories, the goals of the affirmative action program often weren't being met; inequities of these programs were visible to all.

In the digital economy, just as database profiling technologies allow businesses to understand and target consumers based on specific criteria, the government can use these same technologies to target individuals for special treatment based on specific criteria rather than broad categorizations that may or may not meet the intended goals of the program or law. (Of course, we're in the early stages of seeing these technologies applied. In the meantime, the wholesale elimination of affirmative action has created a new set of social problems that have caused yet another backlash. Ultimately, however, technology will help enormously in government's ability to untangle this and other sticky issues.)

The government has new tools and techniques to deliver social services in a more timely and efficient manner. Recently, the government has been applying data-mining techniques developed to reduce mistakes and duplication and eliminate fraud. By cross-referencing such diverse data as welfare roles, social security records, Medicare, Medicaid, IRS refunds, and death certificates, the government is able to catch citizens who are double-dipping or perpetrating other forms of fraud, while increasing the services they provide to citizens truly in need of these services.

As discussed previously, the digital economy and its focus on information as the creator of wealth also result in a new underclass—the information have-nots. The separation between information haves and have-nots often falls along classic social class lines, but addressing this new gap will require a different approach on the part of governments.

Just as governments attempt to improve the bulk of the disadvantaged through job training, education loans, and summer work programs, so they must also develop and expand government programs for the expansion of information access and information management skills. These will be the fundamental tools for future wealth creation for all classes. Putting Internet access into public libraries and public schools is a commendable first step.

Although citizens increasingly rely on the digital marketplace to provide them with the information they need, governments still have a vital role in enabling this distribution, particularly in emerging markets.

For example, in those countries where there is little telecommunications infrastructure or computing capacity, it will be the government's role to create an environment in which the average citizen can become connected. This role is at odds with the philosophies of some countries that would prefer to maintain tight controls over the quality and quantity of information their citizens digest.

Vietnam and China, among other nations, have inconsistent and confusing laws governing the availability and proper use of Internet access for citizens. In the industrial economy, a country's decision to keep its population disconnected from the rest of the world was seen as a political and human rights issue; in the digital economy, it is also seen as an urgent *economic* issue. Governments that don't encourage the free and open exchange of information across their borders will find themselves with an increasingly disadvantaged economy.

Nurturing the Digital Marketplace

The single most critical business-related role for governments in the digital economy is that they must continue creating and enforcing the minimal level of rules, regulations, and infrastructure required for conducting commerce in the digital economy.

What are these *minimal* rules and regulations, however? As we've seen, there's going to be extensive debate about this. Also, there's ample evidence that the government's role need not be as broad or pervasive as it was in the industrial economy. Independent organizations, business cooperatives, and other nongovernmental international organizations, often acting on the behalf of consumers, are taking over many of these roles.

The Internet is the classic example. Nobody owns the Internet, and no single body regulates the Internet. Individual governments' attempts to regulate aspects of the Internet that are beyond their control have consistently failed. Likewise, government attempts to restrict access to the Internet by their citizens have largely failed.

In the digital economy, governments generally must defer to the free market, to international bodies, or to business cooperatives that are better equipped to provide needed infrastructure, oversight, and regulation. However, there *are* specific things that governments must do to nurture the digital marketplace, as we've listed hereafter.

Protect intellectual property rights. As discussed previously, intellectual property will be increasingly important in the digital age. The government must continue in its role as the protector of intellectual property.

Protect the privacy of individuals while protecting the rights of business. Government must protect the rights of individuals while not impinging on the rights of business to use information they rightfully own.

Provide authentication of digital documents and digital personas. Fundamental to the proper functioning of a digital marketplace is the need for buyers and sellers to correctly identify who they are dealing with at any given time. Furthermore, people need to be assured that electronic contracts and electronic transactions are as valid and enforceable as their paper counterparts. To enable these, the government must provide or support through legislation the creation of an electronic notary public function, as well as appropriate consumer digital identification tools.

Support the development of the information infrastructure. The Internet is more than a medium for conducting business, it is a social network for the citizens of the world. The building of the network can't be left solely in the hands of the free market. The role of government is to ensure that the interests of citizens are fully represented as the information infrastructure continues to develop.

Regulate markets and enforce antitrust laws. Although business organizations are increasingly becoming more self-regulated, there will always be a need for governments to ensure that citizens' interests are protected in business affairs. Although we feel many of the recent megamergers are in some ways counter to the operating principles of the digital economy, they point out the ongoing need for vigilant government oversight in mergers and acquisitions.

Support the development of standards. Standards are usually best determined either by relevant business consortia, or through open competition among alternate standards in the market. In some instances, though, the government can speed the development of new markets by setting standards early. For example, the U.S. government's role in setting standards for High-Definition Television (HDTV) in the United States should result in a much quicker launch of HDTV services and equipment.

Securing the Digital Marketplace

Just as a physical marketplace needs physical security, the digital marketplace needs digital security. In the physical marketplace, if something is stolen, you generally know because it is no longer where it physically should be. (The television set used to sit in that corner of the living room. Where is it now?)

In the digital marketplace, however, the illicit and illegal capturing of information is an alarmingly invisible activity. Because the collecting, categorizing, indexing, and combining of information is the primary function of so many companies in the digital marketplace, even "accidental espionage" is possible. Information can be so easily dispersed that the boundary between illegal corporate espionage and legitimate legal market research is often difficult to determine.

There are a number of technologies used to ensure that the private communications and information of a company or individual remain private. Corporate intranets are protected by firewalls that keep out intruders. Personal identification numbers and secured passwords are required to access sensitive data and applications. Control of most of these technologies will remain in the hands of business. One area of security technology that governments have chosen to regulate is that of encryption.

Starting in the 1970s, academics began researching a new form of encryption known as public key encryption. This technology would allow anyone to implement a virtually unbreakable encryption of digital data and communications. Since the early days of public key encryption research, the U.S. government has been unable to come to a coherent stand on it.

For starters, the U.S. government naturally wants to be able to encrypt its own communications with the strongest encryption technology possible. It also wants its enemies (or potential enemies) to only have access to weaker encryption technologies for the obvious reason that they can be more easily broken. Likewise, although the government wants law-abiding citizens and businesses to use strong encryption technologies when conducting business and personal communications, it wants to be able to break those if it suspects criminal activities.

Although public key encryption techniques are a perceived threat to the government's ability to perform law enforcement functions, the public/private key aspects of public key encryption techniques also provide a magic solution. The controllers of the private portion of the keys have the ability to unlock encrypted messages easily. The U.S. government is currently proposing to allow the use of strong encryption algorithms, but that a trusted third party will hold copies of all private keys in escrow that can be released to the government if a proper court order is obtained.

Of course, management of encryption technologies and key escrow databases is clearly something that must be handled internationally if it is to be successful. We'll discuss the futility of unilateral actions later in this chapter.

The European Union has similar concerns about privacy and believes that the legal framework for Web-based trading must be more clearly defined. Encryption technology is available today from U.S. companies, but the U.S. government has placed tight restrictions on its export. European ministers have called for the removal of such restrictions. Visa and MasterCard are addressing some of the issues related to secure credit card transactions over the Web with the secure electronic transaction (SET) payment protocol, which uses a system of public and private keys to encrypt transactions between the trading parties.

INDUSTRY'S ANSWER TO THE ENCRYPTION DEBATE

An attempt to balance the needs of law enforcement officers with the demands of businesses for robust Internet security can be seen in the "private doorbell" approach promoted by a coalition of leading computer companies. Under this model, information traveling over a private or public data network remains secure and private unless a network operator is served with a legal warrant or court order. In that case, the network operator accesses the information.

Thus, law enforcement agencies that go through proper court order or search warrant channels will be given access to Internet messages to and from specific individuals suspected of carrying out illegal activities. The advantage of the "private doorbell" approach (so named because the government must ring the doorbell with a legal document rather than hold the keys and use them at will) is that it requires far less complex infrastructure than key recovery or key escrow methods of security.

Ensuring Global Cooperation

Governments are necessarily local in nature. They are tied to a geography and are supported by the residents of that geography. For this simple reason, governments will always support the best interests of their citizens over the interests of the larger global community.

Businesses, on the other hand, have no such geographic ties. Multinational corporations are answerable to their stockholders, who can reside in multiple countries. As the world becomes a smaller place through the evolution of communications and other technologies, businesses are clearly growing more powerful, often at the expense of the traditional nation-state.

Power isn't merely shifting from governments to corporations. The global economy is forcing governments to relinquish control in areas previously considered the exclusive domain of a single nation-state to other international bodies. Organizations such as the World Trade Organization (WTO), and agreements such as the General Agreement on Tariffs and Trade (GATT), the Maastricht Treaty that formed the European Union, and the North American Free Trade Agreement (NAFTA), are evidence of this shift in control.

The cooperation needed to nurture an increasingly global economy is requiring unnatural acts of teamwork and collaboration among previously adversarial countries. Nowhere is the interlinking of world governments more evident than in financial markets. Government decisions to raise or lower interest rates, change tax laws, or adjust government spending have international ramifications with unintended consequences on world financial markets.

The Asian financial crisis in late 1998 highlighted the complex and unpredictable interactions of financial markets in the digital age. At the onset of the crisis, many governments burned through the majority of their cash reserves in an attempt to prop up overvalued currencies and hold off the decline in local economies. Still, global currency speculators turned out to be a more powerful force than these nations had anticipated, and the result was a catastrophic economic failure that resounded throughout Asia.

Governments will probably try and continue acting autonomously until a few more lessons of this sort are dealt; however, sometimes they will be successful at imposing a local concern on the international community. In 1995, German officials decided that certain materials on the CompuServe network were offensive, and mandated that CompuServe remove the materials. To accomplish this, CompuServe had to remove the materials from its entire network, which it did, but not without great effort. The French government sued Georgia Institute of Technology's French campus in Lorraine for using English exclusively on its web site in violation of the 1994 Toubon law designed to protect France against the growing use of English. The lawsuit was overturned in French court on a technicality, but France is still pursuing the extension of its language laws to the World Wide Web. In general, these types of unilateral moves have resulted in negative publicity for the countries in question. In some cases, the offending businesses simply moved their operations to a friendlier digital marketplace.

Businesses are aggressively looking at multinational growth opportunities. However, globalization in the digital economy does not necessarily imply *physical* relocation. As high-speed communication bandwidth becomes more readily available, virtual offices will become more and more common. Workers will not have to come to a physical work site every day, but can telecommute to an office thousands of miles and even continents away. To take this concept further, it is possible to experience *reverse immigration,* in which workers in a virtual corporation relocate to other countries to minimize their cost of living and taxes.

The dissemination of news, entertainment, and sports has also acquired global dimensions, with the evolution from broadcast TV to satellite transmission. Global content is now available at the flip of a button, and global news networks such as CNN and BBC have audiences estimated in the hundreds of millions. These networks wield tremendous power as information disseminators, both through television and the Internet. The long-term effect on their dedicated following will be a gradual *homogenization* of viewpoints and language. The expectations of the world consumer will rise. Global news content will come to be seen as a necessity, and this expectation will act as a force against government-imposed barriers to information.

For example, after the 1998 Indo-Pakistani nuclear tests, flocks of subscribers accessed the online pages of Indian and Pakistani newspapers, official government press releases, and other official and quasi-official information sources, obtaining their information directly and without relying on news intermediaries. They were able to inform themselves directly of local reaction, view satellite pictures of the test site, and access related information from neighboring countries such as Afghanistan and China to get the local viewpoint as well. In other words, citizens in the West were able to get a comprehensive picture of the crisis between these two countries, perhaps more easily than if they were at the scene itself.

This rapid dissemination of information to the world serves as a catalyst for global education and person-to-person communication without the need for biased middlemen politicians or media interference. It is another example of disintermediation born of the digital economy.

The most obvious thing a government can do to empower its citizens in the global digital economy is to maintain an international policy that encourages the open flow of ideas and information across its borders. You might assume that a democratic nation such as the United States would universally embrace this policy, but this is not necessarily so (as demonstrated by the U.S. government's stubborn policy on the export of encryption software). Foreign policy must be adjusted to encourage multinational corporations to invest capital and share technology and information across national boundaries. Barriers impeding the flow of products, services, and technologies should be broken down. If a nation chooses to insulate itself from the rest of the world, not only will it lose out on information inflows, but it will limit the ability of its citizens to be active participants in the global economy.

Managing Taxation

A government's tax code is a powerful tool for effecting social change. This has always been the case, and will be no different in the digital economy. The U.S. model of taxation, for example, is designed to divert resources from areas of greater concentration to those of lesser concentration. Businesses have traditionally been both targets and beneficiaries of taxation policy. It makes sense to ask whether current systems of taxation will be able to address the demands of the digital economy.

Although we saw an increasing globalization of business in the industrial age, we still have seaports, airports, and national borders where a government could impose its particular regulations and collect whatever taxes it wanted to impose.

In the industrial age, it was fairly easy to use this system: Governments could visibly perceive that ships, airplanes, or other vehicles carrying goods were approaching a national boundary; officials could therefore be waiting to extract the requisite taxes. Taxation was generally in the form of levies and import duties because they were easy to impose and there were few control points that had to be monitored.

In the digital economy, in which the value of goods is measured by their digital content (and that digital content is transmitted electronically), the way in which taxes are collected obviously must change.

Moreover, traditional ways of assessing tax, such as the value-added tax (VAT) method, will no longer apply. Existing VATs levy fees on the various steps that add value to products (usually manufacturing or other forms of physical conversion). This also becomes more difficult in the digital economy. As products obtain more of their value through the addition of intellectual content, the specific value-adding steps become difficult to identify and quantify.

The United States currently comprises more than 30,000 different state and local jurisdictions, each of which has the authority to levy taxes. When one considers the large number of potential tax jurisdictions, the tremendous variations in tax policy that exist within those jurisdictions, and the world-without-borders nature of the Internet, you see the challenges that lie ahead.

It doesn't stop there, either. Companies who sell their goods over the Net face the specter of massive compliance costs. "A company active in every state and local jurisdiction would have to file over 2,600 sales tax returns a year," says Rob Garretson, a tax specialist with KPMG Peat Marwick in Washington, D.C.

Here's an additional complication: Most states do not tax items that they consider intangible. Some states have a narrow definition of tangibility, which includes only physical items that can be seen and touched, and such states consider software downloads to be intangible, and therefore not taxable. Other states have a broader definition of tangible goods that includes software. In these states, a download would be considered a transfer of tangible goods and *would* be taxable.

The value in U.S. dollars of business-to-business commerce on the World Wide Web is expected to reach $327 billion by 2000, up from $8 billion in 1997, according to Forrester Research. It will be interesting to see if tax-free zones, such as the one in Massachusetts, can sustain themselves in the face of such numbers. Most industry observers believe that the best position for legislators to adopt for the short term is taxation neutrality, which means simply applying to the electronic world all the existing tax codes, enabling both large and small ventures to begin engaging in electronic commerce more rapidly. However, a KPMG Peat Marwick study shows that Web businesses have expressed a great deal of frustration with the murky environment created by applying old tax laws to new ways of doing business.

In these days of virtual corporations, an unduly harsh taxation policy on information exchange or digital commerce is likely to induce companies to simply move their headquarters to a place with a more attractive tax environment. The more virtual a company is, the easier it is to make such a move. To provide electronic commerce with a favorable climate, at least for the next two years, the U.S. Senate has enacted a groundbreaking piece of legislation that protects Internet commerce from taxation. Bill S.442 is summarized by the Library of Congress Internet site THOMAS as, "A bill to establish a national policy against state and local government interference with interstate commerce on the Internet or interactive computer services, and to exercise Congressional jurisdiction over interstate commerce by establishing a moratorium on the imposition of exactions that would interfere with the free flow of commerce via the Internet, and for other purposes."

In an attempt to push this even further, Senate bill S.328 seeks to make permanent this ban on taxation of Internet commerce to ensure a robust and growing digital marketplace.

Governors of many states are panicking at the prospect of Washington usurping their right to levy Internet excise taxes. They say states and localities could experience significant erosion of tax revenues if the law is enacted. No wonder. Given the expected magnitude of electronic commerce, and the resultant shift of consumers away from conventional ways of doing business, the inability to tax such purchases could account for nearly one-quarter of all state and local tax revenues, according to the Center on Budget and Policy Priorities, a nonpartisan research organization that conducts research on government policy and programs. The Center adds that the loss of these revenues could significantly impair the ability of some states and localities to meet their funding requirements for education, health care, and welfare programs. Moreover, it's arguable that higher-income families, those who can afford computers and modems, would be the major beneficiaries of any prohibition of taxation on Internet transactions. Therefore, to the extent that states would raise sales and telecommunications taxes to replace the lost revenues on Internet commerce, the increased burden would fall disproportionately on low and moderate-income households, some observers say.

In summary, governments face a dilemma in the taxation area. On the one hand, if they tax the Internet, they will inhibit free information flow, create a barrier to enterprise, and possibly force virtual businesses to relocate elsewhere. On the other hand, if they make the Internet a tax-free zone, most of the burden for funding traditional government services will fall on the most burdened segments of society, assuming that other taxes remain constant.

Obviously, neither outcome is desirable, and a compromise has to be reached. If, as a nation, we can formulate equitable measures for businesses to support education and innovation, then perhaps we can render government interference in the form of taxation unnecessary.

AN ALTERNATIVE APPROACH—THE "BIT TAX"

Some government agencies are addressing this issue in an exceedingly direct manner. In Europe, there is currently a discussion of a "bit" tax—a tax on each of the digital zeros and ones transmitted over the Net. This proposal, from Luc Soete of the University of Maastricht, The Netherlands, is viewed as a way to use taxation to ensure that poorer citizens have equal access to information.

Another view comes from Rishab Aiyer Ghosh, editor and publisher of the *Indian Techonomist,* and managing editor of *First Monday,* the peer-reviewed journal of the Internet. Ghosh writes, "There is no question that there are differences between the economic logic—the application of basic economic principles—on and off the Net. Much of the economic activity on the Net involves value but no money."

Controlling Citizenship

The concept of citizenship is also evolving as a result of the digital age. Frequent international travel, employment assignments abroad, and prolonged leisure stays in foreign countries used to be limited to a handful of privileged or exceedingly well-qualified citizens. Today, employees of multinational corporations routinely travel abroad and take up temporary residences in different nations. The term "citizen of the world" was once used to describe the elite world traveler who had no roots in any single country, but it increasingly represents the common citizen.

Even when we don't travel, we often find that we feel less allegiance to our country than to other sorts of organizations to which we belong to. The interests of our individual families, companies, churches, and social organizations can take priority over national interests. Being a member of a social group centered around common interest, religion, national/ethnic origin, or race can fulfill emotional and psychological needs—and inspire greater loyalty—than the national patriotism that is tied to a specific geography or political state. (Even the once-vaunted "Made in America" label doesn't tug at the heart strings the way it used to.) In short, individuals across the globe are feeling more and more connected to one another, often at the expense of national identity.

How governments will try to manage this sort of identity crisis remains to be seen.

The Model for the New Millennium

Much excitement is ahead for those who will use this book as a guide for transforming products, markets, and organizations. It will also be a very challenging journey, but nonetheless a necessary one for those who expect to be successful, or even exist, in 10, 15, or 20 years from the turn of the millennium. Those businesses that have an energized leadership core and a workforce accustomed to change will find this transition a fairly easy process. Those without either or both components will find it much more difficult. We hope, however, that everyone recognizes by now the inherent value in the digital economy and the immediacy and necessity of the change required to compete in it.

Comments on the Digital Marketplace

ON MARCH 18 THROUGH 20, 1999, A. T. KEARNEY HOSTED A CEO FORUM ENTITLED "MASTER-ing the Digital Marketplace" at the Biltmore Hotel in Coral Gables, Florida. Numerous CEOs were invited to actively participate in the forum and discuss how their companies were dealing with the digital economy. Joining me on the podium were some of the leading thinkers and speakers of today, including Stephen Covey, Nicholas Negroponte, Arno Penzias, Alvin Toffler, Colin Powell, and Elizabeth Mackay. Along with the attending CEOs, these speakers participated in engaging discussions on the topics of intelligent products, intelligent markets, intelligent organizations, and methods for maximizing shareholder value in the digital marketplace. From this forum and subsequent research and discussions, I've developed this Afterword to put some new spin on many of the ideas expressed throughout this book.

To give you some perspective on the level of adoption or buy-in to the concepts of the digital economy among the CEOs, let me relate an observation that Arno Penzias made. During Nicholas Negroponte's discussion, Nick conducted a quick informal poll of the number of processors that were contained in the various products made by several of the CEOs' companies, particularly the consumer products companies. One CEO sheepishly said that his product contained only 5 microprocessors, whereas another CEO said his contained well over 100. When it was Arno's turn to lead the discussion, he pointed out how telling it was that one of the CEOs actually *apologized* for the relatively small number of microprocessors that were in his product. Just think about that. How many years ago would that have sounded ludicrous? How many years ago would the CEOs have not even been able to answer the question, "How many microprocessors are in your product?" As Arno pointed out, this audience was full of CEOs. They were the guys with the pointy hair in the *Dilbert* cartoons, the obstacles to change and technology, the stalwarts of the old regime. Yet, they clearly wanted to have more microprocessors in their products. These are truly amazing times, and I'm thrilled that we were able to organize such an illustrious group of speakers and CEOs to discuss these topics.

On Time and Speed

If there was a single central, overriding theme to the forum, it was that of *speed* and *time* being the drivers of commerce in the digital marketplace. Speed and time impact the way companies deal with consumers and represent an unfulfilled opportunity to grab customer/consumer pocket share, as we discussed with the new time-value proposition in Chapter 2. Speed and time are the drivers of the new extended digital value networks (DVNs) that are forming in the digital marketplace as discussed in Part Three. Optimizing for speed and time is one of the capabilities and requirements for the new value-based organizations (VBOs) discussed in Part Four.

Stephen Covey, well-known author of *The Seven Habits of Highly Effective People* and *The Seven Habits of Highly Effective Families,* spoke at length about how speed and time are transforming both our business and personal lives. Although Stephen agrees that change and the pace of change are intertwined in our lives now, he focused not on the need for speed, but the need to take the time that is really necessary to build a trusting organization. As we discussed in Part Four, "Intelligent Organizations," *trust* is a key ingredient to the successful VBOs of tomorrow. Stephen said, "The problem is, we get on such a pace because of the importance of speed and how valuable speed is in so many ways; it's like dog years—seven for one. It's going at such a rate, but there is something that doesn't go at that rate, and that is the building of a high trust culture." It's easy to get focused on speed of execution, but focusing on speed alone can sidetrack us from doing what we really need to be doing. We can end up focusing on what is *urgent* rather than what is *important* due to the pressure to perform. As Covey put it, "With people, fast is slow and slow is fast. You can't be efficient with people on issues where there are profound differences, where you haven't yet cultivated the criterion around which all of the decisions are made. It takes time. It takes patience. It takes slowing down." Building a culture that will drive the company in a unified fashion is critical to success. A central part of this culture is a shared understanding of the overriding strategy, most often embodied within and expressed as a company's value-added competency (VAC). I'll talk more about this in the later section, "On Intelligent Organizations."

On the Empowered Consumer

In Chapter 1, I expounded on the new empowered consumers, the information they now have, the power they wield over companies, and the decisions they can and do make every day. Although the CEOs attending the forum, as well as the featured speakers, all agreed with this premise, several of the CEOs took a somewhat counterview—which was that while consumers are empowered, that doesn't necessarily mean that they know what they want. The consensus of the group was that what consumers are really looking for is to have their problems solved, their everyday dilemmas addressed, and that providing them with vast quantities of well-organized information and empowering them to make lots of decisions about what widgets they get in what color at what time is only one small part of addressing those dilemmas. Companies can't assume for a second that just because consumers now have access to the vast quantities of information available on the Internet that they will automatically know exactly what they're looking for and will be able to configure it exactly to their tastes based on their own insights.

An interesting case in point was an innovative approach that Maytag has taken recently in really understanding consumers—getting inside their heads and finding out what they really need, not what they say they need through traditional surveys or market research. Through the science of ethnography, they studied how consumers used their products and developed some new insights. As Lloyd Ward, CEO of Maytag, told us . . .

> We put researchers into consumers homes and watch them interact with our appliances. And through those observations we gain insights that then provide a direction for us to pursue in terms of our innovation.
>
> I'll give you a simple example. We're watching a lady load her dishwasher. Before she closes the door and runs the cycle, she walks to the family room that's just adjacent and picks up two durable toys. She comes back, she puts them in the dishwasher, and runs the cycle. Later, the ethnographer says, "Ma'am, I noticed you put the toys in the dishwasher.

Why?" She says, "Oh, you must not have little kids at home, because if you did, you'd know exactly why. Everything my little Suzie picks up, she puts in her mouth. And I put those in the dishwasher to sanitize them clean." And he says, "Well Ma'am, do you realize that dishwashers don't sanitize your dishes?" She says, "Of course they do. Every time I open up the door the steam hits me in the face." He says, "No, they clean your dishes but they don't sanitize your dishes." She said, "They don't?"

And so we got two insights from that. One insight is that consumers expected their dishwashers to sanitize their dishes. We confirmed that in focus groups and further research. Secondly, that consumers were using dishwashers to clean things other than their dishes. Two important insights.

We worked with the National Sanitation Foundation. We developed a sanitation cycle that was time/temperature dependent. We then built it into our high-end Jenn-Air and Maytag dishwashers. It's the kind of innovation that we can charge for at retail because it adds real value for consumers, and the product is flying off the shelves. Consumers get an LED visual read out that tells you your dishes have been sanitized clean when you select that cycle.

The point here is that although I clearly believe we've entered an era that will be and in many cases already is dominated by the new empowered and informed consumer, that's no excuse for companies to throw all decision making and, hence, all innovation over to the consumer. Consumers will still need companies to educate them on their options, and to see past their surface wants to get at their underlying, and perhaps more fundamental, needs. Arno Penzias took this a step further, stating, "I don't believe the world is customer driven because the customers don't know what they want. The customers are far too slow." He used the example of IBM asking their old mainframe customers if they really wanted those silly UNIX RISC boxes, and of course, they didn't, and so the market went to Sun. Once again, listening to your customer and catering to their needs will never obviate the need for companies to innovate and go beyond what their customers think they need today to what they'll really need tomorrow.

On Intelligent Products

In Chapter 3, I introduced the concept of containers and content and how this construct was useful for understanding where value was generated in your product/service offering. Nicholas Negroponte, author of the book

Being Digital and founder and director of the MIT Media Lab, discussed his well-known division of the world into atoms and bits. Nicholas's construct of bits and atoms is very similar to my construct of container and content with container equating to atoms, and content equating to bits. The fundamental difference between atoms and bits as Nicholas described it is that when I sell you something made of atoms (a toaster in the specific example he used), I no longer have the toaster. This may sound rather obvious, but it's very profound in that it points out one of the fundamental differences between bits and atoms. Now, when I sell you some bits (think digital content, a piece of software), you have those bits, but so do I. The marginal cost of creating more bits is virtually zero. This is not a terribly new insight. After all, I've been discussing it with clients for years, and Negroponte's book was published in 1995. Nevertheless, I thought the similarities between our constructs were interesting and complementary.

In Chapter 2, I talked about a new consumer value proposition—time value. In Chapter 4, I talked about the transformation of traditional value propositions including brands. One observation that was made at the Forum, which I didn't articulate clearly in either of these chapters, was the use of brand as a vehicle to deliver the time-value proposition to consumers. Although this may be intuitively obvious, I thought it warranted further mention here. If a consumer can trust in your brand, your brand then becomes a vehicle for delivering time. By eliminating the need to shop, the consumer can save time. Positioning your brand as a time-saver in this way, I'm convinced, will be one of the major components of branding and brand management in the digital marketplace. As Lloyd Ward put it, "I think brands will be a time saver for folks . . . with the explosion and proliferation of information, how do you organize it and deal with it and ultimately make decisions?" His answer (and my answer as well) is often *brands* and the assurance the consumer can have in trusting a brand and realizing the time savings resulting from that trust.

On the topic of intelligent products, Arno Penzias made several interesting observations. The first was his example of a very content atom type of physical product, cement, that has been transformed by a Mexican company. Cemex, a large Mexican cement producer, uses a computer routing and distribution algorithm, along with GPS and mobile communications technology (all forms of digital content), that routes the cement trucks (a traditional physical container) based on both their proximity to the requesting job site as well as the age of the cement. Once cement is in a truck, it has a finite life (measured in hours) before it becomes unusable. When they have a cement truck at a construction site and the site decides for some reason that they don't want the cement, the truck goes right back into the pool for distribution to another site. In using this combination of computing and communications, they've significantly reduced the number of cement trucks, increased profits, and significantly improved their competitive position. With their new technological approach to routing and distribution, they have effectively penetrated foreign markets and positioned themselves as a world leader in their industry. Companies that find innovative ways such as this to incorporate digital content into their traditional physical container offerings will be winners in the digital marketplace.

Arno made one other very insightful remark that I think is worth mentioning. We've all come to expect quality in the products we buy. In fact, it is pretty much universally understood that it is less expensive to make high-quality products than low-quality products due to the costs associated with servicing products. Arno used the example of the universal $10 watch that keeps perfect time. It would just be too expensive to make a $10 watch that didn't keep perfect time. So increasing quality isn't a new imperative for the digital economy—we all already expect and, for the most part, receive high quality. If we can't generate new value through increasing quality, how do we create the ever-increasing value that our shareholders and customers demand? Well, there are the traditional value propositions of brand and price, and the new value drivers of time and digital content. However, there's also a new feature that we can call *networkability*. We're probably all familiar with Metcalfe's Law (the value of the entire network to members increases exponentially as the number of nodes/members on the network increases). The typical examples are fax machines and now the Internet. Arno made the point that just as quality has become pervasive (companies can't afford *not* to make high-quality products), so too we'll see a pervasive adoption of networkable products, because it will just be too expensive to make stand-alone products. At some point, it will actually be *cheaper* to make the product networkable than stand-alone due to the inherent increased value of a networked product to both the customer and the producing company. Just as quality now has a negative cost, in the future so too will the networkability of a product have a negative cost. We can relate this point to what's often called the "knee" in the exponential curve of Metcalfe's Law—the point at which the value of joining the network exceeds the costs associated with joining the network. Now, obviously, there must be a reduction in both the costs of network access electronics as well as growth of the network itself. Nevertheless, it isn't much of a stretch to envision a home network in which a networked dishwasher is cheaper than a stand-alone dishwasher, because the networked dishwasher can cut down on service costs by communicating things like which part is broken before a repairman is dispatched. Anyone can already go to their local computer shop and buy a network interface card for about $10, and many already have broadband IP connections into the home as well as wireless LANs, so it's not hard to see this becoming a reality in the near future.

On Intelligent Markets

There's a major problem with our current marketplace. Although consumers have an incredibly powerful new channel for obtaining content/bits (the Internet), they're still stuck with the same old distribution network for obtaining their containers/atoms. They can either go to a brick-and-mortar store, or they can have someone deliver the atoms to their home, often at considerable expense. As Nicholas introduced the problem and resultant opportunity at the forum, ". . . the world of electronic commerce is going to explode at a rate that will be driven by a number of factors, but one of the biggest factors will be the delivery system. The physical delivery system is going to affect that market dramatically. All you need to do is when you walk out of a supermarket with a shopping cart, look at what's in that shopping cart and ask yourself, do you want every one of those items to arrive at your house separately via Airborne, UPS, FedEx, the Post Office or whatever? You'd have a traffic jam. So clearly it's not that we're all going to be buying everything direct and it's all going to be coming through FedEx or the equivalent, it's that there's going to be a lot of innovation in the transportation systems, so they can physically deliver this stuff." On some days of the week, I have a FedEx delivery, a UPS delivery, a U.S. Postal delivery, and a courier delivery of some kind. Just think about the inefficiencies and costs inherent in that, and you understand the need and opportunity present to develop a new way to move products to the consumer's home.

Elizabeth Mackay, senior managing director at Bear Stearns, in her discussion on shareholder value, highlighted the continued development of the outsourcing market in the areas of transportation, logistics, and distribution. As the Internet enables new retailers to set up shop in record time, the need for efficient distribution of those goods is becoming paramount. Guess who is in a strong position to lead the development of distribution systems for the consumer? Traditional brick-and-mortar retailers and others that have an existing connection to the consumer and the manufacturer. Companies such as Fingerhut, with their long-standing customer relationships and substantial warehousing and fulfillment networks, are receiving lofty stock market valuations as investors realize the role they can (and will) play in efficiently moving products to the consumer through electronic commerce. Other companies, such as Wal-Mart, JC Penney, and other mainline retailers with substantial distribution networks, are positioned to see these networks leveraged in some way as fulfillment arms for the new e-commerce channels to the consumer. Yet, these networks are still reliant on the customer coming to them, or on one of the existing package delivery providers, or in other instances a costly direct-to-consumer delivery model.

This is a topic that has stirred considerable discussion within A. T. Kearney. We've referred to it as the physical "last mile" to the consumer (analogous with the communications "last mile" that has traditionally been owned by the telecoms and increasingly now is being usurped by the cable companies and, in some cases, satellite companies). Clearly, we're in store for some major innovation in the area of product distribution to the consumer. Envision a staging area for the distribution of consumer goods that supports all types and sizes of product storage (dry goods, frozen/refrigerated, large, small, and so on). This new intermediary will receive and inspect all shipments (even U.S. mail) for a consumer, approve necessary payments, handle reject/return of defective merchandise, and store things appropriately. This intermediary could receive discounts on delivery from the package delivery services because they would provide a single point of delivery for numerous households and would be always open—no repeat delivery attempts. These cost savings and others could fund the service at a very marginal cost or no cost to the end consumer. They would deliver the products to the consumer's home at a prearranged time, or on demand, depending on the needs of the consumer. Alternatively, the consumer could stop by a drive-through window on the way home from work or on the weekend. It obviously makes sense to integrate this type of service with traditional retail services, namely grocery, to further enhance the value to the consumer and reduce the amount of time they spend in all shopping. We're seeing companies like Peapod and Streamline providing a subset of these services in specific areas, but none have yet integrated fully with the package provider networks (to my knowledge) to provide a complete link to the consumer, conquering this last physical mile efficiently.

On Intelligent Organizations

Stephen Covey spoke at length about the need for all of the employees of a company to have a central shared understanding of the company's different strategies. That the development of a shared understanding of a company's purpose, its value systems, its VAC, isn't necessarily a fast process. As Stephen put it, "I'm suggesting that the development of the criterion, that is the purpose, the value statement, you go very slow with. Once you have it inside people, then you can go fast in most every other way." In his study of organizations that have won the Demming Prize, Stephen found that the vast majority of the award-winning organizations had a clear and shared understanding of what was important. As Stephen stated, in companies that have ineffective organizations, "there is no deeply embedded cultural criterion about strategy, about what is truly significant. In a sense, there is no compass. There is no common sense of that which represents the value system and also the transcendent purposes or strategic goals of the organization." I would extrapolate from this that often these companies have no clear understanding of their VACs. The process of identifying your company's VACs, and the act of transforming the company into a VBO (shedding noncore activities and fortifying your core VACs), is one process whereby these shared values can be socialized and clearly communicated within the company.

Alvin Toffler led the discussion on intelligent organizations. In his opening remarks, he hearkened back to a type of organizational model that he discussed in his book, *Future Shock,* an *adhocracy*—basically, an organization without borders in which individuals self-organize and operate against a set of shared goals. On thinking about this, I was struck by how similar the concept of an adhocracy is to what I've called a VBO in Chapters 8 and 9 (more specifically, the Lego™ brand building blocks metaphor of a company having distinct competencies and mixing those competencies with external competencies to create a new, unique, and ultimately temporary organization in response to new market conditions). Although the development of the efficient market for all sorts of business services had not matured very far, and information technology (IT) hadn't yet punched holes in the walls of the classic organizations of the time, *Future Shock* did lay down some of the foundations for the VBO. Indeed, a VBO, as I've described it, is a form of adhocracy.

In recounting the history of organizational revolution, Alvin linked the advent of decentralized profit center–based organizations to the adoption of the PC in the early 1980s. However, all this did was copy the bureaucracy that existed within the larger company into the smaller profit centers. Without the proper use of these new networked PCs to effectively communicate and share information, and without the development of an effective and efficient competency-supplier network, the decentralized profit center–based organizations weren't able to deliver their expected value. It wasn't until organizations really began to implement IT to reduce transaction costs within the four walls, to open up the lines of efficient communication, and until the efficient markets started to develop for ever more granular business services that the possibility of the VBO was realized. I place this at sometime in the early to mid-1990s, and we're in the very early stages of this new form of organization.

In the discussions that followed Alvin's presentation, there was agreement that traditional forms of hierarchical organizations will have to be transformed for competitiveness in the new economy. Of paramount concern for many of the CEOs in attendance was again the issue of *trust* being one of the overriding criteria for these new networked VBOs. When an organization becomes highly virtual, when communications are electronic and asynchronous, when decisions must be made quickly, and the resultant actions synchronized for efficiency—all of these require an implicit trust that is perhaps easier to achieve in a traditional organization that is focused within the four walls. It made me think back to Stephen Covey's opening remarks on trust being the absolute requirement before a company, or perhaps more important, an extended organization, can operate effectively. Unfortunately, IT doesn't go very far in building trust. E-mail, voicemail, and EDI transactions may be wonderfully efficient for processing transactions and even facilitating decision making, but they're lousy mechanisms for building relationships and trust because they eliminate the human component of the transaction. Therefore, as companies move into the digital marketplace, as they increase the numbers of partners they interface with, as they virtualize their operations and their workforces, and increasingly sacrifice those inefficient and costly human interactions for faceless ones, they'll have to develop processes and forums to build that most fundamental of business relationships—trust. Much of the "trust-building" activity will likely be centered on things like reliability, responsiveness, flexibility, and exceeding expectations. Companies that live up to these qualities and characteristics will build trust for *what they do* in the digital economy instead of just who they are.

Related to trust is *loyalty,* and more specifically, the lack of loyalty that can result and is resulting in today's dynamic organizations. In an environment in which companies are forming and reforming, hiring and laying off, and acquiring and divesting, it's not easy to build an environment in which employees are secure in their positions and motivated to perform at their best. As one CEO put it, "People, no matter how much we tell them that they need to be modern and flexible and face up to the realities of the new world, are still as eager as ever to have some kind of security and some kind of predictability in their environment. And these old values will not disappear unless we succeed in supplying something to replace that old sense of security and protection." These sentiments were widely held among the CEOs—that while we all understand the dynamics of the new market at some level, the fundamental human (that is, employee) need to belong and to have a sense of security still exists and is not being adequately met by many of these new organizations. Stan Davis and Christopher Meyer talk a lot about the concept of "free agency" in their book *Blur.* This is simply a view of the VBO from the perspective of the individual— an idea I mentioned briefly in Chapters 8 and 9. However, free agency (looking at yourself as a free agent who provides some specific skills/value operating in a free market) is a lonely way to exist and, in some ways, only highlights the concerns expressed by the CEOs at the forum. I think one answer to this dilemma is to apply the "habits" concepts that Stephen Covey discusses in his books. Having a strong sense of self-worth (free agency) must be complemented by a sense of culture and shared purpose within these new digital organizations. One tool to encourage a sense of belonging is stock options. Providing the opportunity for equity ownership and its potential for growth was highlighted by several of the CEOs as a very potent tool for supporting the sense of unity, belonging, and purpose, in addition to encouraging positive attitudes, which, taken together, leads to the desired behavioral outcome.

During the discussion on intelligent organizations, and specifically the VBO, many of the CEOs discussed the disparities that are growing within their organizations related to value creation and more specifically, pay. In software companies, the R&D staff are getting between 10 percent and 15 percent annual raises, whereas the financial/accounting group gets 5 percent raises. Similar disparities were highlighted by other CEOs in other industries. In the past, this might have created consternation within the organizations, but increasingly, employees understand that this is a fact—the market at work within their company. Do you want to get 10 percent to 15 percent raises? Develop your skills and move into R&D. I would hypothesize that organizations that are seeing these types of disparities within their organizations and that aren't dealing well with them are primed to implement a VBO model— to drive down their transaction costs and disintegrate their organizations into their constituent parts, to take these parts that are creating different levels of value and compartmentalize them and shop for the low-value competencies and capabilities from other providers in the marketplace. The real question for the software company might not be, "How do we make our finance/ accounting department happy with 5 percent raises when the software guys get 15 percent?" The more appropriate question might be, "Why do we have a finance/accounting department at all when it's so obviously not our core VAC?" One place where the market is not having as great an effect is within technical programs on university campuses. Although the demand (and, correspondingly, the pay) of students with technical degrees such as engineering and computer science is at an all-time high (and is higher than almost all other disciplines), the percentage of students choosing these programs continues to drop. Unfortunately, this trend is expected to continue, and at this point no solution has been found.

If there is any metric that would indicate a potential shift to what I've called a VBO, it would be the increasing adoption of outsourcing. Implementing a VBO means focusing narrowly on your VACs and obtaining all other competencies required to fashion a valuable offering for the market from other companies, often in the form of outsourcing relationships. Elizabeth Mackay with Bear Stearns highlighted the continued growth in outsourcing, particularly outside of the United States. Not surprising, the largest growth continues to be in IT as companies realize that IT is critical to their success, but that they aren't equipped to deliver the required level of competency. Other areas of outsourcing growth continue to be in transportation, procurement, call center management, human resources, and finance/accounting.

If there is any metric that would indicate whether the VBO is being recognized and rewarded in the marketplace, it would be the stock market valuations of companies that move in this direction versus those that move in the opposite direction. In a recent study of corporate mergers conducted by A. T. Kearney, it was found that the majority of mergers actually hurt shareholder value. Of those mergers that did result in increased shareholder value, the majority were between companies that were in the same or a very closely related business. In a related study, Bear Stearns looked at the share prices of companies that were part of mergers before and after the merger compared with the share prices of companies that were divested or sold off (along with the parent's share price) before and after the divestiture. The result—companies that spin off stand-alone businesses create significantly greater shareholder value than the S&P 500, particularly in the spun-off entity. Companies that are part of mergers produce significantly less shareholder value than the S&P 500. I believe the lesson underlying all of this data is clear. Wall Street is rewarding companies that focus on their core VACs. If companies have multiple competencies that can operate independently, then the parts are valued greater than the combined entity. If a company is going to get bigger through mergers, staying within your narrow competency is rewarded over diversifying (or "deworsifying," as Peter Lynch puts it) into disparate areas or industries. All of this supports the move to the VBO I described in Chapters 8 through 10.

On Intelligent Society

Nicholas Negroponte made considerable commentary on the state of the digital marketplace throughout the world. One point of his that I found particularly interesting was his criteria for countries/societies that will be successful in the digital economy. He laid out three criteria:

1. Citizens have respect for the "small guy," or the underdog. They respect start-ups, entrepreneurs, those that are struggling against the odds.

2. The economy is able to operate in a free, open, and dynamic atmosphere. In many instances, this may have been previously demonstrated in a robust underground economy.

3. Citizens have a "healthy" disrespect for authority. This doesn't mean they want anarchy, but they don't want heavy regulation or "big brother" watching their every move.

Nicholas made the point that countries that exhibit these three characteristics are primed for success in the digital economy. Obviously, this is a very subjective judgment, but I tend to agree with his analysis. Countries such as Italy and the Latin American nations do, indeed, have the social and cultural requirements for success in the digital economy if their telecommunications infrastructure and economic fundamentals can be developed sufficiently to support wide access to the global network.

Negroponte made another interesting observation related to the evolution of our intelligent society. He spoke about the growth of a new class that he termed the "digital homeless." Those that, as he put it, "hadn't done anything wrong except arrive on the planet at the wrong time, and they weren't part of this digital age." I've referred to this group as the *information have-nots* in Chapter 13, but the distinction is the same. Nicholas has observed that in the United States, the digital homeless is a quickly shrinking underclass as access to the Internet penetrates even the most disadvantaged groups. Although the Internet is becoming more accessible to all consumer segments, only 9 percent of the CEOs at the conference responded in the digital marketplace survey that their customers were digitally sophisticated. In short, although their customers (both end consumers and other companies) are increasingly adopting e-commerce and the Internet, the CEOs felt that they are still generally more focused on traditional ways of doing business. It will be interesting to ask the same question again next year and see if the results are the same.

Whereas the United States has a shrinking population of "digitally homeless," this is not the case in much of the underdeveloped world, or even some of the more developed countries, such as France and Germany. As Nicholas pointed out, developed countries, such as France, Switzerland, Austria, and Germany, have very low numbers of personal computers per capita when compared with the United States or the Scandinavian countries. The story here is that although companies obviously must craft channel strategies for the increasingly digitally savvy consumers, much of the global marketplace will continue to be digitally disconnected, or digitally "homeless," well into the first part of the twenty-first century.

If there was one speaker that really drilled on the topic of our intelligent and transforming society, it was Alvin Toffler. Although the CEO Forum was clearly focused on business issues as they related to the digital marketplace, Alvin clearly feels that the societal impacts of the digital marketplace "may turn out to be the most important consequence ultimately of the digital revolution."

In Chapter 13, I discussed the government and how it has traditionally treated people as members of groups, such as rich and poor or black and white. I took the position that the government now has both the technology and the responsibility to no longer treat these groups as groups per se, rather to directly affect the underlying inequities that we are attempting to address through legislation, the classic example being affirmative action. The goals of affirmative action are noble, but legislating the blanket treatment of black versus white, or any minority versus majority, does not inherently get at the underlying inequities. Alvin labeled this trend "demassification" and extended it beyond government to business and all other pieces of the economy and society. The ability to treat people as individuals rather than masses, to target market, and to cater to the needs and desires of each individual person—this is demassification and it is happening on a grand scale as the digital marketplace unfolds. As Alvin put it, "One size misfits all."

Alvin made one other observation that I really liked and I want to share it with you. As companies virtualize their workforces and more and more people begin to work at home, as people begin to shop more and more at home, and as we begin to get more of our entertainment at home, what's the end result? Well, quite obviously, we'll be spending more time at home. In a very optimistic twist on the digital economy, Alvin sees an increase in the ties we develop to our local communities and our families as we spend this additional time at home. It's a nice notion. I certainly hope it comes true.

On Maximizing Shareholder Value

Well, you can't get a group of CEOs together and not talk about shareholder value. It was universal among the attendees that stockholders and their representatives have become increasingly demanding, particularly in the United States, and increasingly throughout the globe. Elizabeth Mackay led the discussion on maximizing shareholder value in the digital marketplace. In Chapter 5 of this book, I highlighted one of the obvious sources of value in the marketplace—the shift in value from hard-asset companies to soft-asset companies. Although it wasn't hard to support that assertion with quantitative data (refer to Figures 5.4 and 5.5), I thought Elizabeth showed two pictures that really drove the point home for me in a very tangible way. In Figure 14.1,

FIGURE 14.1
Table of contents from the 1972 edition of the *S&P Analysis' Handbook*.

INDUSTRIALS

	Page
425 INDUSTRIALS	1
AEROSPACE	2
AIR TRANSPORT	3
ALUMINNUM	4
AUTOMOBILES	5
Excluding General Motors	6
Auto Accessories	7
Trucks	8
BEVERAGES	
Brewers	9
Distillers	10
Soft Drinks	11
BUILDING MATERIALS	
Composite	12
Air Conditioning	13
Cement	14
Heating and Plumbing	15
Roofing and Wallboard	16
CHEMICALS	17
Excluding du Pont	18
COAL—BITUMINOUS	19
CONFECTIONERY	20
CONTAINERS	
Metal and Glass	21
Paper	22
COPPER	23
COSMETICS	24
DRUGS	25
ELECTRICAL EQUIPMENT	26
ELECTRICAL HOUSEHOLD APPLIANCES	27
ELECTRONIC COMPANIES	28
ELECTRONIC MAJOR COMPANIES	29
FINANCE COMPANIES	30

	Page
SMALL LOANS	31
FOODS	
Composite	32
Biscuit Baker	33
Bread and Cake Bakers	34
Canned	35
Corn Refiners	36
Daily Products	37
Meat Packing	38
Packaged	39
FOREST PRODUCTS	40
GOLD MINING	41
HOME FURNISHING	42
HOTEL-MOTEL	43
LEAD AND ZINC	44
MACHINE TOOLS	45
MACHINERY	
Agricultural	46
Composite (Excl. Agricultural)	47
Construction and Material Handling	48
Industrial	49
Machinery & Services—Oil Well	50
Specialty	51
Steam Generating	52
METAL FABRICATING	53
METALS—MISCELANEUOS	54
MOTION PICTURES	55
OFFICE AND BUSINESS EQUIPMENT	56
Excluding IBM	57
OFFSHORE DRILLING	58
OIL	
Composite	59
Crude Producers	60
Integrated Domestic	61

	Page
Integrated International	62
PAPER	63
PUBLISHING	64
RADIO-TV	
Broadcasters	65
Manufacturers	66
RAILROAD EQUIPMENT	67
REAL ESTATE	68
RESTAURANTS	69
RETAIL STORES	
Composite	70
Department Stores	71
Food Chains	72
Mail Order & General Chains	72
Variety Stores	74
SHOES	75
SOAPS	76
STEEL	77
Excluding U. S. Steel	78
SUGAR	
Composite	79
Beet Refiners	80
Cane Refiners	81
SULPHUR PRODUCERS	82
TEXTILES	
Apparel Manufacturers	83
Synthetic Fibers	84
Textile Products	85
TIRES AND RUBBER GOODS	86
TOBACCO	
Cigarette Manufacturers	87
VENDING MACHINES	88

I've included the table of contents from the 1972 edition of the *S&P Analysis Handbook*. Looking at this, you see the concentration in foods (as Elizabeth pointed out, there are categories for both "Biscuit Bakers" and "Bread and Cake Bakers," which seems almost funny now), machinery, all types of equipment, and basic consumer products. Compare this with the 1998 table of contents in Figure 14.2 and we get a very different picture. There's been an incredible shift to computers, health care, services, financial industries and the like—all what we would call soft-asset industries. I've never seen a clearer exhibit of this shift in the U.S. economy and in stock market value. Clearly, a path to creating shareholder value is to understand your soft assets and make sure that they are understood in the marketplace.

So soft-assets, or content/bit-based, companies are obviously primed for increased shareholder value. However, that doesn't mean that you need to be in the computer or Internet industries to have solid stock performance. Integrating leading-edge content through IT is a strategy that is building success in every industry, even the container/atom industries. Going back to Cemex as an example, they quit competing on the quality of their cement long ago. As with the $10 watch, the quality of the cement is a given, but the ability to deliver it at exactly the right time in exactly the right quantity with consistency has allowed Cemex to become one of the largest cement companies in the world, and they did it through IT. Is IT really the answer in and of itself, though? What Cemex actually did is understand that they weren't in the business of making cement, but in the business of delivering that cement to their customers exactly as the customer wanted it (right quantity, timely delivery, the cement wasn't to old/hot, and more). In other words, they understood their core VAC (which happened to be highly reliant on IT), and exploited it to dominate their local market and, increasingly, the global market. In the future, Cemex could conceivably exit the concrete manufacturing business and focus exclusively on this competency of effective delivery.

Perhaps most important, Wall Street understands this and handsomely rewards companies that have developed a strong VAC and then exploit that competency in their industry and even across industries. In her discussion, Elizabeth highlighted that the very way that analysts talk about stocks is changing. The new rules (or perhaps lack thereof) that govern the valuation of Internet stocks are being applied to other industries as well. Present value, discounted cash flow, economic value added, franchise values—these are the new measures that are being used to evaluate stocks in the digital marketplace, and increasingly, these are the measures that CEOs and other executives must monitor and use to drive behavior and decision making. These measures move away from the traditional GAAP accounting and income-reporting processes and, instead, focus on the actual economic earnings, the cash earnings of a business. Another major focus is on the effective, productive use of capital. The return on capital, as measured by economic value added, is increasingly being seen as a more reliable measure of share price.

Closing Comments

If you've read this book, at the very least you understand and probably believe that we're in the midst of a revolution—a sea of change in the way the economy works and the ways that businesses must operate to survive. I've spent the last 280-plus pages giving you my best ideas on how you should change the way you think about operating your business in the digital economy, and I've supported these ideas with evidence and case examples where appropriate. The topics of intelligent products, markets, and organizations were a logical way for me to group and structure these ideas, but things are never quite that clean in the business world, and I suspect you'll have priorities that touch on each of these areas, but in new and interesting combinations.

In my dealings with clients over the past many years, I understand and appreciate how difficult it is to take concepts such as these and make them practical by applying them to real-world situations. I've tried to keep the advice here practical and very doable. As the old joke goes, "Those that can't do, teach." Although I write this tongue in cheek, my intent is to ensure you that I don't underestimate for a second the complexity of the task laid out before you. However, don't believe that these actions are in any way optional, that somehow you can slowly observe and evolve your way into the digital economy without making major changes to your traditional ways of doing business. As with any revolution, there will be those who profit, and then there will be the casualties, especially among those who ignore the wave or move too slowly. Although many of the consulting engagements I've been involved in have been tough, none have been tougher than those intended to prepare clients for the competitive landscape of the digital marketplace. I invite you to visit the web site we've established for this book, to submit your ideas, share your stories, give us your criticism, and certainly to let us know if we can help in any way. You can find us at http://www.atkearney.com/DigitalStrategy.

Appendices

Digital Marketplace Diagnostic

"What's up, Doc?"

—Warner Brothers spokesrabbit Bugs Bunny, c. 1968

THIS DIAGNOSTIC TOOL WAS DESIGNED TO PROVIDE YOU WITH A USER-FRIENDLY WAY TO help you understand your business's "state of digital readiness" along three critical dimensions: marketplace, organization, and products. Once you understand these critical issues, you'll be ready to begin the real work of preparing your organization for the demands of the new digital economy.

Please understand, however, that this tool will *not* give you hard, quantitative results that will, in turn, provide you with some blinding insight. You need consultants for that (shameless plug).

Still, if you take a few moments to go through the following exercises, you'll not only understand your business better, but will also begin to sense what early steps you can take in leading your company toward mastery of the digital marketplace.

The Digital Marketplace Readiness Dashboard

Figure A.1 shows the digital marketplace readiness dashboard.

FIGURE A.1
The digital marketplace readiness dashboard.

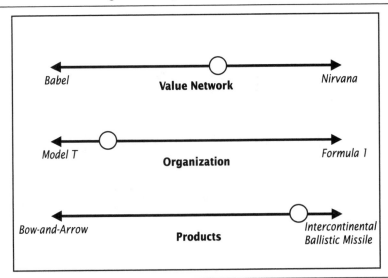

Digital Value Network Positioning Gauge

Let's begin with a discussion of the digital value network (DVN) gauge. At the extremes of this gauge are two states, which we have termed *Babel* and *Nirvana*.

> *Babel.* An organization whose DVN gauge reads "Babel" (as in the Tower of) is currently unable to operate in a digital marketplace. Such an organization employs little information technology (IT) and remains disconnected from potential DVN partners.
>
> *Nirvana.* Organizations whose gauge reads "Nirvana" are well positioned for connectivity in the digital marketplace. Their business model is extendible, and positions them as a value-added player in a DVN. Information on what customers really want is instantly accessible throughout the value network. This kind of organization is well connected and agile enough to adapt to the changing demands of this new environment.

Assessing Your Digital Value Network Positioning

This assessment will help you evaluate how well you are poised for success in the digital economy in terms of your ability to operate effectively in a highly connected digital marketplace. Using the following questions as a guide, plot your organization's position on the DVN gauge.

1. Where in your value network is the lion's share of the value being captured? Who controls the richest base of soft assets?

2. Are any of the DVN roles mentioned in Chapter 3 emerging within your value network? Who (if anyone) is becoming an infomediary? A DFP provider?

3. How are supply chains linking up within your value network to increase its pipeline velocity?

4. Are you threatened by the specter of disintermediation? Where in your value network is disintermediation likely to occur?

5. Is your existing business model imposing location constraints on your growth?

6. Is your emerging DVN at risk from misaligned interests of the container providers and the content providers?

7. Is your organization too vertically integrated? Do you own more of the supply chain than cost-efficiency optimization dictates you should?

8. Is your current role in the value network profitable? Is it sustainable? Is it optimal given your value-added competencies?

9. How good a job are you doing in your current role as a provider of value to consumers? Are competitors better at this role than you are?

Organization Gauge

Next, let's review the organization gauge. At the extremes of this gauge are two states which we have termed *Model T* and *Formula 1*.

Model T. A "Model T" organization will quickly be made obsolete in the digital marketplace. Organizations whose marketplace gauge reads "Model T" currently employ many non-VACs. Such organizations tend to be vertically integrated and use little outsourcing. Additional transaction costs incurred by such an organizational structure lead these organizations to underperform in the digital environment.

Formula 1. A "Formula 1" organization is a well-oiled, high-performance machine poised for success in the digital marketplace. It runs a very lean organization focused on its VACs. These companies work aggressively to reduce transaction costs between VACs and non-core functions, and participate in numerous innovative outsourcing partnerships.

Assessing Your Organization

Evaluate how well your organization is poised for success in the digital marketplace, compared with the theoretical ideal presented in Chapter 8. Using the following questions as a guide, plot your organization's position on the organization gauge in Figure A.1.

1. Are you realizing the benefits of a network organizational structure, or is your organizational structure accurately described as hierarchical, geographic, matrix, product-based, or geography-based?

2. Are your coordination and control processes stifling entrepreneurial incentives?

3. Does the overhead associated with your coordination and control processes outweigh the value-creating benefits?

4. Do you understand your VACs? Have you ever identified them?

5. Are you handling most noncore functionality in-house?

6. Are any of the following manifestations of resistance to change inhibiting your organizational effectiveness?

   - Denial that change is necessary
   - Confusion about how change will solve the problem
   - Fear and anxiety about the outcome
   - Lack of trust in the future
   - Organizational inertia

Products Gauge

Finally, let's review the products gauge. At the extremes of this gauge are two states that we have termed *Bow-and-Arrow* and *Intercontinental Ballistic Missile*. (If the digital marketplace is a battlefield, then a company's products are its weapons . . .)

Bow-and-Arrow. Organizations whose marketplace gauge reads "Bow-and-arrow" do not understand their customers' needs. Such organizations are focused on operational efficiency rather than delivering value to the customer. These organizations also do not employ IT strategically to pursue value-added activities, such as gathering customer intelligence and streamlining product development cycles.

Intercontinental Ballistic Missile. Organizations with products in this extreme state are dynamic, innovative, and plugged into their customers' needs. These organizations understand the transitory nature of customer preferences in the digital economy and employ IT strategically to anticipate and deliver value against those needs.

Assessing Your Product or Service Offering

Evaluate the value proposition of your product or service offering relative to your competition *from the perspective of your customers.* Using the following questions as a guide, plot your position on the products gauge in Figure A.1.

1. Do you have a clear understanding of your product or service offering in terms of its component parts: *container* and *content?* How about your competitors' product or service offering?

2. Do your competitors' products contain inherently more content (embedded intelligence) than yours?

3. How *customized* is your offering compared with that of your competitors?

4. How flexible and competitive is your *pricing strategy?* How closely do you monitor your competitors' changes in price?

5. Relative to competitors, how much *time value* does your product/ service generate for your customers?

6. What does the customer value about doing business with you (consider physical and virtual elements of your value proposition if appropriate)?

Now What Do You Do with the Information on the Dashboard?

A quick glance at the dashboard reveals the greatest opportunities for quick improvement. (Obviously, there is always room for improvement in all three areas; the dashboard simply helps you prioritize strategic initiatives.)

Here, we present a list of thought-provoking questions that will help you get an idea of what to do to improve your competitive position with regard to markets/value network, organization, and products.

Transforming Value Network Positioning

Think about the DVN that is or will soon be emerging around you. Where do you want to position yourself within it? If you perceive your business environment to be Babel, you are essentially admitting that you are *not equipped* to compete effectively in the digital marketplace. Therefore, you will need to focus a great deal of energy on *getting connected* with both your customers and suppliers.

If, on the other hand, you're already surrounded by a Nirvana-like value network, you are looking more to *fortify and perpetuate* your position within your emerging DVN, and should be looking for ways to grow and enhance the entire DVN. You may also look for other DVNs in which to operate. In either case, this list of thought-provoking questions should assist you in formulating a strategy for improving your value network positioning:

1. If your current role in your value network is suboptimal, what role should you be playing in the emerging DVN?

2. In what ways can we apply the Internet and other technologies for competitive advantage? (For example, can we perform any of the following activities electronically: process customer orders, place orders with suppliers, reduce transaction costs, increase customer satisfaction, reduce the cost of customer service, eliminate duplicate tasks, streamlining A/P or A/R functions, skip stops in the supply chain or eliminate intermediate billing, reduce inventory or overhead, improve cash flow, capture and exploit customer preferences, increase revenue through cross-selling, and so forth)

3. What technologies, strategies, or partnerships can be pursued to:
   • Increase pipeline velocity and cash flow?
   • Decrease product development cycle/time to market?
   • Improve your ability to translate customer insight into product or service innovation?
   • Set up a digital function platform (DFP) in the emerging DVN?
   • Initiate infomediary services within the emerging DVN?

4. Which aspects or elements of your business model are reaching economic obsolescence? Look for opportunities to enhance or redefine the digital value chain.

Transforming the Organization

If you characterized your organization as a Model T, then you've certainly got your work cut out for you. You may be *too vertically integrated*. You must push hard to *reduce transaction costs* so that you are poised to outsource noncore functions. You must take a hard look at your VACs from the eyes of the customer.

If, on the other hand, you fancy your organization a Formula 1 racing car, you must *revisit your VACs*. Also, you may consider employing risk management/mitigation strategies in your dealings with your value network partners. For example, you can identify backup partners, develop contingency plans for the core elements of your emerging DVN. In either case, perusing the following steps should assist you in formulating a strategy for improving your organization.

GENERAL STEPS

1. Reorganize to better:
   - Facilitate information flows and decision making.
   - Define the authority and responsibility for work defined by teams, departments, and divisions.
   - Create the desired levels of integration and coordination among these entities.
2. Refocus on:
   - VACs.
   - Reduction of transaction costs.
   - Evolution of efficient markets.
3. Apply IT strategically to reduce transaction costs at the interfaces to noncritical functions and capabilities.

SPECIFIC STEPS

1. Define your organization's current VACs and the skills, technologies, and capabilities that enable them.
2. Move to insource activities that support the VACs, and outsource activities that do not. Refer to Figures 9.6 though 9.8 in Chapter 9 for ideas on how to proceed.

MORE SPECIFICALLY, A SUMMARY OF THE TWELVE-STEP PROCESS

1. Identify your VACs.
   - If you removed your competence from the value chain, would the end consumer perceive a reduction in the product's value?
   - Does your competence add value to the end product that cannot be provided by a competitor at similar cost and quality levels?
   - Is your value proposition significant enough to induce a customer to switch to your product?

- Is the market for the competence increasing, and is your share of that market also increasing?

2. Identify and categorize all non-VAC business activities according to whether they are currently performed in-house or outsourced.

3. Determine the most likely course of action for each non-VAC activity.

4. Design the value-based organization around the critical dimensions of business impact, market complexity, and relative position.

5. Identify the transaction costs between the VAC activities and all other business functions (non-VAC activities).

6. Continually reduce transaction costs between VAC and non-VAC activities through the strategic application of information technology and the implementation of best-practice business processes.

7. Examine the marketplace for more efficient capabilities in which to outsource your non-VAC activities.

8. Continuously identify and develop new value-added competencies in response to anticipated future market/consumer needs.

9. Employ risk management strategies for outsourced capabilities.

10. Continually create and update performance measures.

11. Continuously use information technology to enable business strategy.

12. Undertake change management processes and techniques to ensure successful migration from the current organization to the value-based organization.

Transforming Products

If you rated your product or service offering close to the bow-and-arrow end of the scale, you're simply not focused on innovation. You must get connected to the customer. What are the new value propositions? Can you offer more time value? Perhaps you can discover new mix-and-match opportunities by separating your container from the value-adding content in your offering. The essential strategy is to focus hard on improving the product or service offering, first by listening to the customer (through market research, focus groups, and so on) and then by building more intelligence into their value proposition.

If you are peddling the intercontinental ballistic missile of the market, you would do well to be aware of the transitory nature of your advantage. Look to springboard into nontraditional markets for your product or service offering. In either case, these questions should serve as food for thought for transforming your product or service offering:

1. What can you do to enhance your value proposition (consider physical container and digital content elements of the offering)?

2. What opportunities exist to generate *more time value* for your customers? How can you move to the ultimate way of delivering this value—automatic execution—and achieve zero customer interaction?

3. What opportunities exist for you to improve your value proposition by *increasing the content* (embedded intelligence) of your product or service offering?

4. How can you *streamline your product development* process?
   - By establishing the infrastructure, processes, and culture to continually capture market information?
   - By continuously evaluating technical solutions and the alignment of each to the needs of your customers?

5. How can you gain insight into *new product/service offerings* by separating your product or service offering into its container and content components?

6. How can you best *communicate the value* of your offering in terms of these new value paradigms (container/content and time value)?

7. Is a *mass customization* strategy appropriate for your product/service offering?

Rules for the Road

Once you've gauged your organization's digital readiness, you will find yourself in one of the three following categories.

Complete Overhaul

If your gauges favored the left side of the dashboard, your organization is in need of radical change. Begin with an honest appraisal of your business' value proposition and your organization's capabilities. Next, look outward at both your customers and competition, and ask what action is needed to add value to your customers and distinguish yourself from the competition.

To bridge the gap between these two positions, you will need to employ a fundamentally new approach to connect with your customer, unite and streamline your organization, and position yourself as a player within a DVN.

Tune-Up

If your gauges favored the middle of the dashboard, then you are not currently prepared for the challenges of the digital economy. Improvements on three fronts are needed. First, you should work to build a tighter coupling between your customers' needs and your product's value proposition. Second, you should look for opportunities within your organization to eliminate activities that do not deliver value to your customers. Also, take steps to increase the effectiveness of technology deployed within your organization to both increase the level of enterprisewide coordination, and to develop stronger links with your business partners. Finally, you should evaluate potential roles that your organization could play in a DVN and work to develop capabilities that will help you excel in those roles.

Routine Maintenance

If your gauges favored the right side of the dashboard, vigilance is the operative term for you to protect your current position and continue looking for new opportunities. By leveraging your current position, maintain a watchful eye on the digital landscape for nontraditional entrants and marketplace shifts. Work aggressively to combat complacency and keep your organization motivated. Fully capitalizing on your current success will place you in a prime position to identify and acquire a leading position in the next marketplace opportunity.

Hard-Asset and Soft-Asset Companies in the Digital Value Chain

Price/Earnings Ratio Analysis of Hard-Asset versus Soft-Asset Companies

We compiled the PE ratios for the 10 largest public companies in each of the major subcategories under hard-asset and soft-asset companies (for example, advertising is a subcategory of soft-asset companies—see description below).

Hard-Asset Companies

Raw materials ($216 billion). This includes major raw materials categories, such as agriculture, farming, forestry, livestock, mining, and petroleum.

Intermediate goods ($817 billion). Products that make up other products (subcomponents) are covered by this category, including paper, lumber, chemicals, agricultural fertilizers, plastics, iron, metal, farm materials, industrial machinery, *computers and office equipment,* electrical wiring, trucks, buses, aircraft, and other transport equipment.

Consumer products ($926 billion). This category includes most major consumer goods manufacturing operations, such as food, tobacco, furniture, newspapers, books, drugs (including genetically engineered products for crops when reported under the revenues of a drug company), footwear, housewares, appliances, automobiles, eyewear, photo equipment, and miscellaneous manufacturing (for example, toys).

Retail ($451 billion). The retail segment has giant general merchandisers like Wal-Mart and Sears; grocery stores like HEB, Kroger, and Safeway; as well as wholesale retailers like PriceCostco and Home Depot.

Consumer services ($348 billion). This segment includes all personal services for consumers, including restaurants, hotels, dry cleaning, personal repair, and auto repair.

Soft-Asset Companies

Information services ($524 billion). Information services firms include public accountants, employment services, and consultants.

Media ($130 billion). This includes all broadcast media (radio, television, and film) and magazines, newspapers, and other print publications.

Advertising ($24 billion). This category includes advertising agencies as well as PR firms and consumer market research organizations.

Software/processors and networks ($241 billion). This category includes companies such as Microsoft (software) and EDS (processing services). This also includes telecommunications networks such as AT&T and other long-distance networks, as well as the Baby Bells.

Wholesale ($501 billion). This includes all firms that sell products to retailers. The industry is not concentrated. The top 30 firms account for only 20 percent of all sales.

Freight ($241 billion). The freight sector moves goods from one point to another along the supply chain.

Financial services ($444 billion). This includes the banking, insurance, and securities industries.

Understanding the Input/Output Table Measure

The Input/Output measure only includes the value actually added at a given stage in the supply chain. For example, the "Consumer Products" category, previously described, does not include total revenues. First, the Department of Commerce subtracts the *input* values which consumer products companies receive by purchasing intermediate goods, raw materials, and soft-asset services to arrive at net value added. (*Note:* The Virtual Value Chain in Figure 5.5 does not include GDP for health care, government services, utilities, construction, and education.)

Traditional Organizational Structure Overview

COMPANIES WITH TRADITIONAL ORGANIZATIONAL STRUCTURES ARE THOSE WHOSE ORGA-nizational structure resemble one of the following: functional, product-based, matrix, and geographic/multinational.[1]

Hierarchical functional structure was designed to standardize routine and repetitive tasks so that management could concentrate on handling exceptions. It is prototypical of the industrial age–way of doing business, which worked very well for a hundred years or so.

Product-based structures are designed to align employees along product lines, alleviating the complexity that would exist under a purely functional design in which functional groups would be responsible for handling all of the firm's products (consumer products companies).

Matrix structures normally align employees along both functional and product lines, requiring that they report to two or more superiors. This design is an attempt to become more market responsive, theoretically creating an environment in which the employee is able to make better decisions based on information from both functional and product disciplines (sales forces, high-tech companies).

Geographic structures are organized around regional and district offices (airlines, insurance companies), whereas *multinational structures* are designed to maintain coordination across functions, geographic areas, and products, and resemble matrix structures with the added dimension of geographic responsibilities (oil and gas companies, snack food manufacturers).

More recently, the following organizational structures have evolved.

Horizontal structures are defined as a cross-functional organization designed around the end-to-end work flows of the company's core processes. An essential design principle of horizontal organizations is to formally structure roles, resources, and day-to-day operations around these core processes rather than functional operations. A horizontal organization requires more than just identifying, reengineering, or managing

FIGURE C.1
Organization model analysis.

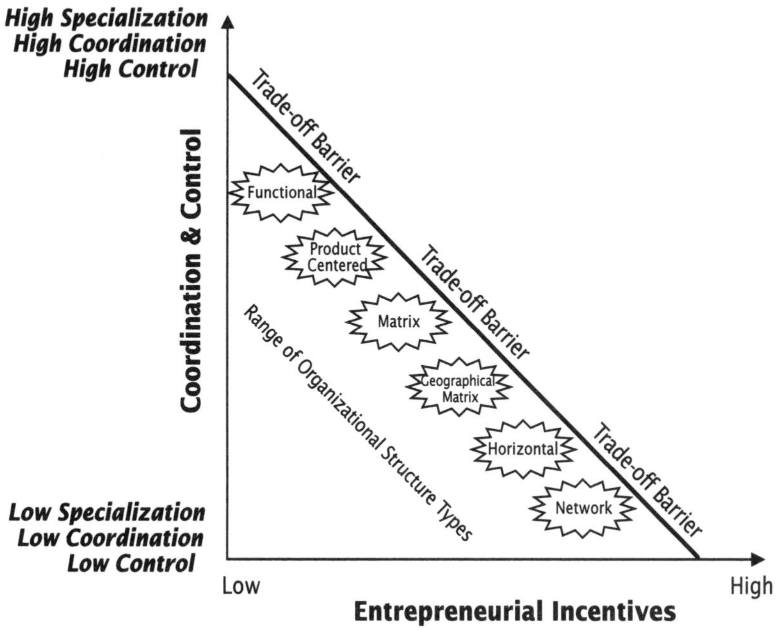

processes; it requires designing and developing formal departments, called *core process groups,* centered on these processes.

Network structures focus on sharing authority, responsibility, and resources among people and departments that must cooperate and communicate frequently to achieve common goals. Network structures consist of individual autonomous groups that have the responsibility of creating value by focusing on specific activities. The central focus of the network design is on the individual employees within a group as drivers of business activity, and it relies on the network of individual groups to create value (see Figure C.1).

NOTES

Chapter 1

1. Tapscott, Don. *Growing Up Digital: The Rise of the Net Generation.* New York: McGraw Hill, 1997.

2. From the A. T. Kearney research study, *Strategic Information Technology and the CEO Agenda,* 1997.

Chapter 2

1. Evans, Philip B., and Thomas S. Wurster. "Strategy and the New Economics of Information." *Harvard Business Review,* September–October 1998: 71.

2. "The Emerging Digital Economy", Secretariat on Electronic Commerce, U.S. Department of Commerce, 1998, p. 14.

3. Bond, James T., Ellen Galinsky, and Jennifer E. Swanberg. *The 1997 National Study of the Changing Workforce.* New York: Families and Work Institute, 1997.

4. *Consumer Pulse* and *Consumer Outlook '98.* New York: Kurt Salmon Associates, 1998. *http://www.kurtsalmon.com.*

5. Hey, Kenneth R., and Peter D. Moore. *The Caterpillar Doesn't Know: How Personal Change Is Creating Organizational Change,* p. 52. New York: The Free Press, 1998.

6. Robinson, John, and Geoffrey Godbey. *Time for Life.* State College, PA: The Pennsylvania State University, 1997.

7. Weber, Alan M. "Are You on Digital Time?" *Fast Company,* February–March 1999: 116.

8. Bianchi, Alessandra. "Innovation: The Ultimate Frequent Flyer." *Inc. Online,* May 1, 1996: 125.

9. Northstar-at-Tahoe Ski Resort web page. *http://www.skinorthstar.com.*

10. Kuusela, Sami. "The Postman Always Clicks Twice." *Business 2.0,* September 1998.

Chapter 3

1. Ford Motor Company archives.

2. Katel, Peter. "Bordering on Chaos." *Wired* magazine, July 1997.

3. Russ, Carey. "OnStar: What Is It?" The Auto Channel, January 15, 1998. *http://www.theautochannel.com/news/date/19980115/news009219.html.*

4. Jensen, Cheryl. "When You Wish Upon OnStar." The Car Connection, April 20, 1998. *http://www.thecarconnection.com/cc_Onsta.htm.*

5. Maier, Dirk E., and Mike D. Montross. "Aeration Technology for Moisture Management." Agribiz.com News and Articles. *http://www.agribiz.com/fbFiles/tNews/grainquality/aeration.htm.*

6. Kahney, Leander. "The Coolest Internet Appliance." *Wired News,* February 12, 1999.

Chapter 4

1. Meeker, Mary, and Sharon Pearson. *Morgan Stanley U.S. Investment Research: Internet Retail,* p. 4-2+. Morgan Stanley, 1997.

2. "The Best Web Sites." *Business Week,* December 21, 1998: 90.

3. "Sun Community Server helps drive traffic to Web sites." Sun Microsystems Press Release, February 2, 1998.

4. Clark, Don. "Intel's Grudging Concession of Chip's Flaws Angers Users." *Wall Street Journal Europe,* November 25, 1994: 8.

5. Kline, David. "Four rules for net success." *Upside,* February 16, 1998: 60.

6. "The Emerging Digital Economy," p. 42. Secretariat on Electronic Commerce, U.S. Department of Commerce, 1998.

7. "Consumer-Direct: Will Stores Survive?" *Progressive Grocer,* May 1997: 30. *www.progressivegrocer.com/consume4.htm.*

8. Ibid.

9. Kaye, Linda. "The Business of Product Development." *Cadence Plugged-In,* 3(3), January 1999.

Chapter 5

1. "Finding Middle Ground," *PC Week,* September 1997.

2. Slywotzky, Adrian J. *Value Migration—How to Think Several Moves Ahead of the Competition.* Boston: Harvard Business School Press, 1996.

3. *Source:* Institute of the Future, A. T. Kearney, and U.S. Department of Commerce Input/Output table.

4. Ibid.

Chapter 6

1. Brandenburger, Adam M., and Barry J. Nalebuff. *Co-Opetition: 1. A Revolutionary Mindset That Redefines Competition and Cooperation; 2. The Game Theory Strategy That's Changing the Game of Business.* New York: Doubleday, 1997.

2. Hagel, John, and Marc Singe. *Net Worth: Shaping Markets When Customers Make the Rules,* Boston: Harvard Business School Press, 1999. (Product Number 8893.)

3. Fabris, Peter. "EC Riders." *CIO Magazine,* June 15, 1997. *www.cio.com/archive/061597_commerce_print.html.*

Chapter 7

1. Bowersox, Donald, and Jim Morehouse. *21ˢᵗ Century Supply Chain.* Sound Business, 1996.

2. *The Economist,* May 1997.

Chapter 8

1. Hellriegel, Don, John W. Slocum, and Richard W. Woodman. *Organizational Behavior,* Eighth Edition, p. 504. Cincinnati, OH: South-Western College Publishing, 1998.

2. Ibid., pp. 500-505.

3. Hamel, Gary, and C. K. Prahalad. "The Core Competence of the Corporation." *Harvard Business Review,* May-June 1990: 79-91.

4. Kaye, Linda. "The Business of Product Development." *Cadence Plugged-in,* 3(3), January 1999.

5. *www.eroom.com.*

6. Coase, R. H., "The Nature of the Firm." Reprinted in *The Firm, the Market and the Law,* pp. 6, 33-55. Chicago: University of Chicago Press, 1988.

7. Ibid., p. 6.

8. Ibid., p. 6.

9. *http://www.contextmag.com/archives/199809/lawanddisorder.asp.*

10. "The Emerging Digital Economy," Secretariat on Electronic Commerce, U.S. Department of Commerce, 1998, p. 21.

11. The Business Case for ANX Service, *www.aiag.com.*

12. Ibid.

13. Ibid.

Chapter 9

1. Quinn, James Brian. "Strategic Outsourcing" *Sloan Management Review,* Summer 1994: 43.

2. *http://www.detnews.com/1998/autos/daimlerchrysler/05150120.htm.*

3. Porter, Michael. *Competitive Strategy—Techniques for Analyzing Industries and Competitors.* New York: The Free Press–Simon and Schuster.

4. *http://www.saffm.hq.af.mil/SAFFM/FMC/ABC/Definition.htm.*

5. Quinn, James Brian. "Strategic Outsourcing." *Sloan Management Review,* Summer 1994: 51.

6. Hamel, Gary, and C. K. Prahalad. *Competing for the Future,* p. 200. Boston: Harvard Business School Press, 1994.

7. Ibid., p. 200.

8. Ibid., p. 199.

9. Ibid., p. 197.

10. *http://www.gm.com/about/info/overview/RD_Center/websiter/intro/98 0425krb.html.*

11. *Harvard Business Review* Case N9-195-142, December 5, 1994, Oticon A/S Consolidated.

12. Byrne, John A. "The Corporation of the Future." *Business Week,* August 31, 1998: 104.

Chapter 10

1. Garner, Rochelle. "Too Much, Too Fast." *Computerworld,* 31 (9), March 3, 1997: 75-76.
2. Beer, Michael. "People Express Airlines: Rise and Decline" (case study). *Harvard Business School,* September 14, 1993: 14. Product Number 490012.

Chapter 11

1. Quinn, James Brian. "Beyond Products: Services-Based Strategy." *Harvard Business Review,* March/April 1990.

Chapter 12

1. *http://www.sec.gov/edaux/searches.htm.*
2. President's Council on Sustainable Development. *Sustainable America: A New Consensus for Prosperity, Opportunity, and a Healthy Environment for the Future,* February 1996. *http://www.whitehouse.gov/PCSD/Publications/TF_Reports/amer-intro.html.*
3. Carnoy, Martin. *The New Global Economy in the Information Age: Reflections on our Changing World.* University Park, PA: Pennsylvania State University Press, 1996.
4. *http://www.ed.gov/updates/7priorities/index.html.*
5. *mbennet@stars.sfsu.edu.*
6. *http://europa.eu.int.*
7. *http://www.worldforum98.org/technology/article_1compu.html.*
8. *http://www.2b1.org/mission.html.*
9. *www.juniorsummit.net.*
10. Board on International Health, Institute for Medicine. *America's Vital Interest in Global Health.* Washington, D.C.: National Academy Press, 1997.
11. *http://www.healthnet.org.*
12. *http://www.healthnet.org/voices/voices19.html.*
13. Ball, David. "Joining medicine takers with medicine makers." *Pharmaceutical Executive.* February 1996.
14. Cockburn, Ian, and Rebecca Henderson. *Public-Private Interaction and the Productivity of Pharmaceutical Research,* Working Paper 6018. Cambridge: National Bureau of Economic Research, 1997.
15. *http://www.irs.ustreas.gov/prod/welcome/ir-98-3.html.*
16. *http://www.irs.ustreas.gov/prod/elec_sus/partners.html.*
17. *http://www.taxrefund.com/what_is_electronic_tax_filing_new.htm.*

Chapter 13

1. *http://www.zdnet.com/zdnn/stories/news/0,4586,2160137,00.html.*

Appendix C

1. Hellriegel, Don, John W. Slocum, and Richard W. Woodman. *Organizational Behavior,* Eighth Edition, pp. 520–522. Cincinnati, OH: South-Western College Publishing, 1998.

INDEX

ABOUT THE AUTHOR

Douglas F. Aldrich is a vice president and managing director of the Strategic Information Technology Practice of the management consulting firm A. T. Kearney. He leads A. T. Kearney's initiatives in electronic business consulting and is responsible for global research into current best practices and future growth opportunities in this expanding arena. Under his leadership, A. T. Kearney is developing extensive e-business tools and capabilities.

Mr. Aldrich has specialized in helping businesses achieve strategic IT advantages in a broad range of industries, including consumer products, financial institutions, and transportation. He has been an industry leader in applying advanced systems tools and techniques in delivering multi-million-dollar, mission-critical applications.

Prior to joining A. T. Kearney in 1993, Mr. Aldrich was one of the founders of the Information Technology Practice at Booz-Allen & Hamilton, Inc., where he led the Southwest Practice. Previously, Mr. Aldrich founded the Advanced Technology Consulting Practice at Arthur Young International (Ernst & Young).

He has served as adjunct professor of business administration at three major uiniversities, and he has served as guest lecturer on IT issues for numerous professional organizations.

Mr. Aldrich earned Bachelor of Science degrees in industrial engineering and computer technology from Purdue University, an MBA in management from Indiana University, and has completed the Harvard University Executive Program.

Mr. Aldrich and his wife, Debbie, have three children and live in Dallas, Texas.